ADOBE® PHOTOSHOP® 7

Introduction to Digital Images

Prentice
Hall

Upper Saddle River, NJ 07458

Library of Congress Cataloging-in-Publication Data

Adobe Photoshop 7: Introduction to Digital Images/Against The Clock
    p. cm. — (Against The Clock Series)
ISBN 0-13-048699-X
1. Computer Graphics. 2. Adobe Photoshop.
    I. Against The Clock Series.

T385 .A358368 2003
006.6'869 — dc21

2002072810

Editor-in-Chief: Stephen Helba
Director of Production and Manufacturing: Bruce Johnson
Executive Editor: Elizabeth Sugg
Managing Editor – Editorial: Judy Casillo
Editorial Assistant: Anita Rhodes
Managing Editor – Production: Mary Carnis
Production Editor: Denise Brown
Composition: Diana Van Winkle, Van Winkle Design
Design Director: Cheryl Asherman
Design Coordinator: Christopher Weigand
Cover Design: LaFortezza Design Group, Inc.
Icon Design: James Braun
Prepress: Photoengraving, Inc.
Printer/Binder: Press of Ohio

Pearson Education LTD.
Pearson Education Australia PTY, Limited
Pearson Education Singapore, Pte. Ltd
Pearson Education North Asia Ltd
Pearson Education Canada, Ltd
Pearson Educación de Mexico, S.A. de C.V.
Pearson Education – Japan
Pearson Education Malaysia, Pte. Ltd
Pearson Education, Upper Saddle River, New Jersey

10 9 8 7 6 5

ISBN 0-13-048699-X

Contents

Purpose

The Against The Clock series has been developed specifically for those involved in the field of computer arts, and now — animation, video, and multimedia production. Many of our readers are already involved in the industry in advertising and printing, television production, multimedia, and in the world of Web design. Others are just now preparing for a career within these professions.

This series provides you with the necessary skills to work in these fast-paced, exciting, and rapidly expanding fields. While many people feel that they can simply purchase a computer and the appropriate software, and begin designing and producing high-quality presentations, the real world of high-quality printed and Web communications requires a far more serious commitment.

The Series

The applications presented in the Against The Clock series stand out as the programs of choice in professional computer-arts environments.

We use a modular design for the Against The Clock series, allowing you to mix and match the drawing, imaging, and page-layout applications that exactly suit your specific needs.

Titles available in the Against The Clock series include:

Macintosh: Basic Operations
Windows: Basic Operations
Adobe Illustrator: Introduction and Advanced Digital Illustration
Macromedia FreeHand: Digital Illustration
Adobe InDesign: Introduction and Advanced Electronic Mechanicals
Adobe PageMaker: Creating Electronic Documents
QuarkXPress: Introduction and Advanced Electronic Documents
Microsoft Publisher: Creating Electronic Mechanicals
Microsoft PowerPoint: Presentation Graphics with Impact
Microsoft FrontPage: Creating and Designing Web Pages
HTML & XHTML: Creating Web Pages
Procreate Painter: A Digital Approach to Natural Art Media
Adobe Photoshop: Introduction and Advanced Digital Images
Adobe Premiere: Digital Video Editing
Adobe After Effects: Motion Graphics and Visual Effects
Macromedia Director: Creating Powerful Multimedia
Macromedia Flash: Animating for the Web
Macromedia Dreamweaver: Creating Web Pages
Preflight and File Preparation
TrapWise and PressWise: Digital Trapping and Imposition

You will see a number of icons in the sidebars; each has a standard meaning. Pay close attention to the sidebar notes where you will find valuable comments that will help you throughout this book, and in the everyday use of your computer. The standard icons are:

The Hand-on-mouse icon indicates a hands-on activity — either a short exercise or a complete project. The complete projects are located at the back of the book, in sequence from Project A through C.

The Pencil icon indicates a comment from an experienced operator or trainer. Whenever you see this icon, you'll find corresponding sidebar text that augments the subject being discussed at the time.

The Key icon is used to identify keyboard equivalents to menu or dialog box options. Using a key command is often faster than selecting a menu option with the mouse. Experienced operators often mix the use of keyboard equivalents and menu/dialog box selections to arrive at their optimum speed of execution.

The Caution icon indicates a potential problem or difficulty. For instance, a certain technique might lead to pages that prove difficult to output. In other cases, there might be something that a program cannot easily accomplish, so we present a workaround.

If you are a Windows user, be sure to refer to the corresponding text or images whenever you see this Windows icon. Although there isn't a great deal of difference between using these applications on a Macintosh and using them on a Windows-based system, there are certain instances where there's enough of a difference for us to comment.

For the Reader

On the CD-ROM, you will find a complete set of Against The Clock (ATC) fonts, as well as a collection of data files used to construct the various exercises and projects. The ATC fonts are solely for use while you are working through the Against The Clock materials.

A variety of resource files are included. These files, necessary to complete both the exercises and projects, may be found in the **RF_Intro_Photoshop** folder on the Resource CD-ROM.

For the Trainer

The Trainer's CD-ROM includes various testing and presentation materials in addition to the files that are supplied with this book.

- **Overhead presentation materials** are provided and follow along with the book. These presentations are prepared using Microsoft PowerPoint, and are provided in both native PowerPoint format and Acrobat Portable Document Format (PDF).

- **Extra free-form projects** are provided and may be used to extend the training session, or they may be used to test the reader's progress.

- **Test questions and answers** are included on the Trainer's CD-ROM. These questions may be modified and/or reorganized.

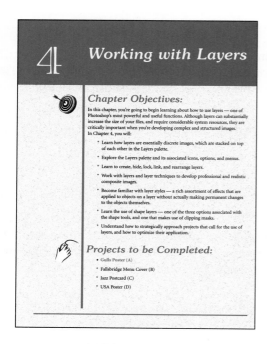

Chapter openers provide the reader with specific objectives.

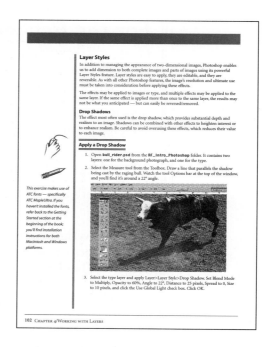

Sidebars and hands-on activities supplement concepts presented throughout the book.

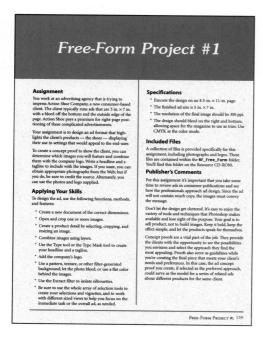

Free-form projects allow readers to use their imagination and new skills to satisfy a typical client's needs.

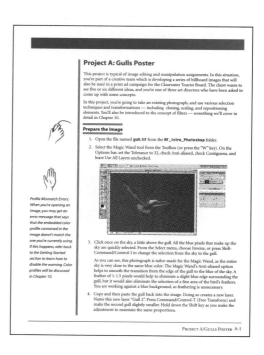

Step-by-step projects result in finished artwork — with an emphasis on proper file-construction methods.

Project A: Gulls Poster

This project represents a typical "concept development" assignment. A tourism client has retained the services of your design firm to help them develop a graphic treatment that will ultimately be used in several ads, mailings, and promotional brochures. You're going to create one of several different pieces that will be used for the next presentation. You'll make use of complex selections, transformation techniques, and filters in the construction of your work. You'll start with a simple image, and turn it into a work of art.

Project B: Fallsbridge Menu Cover

Two of your friends are the proud new owners of an historic New England bed and breakfast inn. Your job is to develop a graphic that can be used as their new menu cover. You'll begin with an image of a 100-year old covered bridge that has already had several effects applied to it. You will complete the image by adding foliage and further repairing the photo. Then you'll add type elements and use an imported line-art graphic to enhance the final piece.

Project C: Jazz Postcard

The client for this project is an ownership group that operates a dinner and concert cruise line. The graphic will be a cross-purpose image that is designed to attract tourists, and appeal to local customers who are already familiar with the event. Most of the components in this image will be created from scratch, including a star-filled sky and descriptive type elements. To complete the artwork, you'll make use of imported images and compositing techniques, including masks and custom alpha channels.

Project D: USA Poster

This is the last — and most challenging — project in the book. Your assignment is to create a large, high-resolution poster for a civic organization. Completing the task requires the use of many advanced techniques. You will start with vector artwork created in Adobe Illustrator, and apply a number of different compositing techniques. You will then work through the creation and application of custom displacement maps. These maps will help you to achieve a totally realistic background texture for the vector artwork. You'll also combine photographic and text elements using masks and alpha channels.

ACKNOWLEDGMENTS

I would like to give special thanks to the writers, illustrators, editors, and others who have worked long and hard to complete the Against The Clock series.

A big thank you to the dedicated teaching professionals whose comments and expertise contributed to the success of these products, including Carin Murphy of Des Moines Area Community College, Nicole Marcisz of Purdue University, Calumet, Russel Kahn, Ph.D of State University of New York, Utica/Rome, Tara Gray of Allentown Business School, and Chris Collins of The International Academy of Design and Technology.

Thanks to Laurel Cucchiara, copyeditor, and final link in the chain of production, for her help in making sure that we all said what we meant to say.

A big thanks to Denise Brown and Kerry Reardon, for their guidance, patience, and attention to detail.

— *Ellenn Behoriam, July 2002*

Our History

Against The Clock (ATC) was founded in 1990 as a part of Lanman Systems Group, one of the nation's leading systems integration and training firms. The company specialized in developing custom training materials for such clients as L.L. Bean, *The New England Journal of Medicine*, the Smithsonian, the National Education Association, *Air & Space Magazine*, Publishers Clearing House, the National Wildlife Society, Home Shopping Network, and many others. The integration firm was among the most highly respected in the graphic-arts industry.

To a great degree, the success of Lanman Systems Group can be attributed to the thousands of pages of course materials developed at the company's demanding client sites. Throughout the rapid growth of Lanman Systems Group, founder and general manager Ellenn Behoriam developed the expertise necessary to manage technical experts, content providers, writers, editors, illustrators, designers, layout artists, proofreaders, and the rest of the chain of professionals required to develop structured and highly effective training materials.

Following the sale of the Lanman Companies to World Color, one of the nation's largest commercial printers, Ellenn embarked on a project to develop a new library of hands-on training materials engineered specifically for the professional graphic artist. A large part of this effort is finding and working with talented professional artists, authors, and educators from around the country.

The result is the ATC training library.

About the Authors

Win Wolloff, is the President and founder of The PhotoShop, a digital imaging and retouching center. Win holds degrees as a master photographer and photographic craftsman from the Professional Photographers of America, the nation's largest and most respected trade organization.

Among Win's recent assignments was the position of Digital Director of Eagle Photographics, a Tampa-based color lab. Currently, Win brings his 25+ years of real-world experience to the classroom where he instructs art students at The International Academy of Design and Technology in Tampa, Florida.

Michael Baumgardt is Germany's most respected author on Web design and desktop publishing. One of the first designers to adopt desktop publishing, he made the leap into designing for the Web in 1996 and works today as Web designer/consultant. His most well-known book on Web design is *Web Design with Photoshop 7*, published by Peachpit Press/Adobe Press.

Gary Poyssick, co-owner of Against The Clock, is a well-known and often controversial speaker, writer, and industry consultant who has been involved in professional graphics and communications for over 15 years.

A respected author, Poyssick penned the highly-popular *Workflow Reengineering* (Adobe Press), *Teams and the Graphic Arts Service Provider* (Prentice Hall), *Creative Techniques: Adobe Illustrator*, and *Creative Techniques: Adobe Photoshop* (Hayden Books), as well as many of the titles that make up the Against The Clock library.

NOTES

Getting Started

Platform

The Against The Clock (ATC) series is designed for both the Macintosh and Windows platforms. On the Macintosh, Photoshop 7 requires Mac OS 9.1, 9.2, or Mac OS X 10.1.3. The Windows version runs on Windows 98, Windows NT, Windows 2000, Windows ME, and Windows XP.

Prerequisites

This book is based on the assumption that you have a basic understanding of how to use your computer. This includes standard dialog boxes with OK and Cancel buttons. In the case of many exercises, it is assumed that you will click the OK button to change the values of a dialog box according to the instructions provided.

You should know how to use your mouse to point and click, as well as to drag items around the screen. You should be able to resize and arrange windows on your desktop to maximize your available workspace. You should know how to access pop-up menus, and understand how check boxes and radio buttons work. Lastly, you should know how to create, open, and save files. It is also helpful to have a firm understanding of how your operating system organizes files and folders, and how to navigate your way around them.

The CD-ROM and Initial Setup Considerations

Before you begin using your Against The Clock book, you must set up your system to have access to the various files and tools to complete your lessons.

Resource Files

This book comes complete with a collection of resource files, which are an integral part of the learning experience. They are used throughout the book to help you construct increasingly complex elements. These building blocks should be available for practice and study sessions to allow you to experience and complete the exercises and project assignments smoothly, spending a minimum of time looking for the various required components.

All the files that you need to complete the exercises and projects in this book are located on your Resource CD-ROM, and contained in a folder named **RF_Intro_Photoshop**. It's best to copy the entire folder onto your hard drive – if you have 450 megabytes or more of available space. If not, you can work directly from the Resource CD-ROM.

The Work In Progress Folder

Before you begin working on the exercises or projects in this book, you should create a folder called **Work_In_Progress**, either on your hard drive or on a removable disk. As you work through the steps in the exercises, you will be directed to save your work in this folder.

If your time is limited, you can stop at a logical point in an exercise or project, save the file, and later return to the point at which you stopped. In some cases, the exercises in this book build upon work that you have already completed. You will need to open a file from your **Work_In_Progress** folder and continue working on the same file.

Locating Files

Files that you need to open are indicated by a different typeface (for example, "Open the file named **clouds.psd**."). The location of the file also appears in the special typeface (for example, "Open **chairs.psd** from your **Work_In_Progress** folder.").

When you are directed to save a file with a specific name, the name appears in quotation marks (for example, "Save the file as "blends_practice.psd" to your **Work_In_Progress** folder.").

In most cases, resource files are located in the **RF_Intro_Photoshop** folder, while exercises and projects on which you continue to work are located in your **Work_In_Progress** folder. We repeat these directions frequently in the early chapters, and add reminders in sidebars in the later chapters. If a file is in a location other than these two folders, the path is indicated in the exercise or project (for example, "Open the file from the **Images** folder, found inside your **RF_Intro_Photoshop** folder.").

File Name Conventions

Files on the Resource CD-ROM are named according to the Against The Clock naming convention to facilitate cross-platform compatibility. Words are separated by an underscore, and all file names include a lowercase three-letter extension that you see as part of the file name.

When your Windows system is first configured, the views are normally set to a default that hides these extensions. This means that you might have a dozen different files named "myfile," all of which may have been generated by different applications. This can become very confusing.

On a Windows-based system, you can change this view. Double-click on "My Computer" (the icon on your desktop). From the View menu, select Folder Options. From Folder Options, select the View tab. Within the Files and Folders folder is a check box for Hide File Extensions for Known File Types. When this is unchecked, you can see the file extensions.

It's easier to know what you're looking at if file extensions are visible. While this is a personal choice, we strongly recommend viewing the file extensions.

Photoshop is unique among programs in the sense that it's capable of opening dozens of different file formats – and equally adept at exporting images in multiple formats. The native Photoshop extension is .psd. Other file types include .tif (TIFF), .jpg (JPEG), .gif (GIF), and others, depending on the intended use of your images. You should always add the proper extension to your file names.

Fonts

You must install the ATC fonts from the Resource CD-ROM to ensure that your exercises and projects work as described in the book. These fonts are provided on the Resource CD-ROM in the **ATC_Fonts** folder. Specific instructions for installing fonts are provided in the documentation that came with your computer.

We strongly recommend that you install a font-management utility program on your computer. Installing fonts at the system level can be cumbersome, and can significantly affect your computer's performance if you install too many fonts.

If you choose not to install the fonts, you will receive a warning dialog when you attempt to open a document containing the ATC typefaces.

Key Commands

We assume that most people using this book have an extended keyboard, and can use the function keys, modifier keys, and the numeric keypad. If you are using a laptop computer, or other computer with an abbreviated keyboard, some of the key commands discussed in this book may not be available.

There are three keys that are generally used as modifier keys — they don't do anything by themselves when pressed, but they either perform some action or type a special character when pressed with another key or keys.

We frequently note keyboard shortcuts that can be used in Photoshop 7. A slash character indicates that the key commands differ for Macintosh and Windows systems; the Macintosh commands are listed first, and then the Windows commands. If you see the command "Command/Control-P", for example, Macintosh users would press the Command key and Windows users would press the Control key; both would then press the "P" key.

The Command/Control key is used with another key to perform a specific function. When combined with the "S" key, it saves your work. When combined with "O", it opens a file; with "P", it prints the file. In addition to these functions, which work with most Macintosh and Windows programs, the Command/Control key can be combined with other keys to control specific Photoshop functions. At times it is also used in combination with the Shift and/or Option/Alt keys.

The Option/Alt key, another modifier key, is often used in conjunction with other keys to access special typographic characters. On a Windows system, the Alt key is used with the number keys on the numeric keypad. For example, Alt-0149 produces a bullet (•) character. The Alt key can be confusing because not only do you use it to type special characters, you can also use it to control program and operating system functions. Pressing Alt-F4, for example, closes programs or windows, depending on which is active. On a Macintosh computer, the Option key is often used with a letter key to type a special character.

The Shift key is the third modifier key. While you're familiar with using this key to type uppercase letters and the symbols on the tops of the number keys, it's also used with Command/Control and Option/Alt in a number of contexts.

Color Management

In today's demanding workplace, consistent, repeatable color is very important, and many artists and designers make use of color management techniques to ensure that the images they see on their monitors reproduce properly. One of the ways this is accomplished is through the use of Profiles.

Profiles are designed to provide Photoshop with accurate descriptions of how different monitors, color printers, scanners, and printing presses reproduce specific colors. By having a profile for the monitor, scanner, and target printing press, a designer can be reasonably certain they're going to get the results they expect when their work is reproduced.

If an image has a particular profile attached, and your computer is using a different profile than the one used to create the image, you will get an error message whenever you attempt to open one of the resource files from the **RF_Intro_Photoshop** folder.

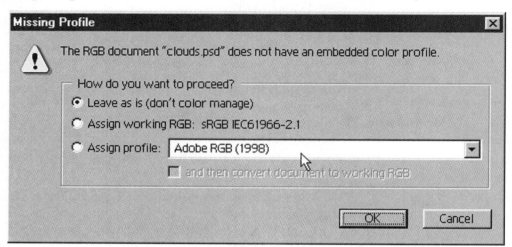

Color management is a fairly advanced topic, and managing the color consistency of the resource images supplied with this book isn't important. This message will prove quite distracting if it appears every time you open an image from now until the time you finish the last exercise in the last chapter. It is highly recommended that you turn off this warning.

Turn Off the Missing Profile Warning

1. To turn off the message, start Photoshop. Without any documents open, select Color Settings from the Edit menu.

2. Click the Advanced Mode button. In the middle of the dialog box, you find a section labeled "Color Management Policies." Use the pop-up menus to turn off Color Management for all three color models (RGB, CMYK, and Gray).

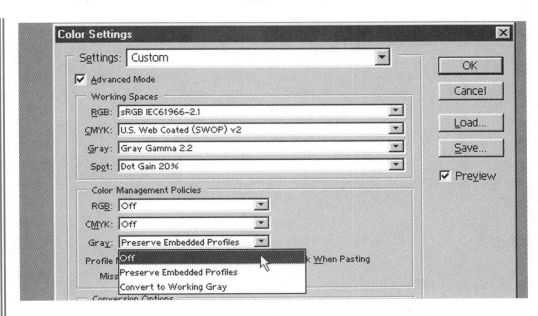

3. Uncheck the check box labeled Profile Mismatches. This turns off the warning dialog box.

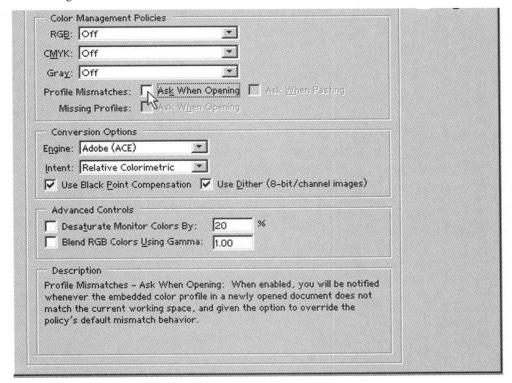

System Requirements for Photoshop

Macintosh:

- PowerPC® processor (G3, G4, or G4 dual)
- Mac OS software version 9.1, 9.2, or Mac OS X version 10.1.3
- 128 MB of RAM (192 MB recommended)
- 320 MB of available hard-disk space
- Color monitor capable of 800 × 600 pixel resolution
- CD-ROM drive

Windows:

- Intel® Pentium® III or 4 processor; fully-compliant alternative processors
- Microsoft® Windows® 98, Windows 98 Second Edition
- Windows Millennium Edition, Windows NT® with Service Pack 6a
- Windows 2000 with Service Pack 2, Windows XP
- 128 MB of RAM (192 MB recommended)
- 280 MB of available hard-disk space
- Color monitor capable of 800 × 600 pixel resolution
- CD-ROM drive

Introduction

This book was designed to familiarize you with the fundamentals of Photoshop 7, the standard program for creating and editing images — both for the printed page, as well as for the Web.

First and foremost, Photoshop is used for image editing. Image editing is the process of making changes to existing images. These are usually scans taken from original transparencies or prints. They might be color, grayscale, or black-and-white images. Image editing is sometimes referred to as "retouching." You can combine images to create a composite image, or montage, to which you may add special effects.

Photoshop is also used as a painting program. Its paintbrushes, color palettes, and specialized tools allow you to create original artwork from scratch. In addition, you can combine painting, airbrushing, and other Photoshop techniques with art created in other programs, or combine Photoshop images with type created in other programs, such as Adobe Illustrator or Macromedia FreeHand.

Photoshop is capable of making color corrections — very fine adjustments to specific colors or tones in an image. The color corrections can be as minute as altering a color shift on the overall image, or as extreme as colorizing a black-and-white photo. Photoshop provides calibration tools to synchronize your scanner, monitor, proofing printer, and even an external device (such as a printing press), to obtain consistent, predictable results throughout the printing process.

In addition, the program provides many tools specific to the prepress function. These include controlling halftones, generating color separations, controlling ink densities, creating traps, and many other production-specific functions. Color correction and prepress activities are normally performed by professionals with skill and experience in producing high-quality digital images.

Photoshop is very well suited for the printing process, and the program is also invaluable for producing graphics for the Web. They may range from simply creating compressed file formats, such as GIF and JPEG, to creating animated files to add a bit of entertainment to a Web site. Photoshop files may be saved in Adobe's PDF format for distribution in either print or electronic form.

Photoshop has an extensible format. Third-party developers write programs that actually work within Photoshop to extend its capabilities, or to make it much easier to achieve complex effects. These extensions, called "plug-ins," may be designed to remove the tedium from tasks that are not difficult in and of themselves, or they may combine a series of actions to achieve special effects that require a deeper understanding of the program than many are willing to attain. Relying too heavily on plug-ins often means that the user doesn't learn to effectively use the program; this could lead to disappointment when new versions of the product are released, and the plug-ins no longer work.

Photoshop also has built-in automation functions, so you can quickly perform repetitive, tedious processes.

The focus of this book is to introduce you to Photoshop as an image-editing and painting tool set, to demonstrate methods for adjusting tonal range in photographic images, to learn techniques of managing the elements of complex images, and to teach you some basic special effects that are suitable for both offset printed pieces and multimedia applications.

1   *Images*

Chapter Objectives:

As you read this chapter, you will gain an overall understanding of how to manipulate source images using Photoshop's drawing and painting tools. In today's multipurpose working environments, it is often necessary to use one graphic for many purposes — for print and/or Web distribution. With Photoshop, it is a simple task to generate an image in one color mode, save it to another, and then use copy for a different deliverable. In Chapter 1, you will:

- Learn the difference between analog and digital source images.

- Find out about the file formats and resolution settings that are used for print and Web distribution.

- Learn about the many color modes, and to what type of deliverable each color mode is applied.

- Discover the reason why it became important to develop a standard for naming colors.

- Understand the difference between 1-bit, 8-bit, 24-bit, and 32-bit images.

- Find out why bit depth is important for "photo-realistic" images.

- Gain a basic understanding of tonal ranges and image correction.

Projects to be Completed:

- Gulls Poster (A)

- Fallsbridge Menu Cover (B)

- Jazz Postcard (C)

- USA Poster (D)

Photoshop can "capture" images from a variety of sources, including digital cameras, scanners, and digital video devices. Check with the manufacturer of your device to see if the necessary plug-in is available. They're usually included on the CD that came with the scanner or camera.

Line art is defined as images containing only two colors – black and white. Examples include logos, pen and ink drawings, and other graphics that don't contain any shades or tones. Flat art is artwork that contains only solid colors. Examples include icons, certain logos, and simple cartoons.

Images

The images brought into Photoshop come from two primary sources. A *digital image* is one that already exists in electronic form: it can be a CD image; an image that has its origins in a painting or drawing program, such as Adobe Illustrator or Macromedia FreeHand; or the image may have originated on a digital camera. An *analog image* begins its life as a physical object: a photograph, illustration, or painting. In order to work with an image in Photoshop, it must first be converted into a digital image. This is accomplished with a scanner or similar digital-capture device.

Analog Images

The most common type of image used in today's publications is photographic (prints or transparencies) — although the increasing capabilities and popularity of digital cameras is resulting in an expanding reliance on digital originals. The color, contrast, density, and sharpness of each photo varies, depending on many factors, including the camera, type of film, lighting, and, of course, the ability of the photographer. Other analog image sources include paintings, pastels, charcoal, and pencil drawings.

All these images are called *continuous tone* images because the colors or shades blend smoothly from one to another. Black-and-white photographs and certain types of charcoal or pencil illustrations — ones containing intermediate shades of gray — are referred to as *grayscale* images. The other categories include *line art*, containing only black and white, and *flat* artwork, containing only solid colors. You can use Photoshop to manipulate any of these image formats — assuming they've been converted into a digital format.

The image on the left is a scanned photograph; the one on the right is an icon created in Adobe Illustrator and opened with Photoshop. It's considered flat art because it only contains solid colors.

Digital Images

In addition to analog images that are converted to digital form, many images are readily available as digital data. Photo images are available for downloading from online sources, or may be purchased on CD from stock photo houses. Digital cameras produce images ranging in quality comparable to those from professional large-format cameras, to quality approximating that available from an inexpensive consumer camera. Video capture equipment provides similar capabilities.

Photographs comprise the majority of images brought into Photoshop for manipulation, although original artwork created in drawing and painting programs also plays a role. It is often easier to make adjustments to these images in their originating programs, but images from dissimilar sources are often merged in Photoshop to create composite images.

Digital Cameras

Digital cameras have come a long way since the first models were introduced. Where they once were suitable solely for Web use or lower-quality printing projects, they're now found in the most demanding applications — in many cases even for high-end product and fashion photography.

There are a number of factors that impact the quality (and therefore the cost) of digital cameras, and there are many devices available, ranging in price from under $100 to well over $25,000.

The first — and arguably the most important quality consideration — is related to how much data the camera captures when you engage the "shutter." Resolution is measured in how many specific data points are read from the scene and stored in the device's memory — something the manufacturers refer to as *megapixels*. A camera that captures 4 megapixels naturally produces more data (and larger files) than one rated at 2 megapixels. At the time we wrote this book, you could buy an excellent 4-megapixel camera for under $1,000 — and a totally acceptable device for Web graphics for under $250.

Canon is only one of several manufacturers of high-quality, cost-effective digital cameras.

The intended use of digital camera images (and all digital images, for that matter) determines resolution requirements. Web pages require the least; newsprint (and other low-end printing, such as flyers) requires a little more; and high-end materials, such as magazines and color product catalogs, require the most. You'll learn more about the relationship between resolution and output requirements as we move forward.

There is a direct correlation between image quality and resolution – both on the Web and in print. Resolution impacts every imaging project you work on, so it is a factor you'll see discussed throughout the book.

The higher the megapixel rating, the more data the camera captures per square inch. The more data it captures, the larger the image. A camera that offers 1.2 megapixels captures an image that can be reproduced on the Web at approximately 6 in. × 9 in.; if you print the same image, quality begins to suffer at any size greater then 1.5 in. × 2.25 in. The size (weight) of the image is about 1 megabyte.

A camera capable of delivering 6 megapixels creates an image that can be printed — in a quality, four-color magazine — at the full size of the page (8.5 in. × 11 in.). This is far more resolution than you'll ever need for delivery on the Web, but perfect for commercial print production. The size of the high-quality image is almost 18 megabytes. For posters and other large-format printing projects, you could easily find yourself working with an image that weighs in at more than 100 megabytes.

Digital Art

Digital art is usually defined as artwork created in Photoshop or other image-editing applications (you can also import a wide variety of file formats into Photoshop). Within the Adobe family of graphic applications, Illustrator, Dimensions, Atmosphere, and Premiere can also produce images that are compatible with Photoshop.

Stock Photography

We remember spending endless hours looking through what were called *stock books* — catalogs of available images sold through businesses known as *stock houses*. These companies maintained the rights to a wide variety of photographic and artistic copyrights, and managed the licensing of those images for the original creators or owners. If an ad agency, for example, wanted to use a photograph of jazz great Dizzy Gillespie, or a photograph of Elvis Presley, or a picture from the Ufizzi museum in Florence, Italy, they paid a fee to the stock house that offered the photograph. In turn, the stock house took its percentage of the fee, and paid the balance to the copyright owner.

Using stock photography has many advantages. Even though costs for one-time usage (the most common type of license available for stock imagery) can be expensive, setting up a physical camera shoot to create the images envisioned by the designer can be even more so.

In recent years, largely due to the explosion in digital imaging technology, a new form of stock image has emerged. Many of the images used in our books, for example, come from a stock house called Photospin (http://www.photospin.com). For a small annual fee, an artist can gain access to thousands of photographs, already organized into logical categories, and available directly from the company's Web site.

Although conventional (and usually expensive) stock houses still exist, they're under tremendous pressure as more cost-effective digital stock houses continue to expand on the Internet. Some digital stock houses offer extensive collections of related images on CD (in categories such as business, people, animals, landscapes, sports). Most provide multiple usage rights, but you can't sell them to anyone else. Depending on the licensing agreement, you may also have to mention the stock house somewhere in the piece you're publishing.

Try visiting photospin.com. The company offers a wonderful collection of images for a reasonable annual subscription fee. Many of the images from our books come from their site..

Scanners

There are many types of scanners. They differ in their methods of collecting the image data, the type of media they can scan, and how accurately they reproduce the image in digital form.

All scanners share the same principle of operation: they convert images into a pattern of squares called *pixels* (stands for picture elements). A pixel is the smallest distinct unit of an image that can be recorded or displayed by a digital device at any given resolution.

Types of scanning devices include the following:

- **Sheet-Fed.** The user inserts a page into this scanner and the page moves through the device. The drawbacks to this method are similar to those of a fax machine. The original may be mutilated, or it may slip, stretch, tilt, or jam. Resin-coated or glossy photographs are more likely to slip than uncoated paper stocks. Sheet-fed scanners are usually reserved for optical character recognition (OCR) conversion of typed or printed information into text that can be edited in a word-processing program.

- **Flatbed.** This scanner is similar in operation to an office copy machine. The page or book is placed face down on a clear glass sheet and the cover is lowered. The movable sensing device glides back and forth beneath the glass, recording the image. The original is immobile and the recording process is automatic, so this method is capable of producing excellent results from reflective copy. Some very good, high-quality color scanners now use flatbed design. Some flatbed scanners are also designed to scan slides with good results.

Before the advent of digital cameras, scanners provided the only way to create a digital image from an analog source. They're still very popular. Seven or eight years ago a decent scanner cost more than $2,500; today they're available for under $100.

- **Slide or Transparency**. These devices accept 35mm mounted slides, filmstrips, and, in some cases, larger format film. They range in price from under $1,000 to over $10,000. Several excellent 35mm and medium-format models at about $1,000-$3,000 provide professional-quality scans. Projecting light through the transparency or negative and scanning the transmitted light of the image allows a greater range of tones to be captured. Due to advances in Charge Coupled Device (CCD) technology, these units are generally capable of producing very high-quality images. There are slide adapters available for consumer-level flatbed scanners, but the image quality is generally not very crisp.

- **Drum.** Drum scanners offer the highest quality of all three types, and range in price from $10,000 to over $100,000. Either transparencies (removed from their mountings) or reflective originals (prints) are attached to the surface of a spinning drum. Even though these scanners generally have very high resolution, the high-quality scan they produce is the reason for their use. Their higher-quality Photomultiplier Tube (PMT) sensors have a much better dynamic range of sensitivity than do many Charge Coupled Device (CCD) sensors used in less expensive flatbed scanners and digital cameras.

Other factors in scanning include color capabilities and image resolution. These factors will be discussed later in the book.

Digital Video

Video capture is another means of digitizing images. The source of the image may be a VCR, video camera, or a laser disc player. The computer must be equipped with a video board to accept the video input and convert it to digital format. Such a card can capture a single frame from a movie and load it into a window in Photoshop. Resolution is generally lower than conventional scanners.

Image File Formats

There are dozens of file formats that have enjoyed varying degrees of popularity over the years. Some originated as proprietary formats that could only be used on a specific platform, or with a specific software application; others evolved as generic formats that were meant to be used on a variety of platforms and imaging devices. Depending on the nature of your assignments and environment, you may find yourself working with some of the more archaic formats. In most of today's environments, however, you only have to concern yourself with a few: Photoshop, TIFF, EPS, and JPEG formats for print applications; and JPEG, GIF, and PNG formats for Web graphics. If you need to, you can use this table as a reference for other types of formats.

Photoshop's File Formats	
Photoshop	Default format for newly-created images; supports all available image modes, guides, channels, and layers.
Photoshop 2.0	(Macintosh only.) Used for applications supporting only Photoshop 2 format. Flattens the file and discards layer information.
BMP	Windows Paint's BMP (Windows Bitmap), the native format of Microsoft Paint, is the standard image format for DOS and Windows-compatible computers. Supports RGB, indexed, grayscale, and bitmap modes.
CompuServe GIF	GIF (Graphics Interchange Format) is used for images for the World Wide Web. Its 8-bit images may be grayscale or indexed color. 8-bit images can produce 256 colors or shades of gray.
Photoshop EPS	Encapsulated PostScript allows combining both vector and raster (bitmap) graphics in the same file. It supports all color modes, and is the preferred format for producing images with clipping paths. Macintosh preview includes a PICT file, and can only be viewed on a Macintosh; a TIFF preview can be viewed on Macintosh or Windows.
Photoshop DCS	Desktop Color Separations are a subset of the EPS format. DCS 1.0 supports CMYK, and does not support alpha channels. It preseparates the files into a preview, plus four plates. DCS 2.0 supports multichannel files, and CMYK with a single alpha channel, and multiple spot channels. It does not preseparate the file.
JPEG	This lossy compression format was created by the Joint Photographic Experts Group. It is commonly used on the World Wide Web. It sacrifices some image quality to achieve higher levels of file compression.
PCX	PC Paintbrush's native format is commonly used on PC-compatible computers. It uses a standard VCA palette.
Photoshop PDF	Portable Document Format can represent both vector and raster graphics and can contain electronic document search and navigation features. It supports all color models, but does not support alpha channels.
PICT File	Macintosh system software's native graphic format. It supports RGB, indexed, grayscale, and bitmap color modes.
PICT Resource	(Macintosh only.) Used for storing splash screens and Scrapbook contents. It supports RGB, indexed, grayscale, and bitmap images.
Pixar	Pixar workstations produce high-quality animation. This format supports RGB and grayscale images.
PixelPaint	This file format is used with the PixelPaint 1.0 and 2.0 program. Pixel Paint files may be grayscale or indexed color.
PNG	Portable Network Graphics is a lossless compression format that supports RGB images and produces background transparency.
Raw	This binary format supports all color modes.
Scitex CT	Scitex Continuous Tone format supports RGB, CMYK, and grayscale color modes. Scitex is a high-end color scanning system.
Targa	Targa (TGA) is used in many video and modeling applications. It supports RGB, indexed, and grayscale color modes.
TIFF	Tagged Image File Format is the most common raster file format. It is cross-platform compatible.
Wavefront RLA	This format is used for Alias/Wavefront high-end 3D rendering software.

Using Images

It is as important to know how your images will be used as it is to understand where they originated. Digital files are either converted to analog images (as printed documents) or remain in digital form for distribution on the World Wide Web, on CD-ROM, shown directly from a computer monitor in presentations, or retained in a file as an electronic document.

Printed Documents (CMYK)

Different distribution models require different types of images; printing projects usually call for large, high-resolution files; Web images need to be much smaller, and there are limitations on the colors that can be used. If there's even a remote chance that you might need to use one image for both distribution methods, be sure to maintain the original and generate copies for each component of the project.

When considering the printing process, it is critical to remember that all devices — no matter what technology they use — lay down one color at a time, and that color is solid. The most common type of color printing used today is called CMYK printing, where four colors of ink are laid down in a pattern of dots to simulate a vast array of colors. Use a magnifying glass to closely inspect a color photograph in a newspaper and you'll see what we mean. We'll talk more about CMYK a little later.

RGB Printers

Innovations in the printing industry include producing small quantities with ink jet and toner-based printers. These printers offer a wider range of color than traditional lithographic presses. They often use RGB files, and then convert them to their proprietary CMYK range.

Recently, many professional-level color labs and even some consumer-oriented mini labs have added light-based photographic imaging devices. These use laser or LED (light-emitting diode) light to expose silver-based photographic paper, and are genuine RGB devices. They also offer a wider color range than any CMYK device, and fit well into the workflow of many photographers.

Electronic Documents

Today, many documents are prepared for the World Wide Web, for distribution on CD, and for corporate (or private) intranets. These documents need to use the widest range of color available, so they're prepared using the RGB color gamut. A primary drawback of electronically distributed documents is that their display depends on how the recipient's monitor is set up. Chances are good that colors will not be "true"; they will use each monitor's display gamut.

Photographs prepared for electronic distribution need only enough resolution to accommodate a computer monitor or a moderate-resolution printer. As a result, files are much smaller. Compressed formats, such as GIF, JPEG, and PNG are used for electronic distribution because the object must display quickly to keep the viewer's interest. Web designers employ a number of techniques to obtain quick display of graphics on the Internet.

All Photoshop images that make their way to paper are converted into dots — whether the image is being reproduced in color or black and white.

The medium doesn't wiggle or stretch as paper does, so there is no need to employ trapping. Since monitors are capable of displaying grayscale and continuous tone color images, the problems associated with printing dots no longer exist.

Compression technology is important when creating electronic documents in order to present the image well and to fit enough data on the medium. Images must also display in a reasonable amount of time.

When publishing to the Internet and to intranets, the same compression issues arise, but the difficulties are even greater. People won't wait even one minute for an image to display; if an image takes too long to download, visitors will simply move on to another page or site. This creates a variety of compression issues, including the compression of the color gamut, which occurs when creating GIF images. In addition, different computers support different color spaces — and most designers want color displayed accurately. The potential number of problems is monumental.

Resolution, Image Sizes, and Color Models

There are several factors that affect the size of a Photoshop image. An image is impacted by all of the factors, so they must be considered collectively:

- **Physical Dimensions**. Physical dimensions of the image (width and height), usually measured in pixels, inches, or picas.

- **Resolution of the Image**. Depending on the platform, the video card, and the manufacturer, computer monitors display between 72 and 96 pixels per inch. A digital image that will be output to print is normally between 266 and 350 pixels per inch. Resolution is the measure of accuracy of a device, file, or process. The abbreviations DPI (dots per inch), LPI (lines per inch), and PPI (pixels per inch) all represent resolution in one way or another — either on a monitor or on paper.

- **Bit Depth**. Bit depth is a technical term referring to the number of colors attainable in a specific file. A black-and-white (bitmap) image is a 1-bit format; each pixel is either on or off. Images containing 8 bits of data are capable of displaying 8 different values for each pixel, and can contain 256 shades of grays or 256 different colors. Full-color images contain 24 separate values for each pixel, and can display more than 16,000,000 colors. Printing processes cannot reproduce the entire range of a 24-bit image — but a monitor can.

- **Complexity**. Layers and alpha channels (which we'll discuss later in the book) can increase both file size and the amount of RAM required to edit the image. Masks and clipping paths also impact a file's complexity and can increase the time it takes to print.

- **File Size**. This is the amount of disk space the image occupies on your hard drive. Some formats offer compression; as a result, these images may require less space on your hard drive than the memory required to open the document.

- **DPI**. DPI, or dots per inch, is a measurement of the resolution of an output device — usually a laser printer or image setter. A *dot* in this instance is the smallest printable element a device can produce. For example, on a 300 dpi laser

*A **pixel** is the smallest element of an electronic image.*

*A **silver grain** is the smallest element of a conventional photographic image*

Adobe recommends that the amount of RAM and hard disk space be at least twice the size of your image, and for some operations, the factor can be 3 to 5 times image size; surveys indicate, however, that 75% of printed images are smaller than 10 megabytes (and Web graphics are much smaller). Despite this, the general rule is to buy the biggest, fastest machine you can afford.

printer, the smallest element would be a square pixel that is 1/300 of an inch in size. DPI is sometimes referred to as "SPI," or spots per inch; a *spot* is the technical term for an imaging device's dot.

Smaller halftone dots simulate lighter shades of gray, while larger dots simulate darker tones.

- **PPI.** PPI, or pixels per inch, denotes the resolution of a scan. Each pixel is a coordinate for a point in an image with color information attached. Data in scanned images such as TIFF files includes height and width in pixels and the number of pixels per inch. Photoshop uses these numbers to determine the height and width in inches to display the image.

The Relationship Between PPI and Line Screens

You may already understand the concept of a *line screen*, or *line ruling*. This refers to the number (also called *frequency*) of halftone elements (usually dots) per inch used to create a halftone.

Since the offset printing process cannot print shades of ink (only solid areas of ink), a method was developed to represent the gradation of tones in a photographic image. This is *halftone screening*, which represents areas of lighter tone by a field of small dots, and areas of darker tones by fields of larger dots. These variations in dot size create an optical illusion that fools the human eye into seeing a continuous tone image.

The large and small dots are generated on consistent spacing called *line screen frequency* or *line ruling*. Common line rulings range from around 85 lines per inch (lpi) for newspapers and other very porous stock being run on high-speed Web presses, all the way to 200 lpi (and higher) on glossy stock being run on slower, highly-accurate, sheet-fed presses. The finer the line screen frequency, the better the optical illusion.

This book doesn't delve deeply into the science and art of image reproduction (and it is both science and art). There is, however, one very important factor that must be discussed early on in your training: the relationship between the resolution of the image and the line ruling at which the image will be output.

For every halftone dot you require, you must begin with 1.5 to 3.5 pixels of image information. This is called the *quality factor* (QF). Although certain output conditions might produce a totally acceptable halftone using only 1.5 pixels for each halftone dot, you should generally use a factor of 2. The drawback to this approach is that each image is larger than it would be if you reduced the factor, and therefore it occupies more disk space and slows down the machine (this is much less of a problem in these days of fast CPUs, cheap RAM, and large hard drives). The selection of a quality factor depends in part upon the composition of the image. An image with sharp diagonal lines (shingles or fabric) or subtle skin tones requires a higher QF, perhaps from 2.5 to 3.5; a landscape or softened image may reproduce well with a QF of about 1.5.

Here are some of the common line screen rulings and the resolutions at which images should be scanned or created to produce quality halftones:

Line Ruling	QF=1.5	QF=2.0	QF=3.5
85 (newsprint)	128 ppi	170 ppi	298 ppi
100	150 ppi	200 ppi	350 ppi
133 (common sheet-fed)	200 ppi	266 ppi	466 ppi
150 (most common line screen)	225 ppi	300 ppi	525 ppi
175 (high quality, gloss stock, sheet-fed)	263 ppi	350 ppi	613 ppi
200 (coffee table book quality)	300 ppi	400 ppi	700 ppi

Scanning at the correct size and resolution is the single most important factor impacting image quality. Resizing an original rarely, if ever, provides the same results. If a design requires that you reduce or enlarge an image more than about 15% or 20%, re-scan the image at the proper resolution.

These QF values assume that the image will not be significantly resized before the final output. If resizing is expected, an additional sizing factor (SF) must be applied to calculate the proper scanning resolution. The sizing factor is the percentage of the original to which the image will be sized. If it will be reduced to 80%, multiply the ppi by 0.8. If it will be enlarged to 110%, multiply the ppi by 1.1.

The Image Size Command

Images may be resized by changing their dimensions, as discussed above. The Image Size command (Image>Image Size) allows you to change the image's size and resolution interactively. You can also change either the size or resolution independent of one another.

Resize an Image

1. Start Photoshop. From the File menu, select Open, and navigate to the **RF_Intro_Photoshop** folder. Open the file named **oranges.tif**. From the Image menu, select Image Size.

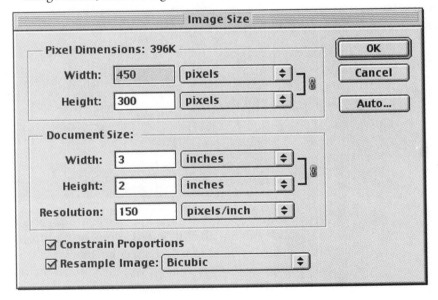

*A **halftone** is an image generated for use in printing. A range of continuous tones is simulated by an array of dots that create the illusion of continuous tone when seen at a distance.*

2. If necessary, change the Document Size units to inches. You can see in Document Size that the image is 3 inches wide by 2 inches high, with a Resolution of 150 pixels/inch. This refers to the size to which the image will default when printed or imported into another application.

3. Notice the Pixel Dimensions section. At the current size, the image size on disk is 396 KB; the dimensions in pixels are calculated according to the print size.

When an image is resampled, pixels are added to or removed from the image. When pixels are added, they are said to be "interpolated" — Photoshop determines the size and color of an inserted pixel based on the properties of the pixels on either side of it. For example, if a pixel were inserted between a yellow pixel and a red pixel, Photoshop would determine that it should be an orange pixel. Sometimes this "best guess" is correct. More often, it's just far enough off to deteriorate the quality of the image.

4. Make certain the Constrain Proportions box is checked. This way you only have to change one setting, for Width or Height; the other dimension changes proportionally. With Resample Image selected (checked), change the Resolution to 300, and notice the size next to the Pixel Dimensions section. It jumps to 1.54 MB. Note that the Width and Height in the Pixel Dimensions section doubled.

5. Change one of the dimensions in the Pixel Dimensions to Percent. It reads 200.

6. Click the Resample Image check box to deselect it. Notice that the Resolution stays at 300, but the dimensions are reduced to 1.5 in. × 1 in. The size of the file is reset to its original size of 396 KB.

7. Change the Resolution to 150. Observe the Width and Height dimension boxes. Type "200" in the Resolution box. Note how the dimensions change as you type different numbers into the Resolution box, but the size stays the same. Change the Resolution to 72 dpi; the dimensions change again.

8. Click the Resample Image check box to select it.

9. Resize the image to fit 8-in. wide at a Resolution of 150 pixels per inch. Click OK.

10. Double-click the Zoom (magnifying glass) tool icon to make certain you are viewing the image at 100%. Look closely at the detail in the oranges. You can see a noticeable degradation in image quality and sharpness.

11. From the Filter menu, select Sharpen>Sharpen More. Some of the detail comes back, but not all of it. Press Command/Control-Z a few times to Undo and Redo the sharpening so you can see the difference. If you have to increase the size of an image to this degree (and you can't rescan the image), then be certain to check the details closely, and sharpen, if necessary. Don't oversharpen the image, though — this causes color loss.

12. Save As a copy to your **Work_In_Progress** folder. Name the file "oranges_1.tif". Select Revert from the File menu, and leave the file open for the next exercise.

Size with the Cropping Tool

1. The Cropping tool allows you to size an entire image (or just a portion of it) and determine the resolution of the crop at the same time. In the open file, press the "C" key to change to the Cropping tool.

2. In the Cropping tool Options toolbar (at the top of the screen), set the Width and Height to 2 in. and the Resolution to 266 pixels/inch. Drag the Cropping tool across the image while depressing the mouse button. Whatever portion of the image you select is automatically resized to the new size and resolution you selected in the Cropping tool Options toolbar.

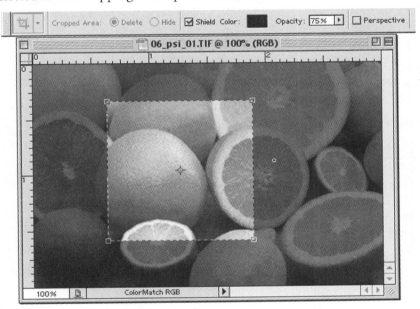

3. You can adjust the size of your cropping box by repositioning the handles at the corners of the box. Also note the changes in the Options toolbar when the crop preview is on.

4. You can also reposition the box to another part of the picture. Move the marquee box to a new location by clicking inside the box and dragging.

5. Rotate the cropped area by clicking the mouse just outside the cropping box handles and dragging; the cursor turns into a curved, double-headed arrow.

6. To finish the crop, press the Return/Enter key.

7. From the Image menu, select Image Size to check the size of the image you cropped. It should now have a 2-in. Width/Height and a Resolution of 266 pixels per inch. Click Cancel, and then press Command/Control-Z to undo the cropping.

8. In the Options toolbar, select the sizes and resolutions you typed in, and press the Delete/Backspace key for each field.

9. Close the file without saving.

The Canvas Size Command

Another way to change the physical size of your image without changing the resolution is to use the Canvas Size command. Canvas Size adds a specified amount of blank image area around your document. The resulting empty space is set to the background color if you are working on the Background layer, or to transparent when you are working on any other layer. This command is useful for framing an image or when you need more room to build a composite of several images.

Use Canvas Size

1. Create a new document. Make it 2-in. square, at a Resolution of 75 ppi, in the RGB Color Mode. Set the Contents to White. Click OK.

2. Press the "D" key to reset the color swatches to their default colors, then press the "X" key to swap (eXchange) the foreground and background colors so the background color is black.

3. From the Image menu, select Canvas Size. The Canvas Size command allows you to enlarge the available image area without resizing the existing image data. The size of the area can be set in the Width and Height boxes. The Anchor specifies the position of the existing image data in relation to the final document size.

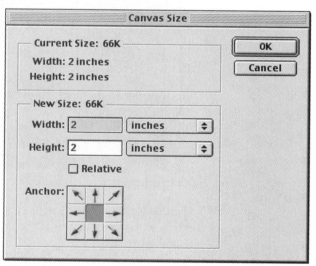

For example, if you click on the center of the Anchor grid (the default), the canvas is added equally all around the image; if you select the upper-left square, the extra canvas is added to the right and bottom of the image.

4. Set the Width and Height to 5 in. Click the upper-left square in the Anchor placement grid. Click OK. Notice the placement of the image with the new canvas size. Press Command/Control-Z to undo.

5. Select Image>Canvas Size again. Set the Width and Height to 5 in. Click the right-center square in the Anchor placement grid. Click OK. Notice where the image was placed. Press Command/Control-Z to undo.

6. Select Image>Canvas Size once more. Set the Width and Height to 5 in. Let the Anchor placement grid default to the center square. Click OK.

   The image is surrounded by a black (or whatever the background color is set to) border that is equal on all sides. Be aware that if you add different amounts to the existing Height and Width, the top/bottom and left/right borders will vary accordingly.

7. When the Relative box is checked, the fields are reset to 0. Typing a number into the fields adds that amount to the existing dimensions of the image. Close the file without saving.

Calibration and Color Models

Calibration is the process of adjusting the monitor, software, and printer so what is seen on the screen more closely matches what can be printed. It is a very complex topic and beyond the scope of a beginner's book. It is important, however, to understand the terminology and know what to expect when producing images using Photoshop.

Color Space

A *color space*, or *color model*, is a mathematical representation of a set of colors that can be produced using a particular process or device. The range of colors that can be produced within a given model is known as the *gamut*. The visible spectrum consists of all colors normally perceived by the human eye. Within this spectrum, we'll concentrate on the additive and subtractive color models while using Photoshop.

An *additive color* model contains colors created by adding together different wavelengths of light. A good example of an additive color device is a computer monitor. All of the colors the monitor shows are created by light emitted from three guns — red, green, and blue — at varying intensities.

Subtractive color models encompass colors that are created when light strikes an object or image, and certain wavelengths are absorbed or subtracted. The light that is reflected back is perceived as a particular color. Subtractive color models include all color in printed materials. They are comprised of dyes and pigments.

These models overlap, but they do not coincide exactly. For example, there are man-made pigments that do not appear in nature; and there are many colors in nature that can't be emulated on a monitor or printing press. More importantly, for the purpose of our discussion, there are many colors that do not appear in both the large additive model (the monitor) and the much smaller subtractive model (the printed page).

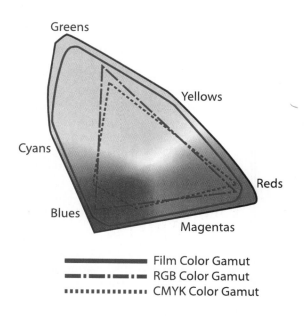

A graphic representation of the RGB and CMYK color gamut inside
the range occupied by color film and the overall CIE L*a*b color space.

RGB Color

Colors in the RGB color model are created by combining red, green, and blue light. As mentioned above, this additive color model is used to describe the colors produced by the monitor. Other examples of devices that use the RGB color model are spotlights with colored gels, and film recorders, such as those used to create slides and transparencies.

Scanned RGB images are also known as "24-bit" or "true color" images. Each pixel contains 8 bits of information for each color channel (8 each for red, green, and blue). In the RGB model, 100% each (256 levels) of red, green, and blue light combine to make white; 0% of each define the absence of color, or black.

CMYK Color

The CMYK color model is defined as the range of colors that can be created using the process printing colors cyan, magenta, yellow, and black. Each set of CMYK inks has a different color gamut. This color model is also referred to as "four-color process," and is used in commercial printing and for most color desktop printers.

CMYK is a subtractive color model. Zero percent (0%) each of cyan, magenta, yellow, and black — that is, no pigment on a page — produces white in the CMYK model. CMY is the mathematical opposite of the RGB model. Theoretically speaking, just as 100% each of RGB combine to make white, 100% each of CMY should combine to make black. In reality, printing pigments are impure. For example, most magenta reflects some cyan and a little yellow, as well as the magenta component of light. The result of mixing 100% of these colors is usually a muddy, purplish brown. Consequently, black is added to produce a true black, add depth to shadows, details to edges, and to reduce the total amount of ink on the printed page.

An image in the CMYK color space yields a file 33% larger than an RGB file — it uses 8 bits of information per color channel, just as an RGB file does, but it has 4 channels of information (C, M, Y, and K), totaling 32 bits of information as compared to 24 bits for RGB.

Indexed Color

An Indexed color image is yet another 8-bit-per-pixel format. Like an 8-bit grayscale image, each pixel is represented by a value from 0 to 255. Instead of a shade of gray, however, the value refers to a position on a color look-up table. Each position on the table contains a specific color, with 0 (zero) as black, and 255 as white. Indexing is often used as a method of reducing the range of colors stored in an image to only those actually used — storing, for instance, 4 or 5 colors instead of 256 or 16,000,000. When a particular color is not found, the Indexed color option finds the color closest to it in the Index palette.

Most page-layout programs won't separate Indexed color images, which must originate as RGB; make certain you convert them to CMYK before sending them to an imagesetter if you intend to use your graphic in a print project. In addition, once an image is converted to Indexed color, much of the continuous tone detail is lost. When possible, convert to CMYK from the original RGB image.

Convert Between Modes

1. It's simple to convert images from one color mode to another using the Image>Mode menu in Photoshop. Open the image **lineworker.tif** from your **RF_Intro_Photoshop** folder. This is an RGB image. Examine it by selecting the Image>Mode menu. You'll see a checkmark next to RGB Color. Notice that the selections for Duotone and Bitmap aren't available to you.

2. Create a copy of the image by choosing Duplicate from the Image menu. Name the copy "lineworker_cmyk.tif", and save it in your **Work_In_Progress** folder.

3. Select Mode>CMYK Color from the Image menu. This converts the image from RGB to CMYK. You will probably see a shift in the color on the screen. Notice, too, that the Title bar of the Image window displays the new color mode next to the Image title.

4. Click the Image>Mode menu; Bitmap, Duotone, Indexed Color, and Color Table are still unavailable.

5. Make a copy of **lineworker_cmyk.tif** by choosing Duplicate from the Image menu. Name the copy "lineworker_grayscale.tif".

6. Select Grayscale from the Mode menu. Click OK when the warning dialog box asks if you want to discard all color information. This converts the image from CMYK to Grayscale. Click on the Mode menu, and you'll see that now all of the options in the Mode menu are available for a grayscale image.

7. Save this image as "lineworker_grayscale.TIF" in your **Work_In_Progress** folder. Close the image. Close **lineworker_cmyk.tif** and **lineworker.tif**.

L*a*b Color Space

To bring these different color spaces together, a larger color space incorporating both CMYK and RGB models is needed. This was discovered in the late 1920s, as color printing became more prevalent. It became obvious that a standard for color description was needed. If 2 colors appear the same, they should be described in the same manner. For example, we might define "pure red" as R-255, G-0, B-0 using RGB color space, or C-0, M-100, Y-100, K-0 using CMYK color space. Of course, someone else might simply call it "bright red."

Different programs and monitors describe color differently, and printing devices create it differently, resulting in widely divergent definitions for the same color. This is particularly so if we describe the color in one space (RGB) and reproduce it in another (CMYK).

In 1931, CIE (Commission Internationale de l'Éclairage) developed the first widely used independent color space, known as *CIE XYZ*, named for the 3 axes used to describe the location of the colors. The values in this color space are derived from the relative amounts of RGB present in the color, and expressed as a percentage of luminance, together with 256 levels (ranging from −128 to +128) across 2 axes. In 1976, CIE XYZ was redefined and renamed *CIE L*a*b*.

This does not mean that you can now see colors on your monitor that you couldn't see before, even though a small portion of the CMYK space extends outside of the RGB space; it means that you can describe that space so it's printable. It also means that you can, by creating a profile of input and output devices, reduce the color space of your monitor to match the imageable colors of your printing device.

Understanding Tones and Image Formats

The more shades of gray or color an image can display, the more "photo-realistic" it appears. The eye cannot distinguish between adjacent tone levels if the steps or gradations are fine enough.

An image that contains 1 bit of tone data per pixel can only display black or white. Adding bit depth increases the number of tones that can be displayed by an image. While 8-bit images appear to be continuous in tone with 256 levels (2^8), a 7-bit image may look banded with only 128 tones.

The standards-making body, Commission Internationale de l'Éclairage (CIE), has defined device-independent color spaces, modeled on the way the human eye sees color.

Bitmap (left) images contain only 1 level of tone data. Grayscale images (right) contain 256 levels.

Bitmap Images

Also known as 1-bit images, bitmap images are black-and-white pictures. Each pixel can be only black or white — no grays, no colors. This format is used mainly for high-resolution line art and multimedia projects. Many page–layout programs can colorize and over-print bitmap images without affecting the other graphics behind them.

To convert an image to a bitmap, you first have to change it to a grayscale image. Once you've done that (or if you're working with an image that's already grayscale), the Bitmap mode becomes available (Image>Mode>Grayscale).

There are five options for bitmap conversions:

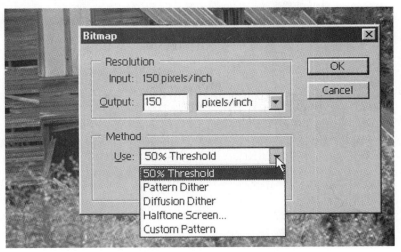

- **50% Threshold**. Every pixel darker than 50% gray turns to black, and every pixel lighter than 50% gray turns white.
- **Pattern Dither**. A pattern of white and black dots is mixed up to form the image.
- **Diffusion Dither**. This option is similar to looking at an image through a window screen. This method usually produces a better-looking result than the Pattern Dither.

- **Halftone Screen.** This option creates a pattern that simulates a printed halftone. You can also choose the shape of the halftone "dot" — including diamonds, lines, and round dots.
- **Custom Pattern.** This option allows you to use a pattern from another image or from part of the current image to create the dither effect.

Grayscale Original

50% Threshold

Pattern Dither

Diffusion Dither

Round Screening (85 lpi)

When preparing bitmaps for printing, the image resolution should match the printer resolution if possible. Otherwise, the imagesetter has to guess whether to make a pixel black or white, which results in undesirable "stairsteps" or "jaggies."

Grayscale

Grayscale images in Adobe Photoshop use up to 256 shades of gray, including black and white. Each pixel uses 8 bits of memory to store a number ranging from 0 (black) to 255 (white), resulting in about a 0.4% difference between each shade of gray. While a 0.4% difference is impossible to see with the human eye, many types of film and density calibration equipment can recognize this minute difference. Some page-layout programs can *colorize* grayscale images, but they cannot usually transparently overprint them; the image *knocks out*, or prevents the printing of items that are beneath it. Grayscale images are the basis for many special effects in Photoshop.

Duotones

Duotones are grayscale images that are printed using two colors of ink. The black plate is typically used to emphasize highlight and shadow areas, and the color emphasizes the midtones. They can only be created from images in Grayscale mode. Duotones are usually used in two-color printed documents to save money while adding interest to the photos.

Photoshop's Duotone mode actually includes monotones, duotones, tritones, and quad-tones, which use one, two, three, and four inks, respectively. Pixels are colorized with a percentage of each ink, depending on their original grayscale values. The curve/ink combination modifies the output without affecting the original grayscale image. The curve data is PostScript information, so duotones can only be printed as EPS files; the actual grayscale pixel color information is stored in 8 bits. While any color may be assigned to the inks, be aware that on-screen colors won't match printed output in most cases.

Gamma

Gamma represents the contrast in the midtones of an image. The monitor's gamma is linear: when viewing a white-to-black gradient on a monitor that has not been color-corrected, the eye perceives the darker shades as encroaching far into the lighter shades. The human eye perceives gamma in a logarithmic fashion, with the darker shades compressed.

Linear gradient (above) and logarithmic gradient (below).

Calibration

The differences in color models mean that it is impossible to get an exact match between the printed page and a computer monitor. For example, true cyan cannot be reproduced on the monitor, and many CMYK greens are very difficult to reproduce on-screen; the monitor can produce a wide array of blues, while the CMYK model is strongly lacking in these hues.

To compensate for the lack of a one-to-one relationship between colors in each model, Photoshop has several methods to control the way it converts between RGB and CMYK and how it adjusts monitor gamma. If a monitor is not gamma-corrected, colors can appear much lighter or darker than they actually print.

Photoshop includes options to adjust the monitor display and to match ink sets used by different color printers or offset presses. For the purposes of this book, the default Photoshop values are fine, but be aware that what is displayed on the screen isn't necessarily what prints.

Calibration is becoming more affordable and accessible to the small design shop or photographer. Several companies offer hardware and software packages that allow you to create your own color profiles. These packages range in price from several hundred to several thousand dollars. The initial cost is soon covered by the increased accuracy of your files and reduced number of proofs or do-overs that are needed to produce accurate color.

Finally, it's important to realize that the purpose of color calibration is not to attempt to rectify all differences between monitors and the printed page; due to the physics of color, it's impossible to create an absolute match. Instead, it is used to create a stable system from which to gain enough experience to allow you to predict how graphics will appear when printed.

Calibrating your monitor to input and output devices is not a replacement for becoming adept at reading color by the numbers provided in the Info palette. Color on your monitor can be skewed by lighting, the reflected color of clothing, temperature, and even your mood.

Converting Between RGB and CMYK

For a decade or more, digital designers have been able to use desktop scanners to place images in their layouts. Recent advances in the quality of desktop scanners and a growing availability of digital stock photography have made the quality of desktop color separations (conversion from RGB to CMYK) much better. As the amount of printed material being repurposed for multimedia grows, more artwork is being converted from CMYK to RGB, as well.

The most important factor in determining when to convert from one color mode to another is knowing where the color is most critical. In today's workflow, many image-makers need to have an excellent RGB file as well as an excellent CMYK file due to the variety of output options available. To achieve this goal, color correcting in RGB, converting to CMYK, and then applying final tweaks is the best method.

A CMYK image has a smaller gamut than an RGB image, but allows for smaller variations in color of the shades it produces. Simply put, images that are converted to and modified in CMYK are going to be different from the same images modified in RGB. The differences between CMYK and RGB begin to stack up as more color changes are made to an image. Consequently, you should never convert back to RGB after converting an image to CMYK.

Techniques such as removing color casts, improving brightness and contrast, revealing fine details, repairing damaged originals, and combining (or compositing) multiple images are all dependent on a knowledge of tones and tonal values.

The difference between the brightest and darkest tones required to reproduce an image is called the tonal range.

Understanding Tonal Values

A vast majority of the images you'll work with — both in this book and as a creative professional — are created from a range of different *tones*. This is true whether they're grayscale images destined for use in a one-color newspaper or flyer, or professional-quality photographs for a full-color magazine. Regardless of their final purpose, tonal values define the nature of all images.

Most advanced techniques and applications relative to tonal values are beyond the scope of this book. The underlying concepts, however, are easily understood.

Light and Dark, Day and Night

Think about the wide variety of scenes we can encounter in our daily lives: a cold, clear winter morning on a ski slope; the brilliance of the stars in the night sky, far from the lights of the city; sea fog drifting ashore on a rainy October afternoon; the dark, rich tones of a leather-bound book.

The point of these exacting details is that some images are very bright, others gray and colorless, and others dark and deep — they're all examples of different *tonal ranges*.

Images contain three primary tonal values: highlights, midtones, and shadows. Let's briefly discuss each of these values:

- Highlights are the brightest areas of an image that actually contain details. The key word in the definition is *details*. A flash of sunlight reflecting from a chrome car bumper isn't a highlight in the true sense of the word (it's actually called a *specular* highlight, but that's for a later discussion). Think of a white rose on a white satin sheet; this is an example of a picture that's made mostly of highlights. This type of bright image is known as a *high key* image.

- Midtones are those tones and shades that fall in the middle of the range — neither totally black nor totally white. Most images — the vast majority of the ones you see in print and on the Web — contain a smooth balance of tones across the midtones range.

- Shadows are the tones that make up the darker areas of images. As is the case in the highlight range, the darkest shadow area is one that contains a certain amount of detail. If an area of an image is totally blacked out, then it's outside the range of the shadow tones. An image that contains most of its tonal values in the shadow region is known as a *low key* image.

Let's take a minute to explore a few different images, and find out how tonal ranges and values differ from one to another.

Look at Tonal Values

1. Start Photoshop. From the File menu, select Open, and navigate to the **RF_Intro_Photoshop** folder. Inside, you'll find an image named **books.psd**. Open the file. It's a picture of some leather-bound books on a shelf.

2. Press Command/Control-L. This command activates the Levels dialog box. Move the dialog box down so it's does not completely obscure the image.

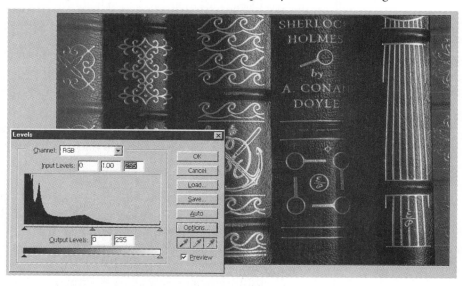

3. Keep both the dialog box and the image open so you can refer back to them as necessary.

Levels

The values of the tones in your image are measured as a series of *levels*. These levels are presented in a graphic called a *histogram* — which is actually visible on your monitor as a component of the Levels dialog box. The histogram is an area chart in the center of the dialog box. Right now, the majority of the tones are on the left (shadow) side of the graph because you're looking at a low key (dark) image.

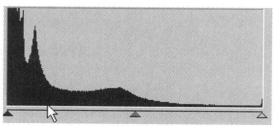

View Different Tonal Values

1. Close both the Levels dialog box (by clicking OK) and the open document (by pressing Command/Control-W or by choosing File>Close). Open the **clouds.psd** file from the **RF_Intro_Photoshop** folder. Activate the Levels dialog box again (press Command/Control-L). This image is built primarily from highlight tones (a high key image), so all the tonal ranges are on the right side of the histogram.

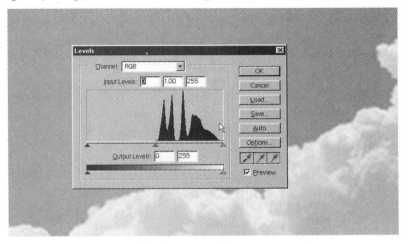

2. Close the Levels dialog box (click OK) and the open file. Now open the file named **ramp.psd** from the **RF_Intro_Photoshop** folder. It's a simple blend that goes from black in the upper-left corner to white on the lower-right corner. Press Command/Control-L access the Levels dialog box and view the histogram.

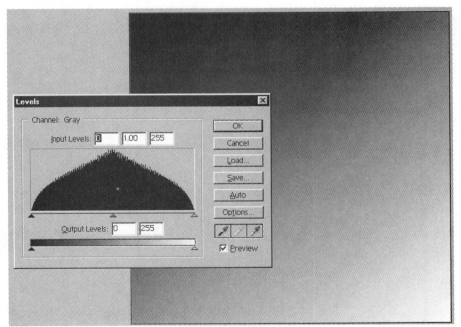

3. You can see that the tones are evenly spread over the entire histogram. Close the Levels dialog box and the image.

As we've already stated, there's a great deal to learn about tonal ranges — although the basic concept is to try to balance the tones in an image so the shadows aren't too dark and the highlights aren't so bright they lose their details (something called being *washed out*).

Automatic Correction

It's going to take some time for you to learn the intricacies of image correction and tonal balance. For now, it's fine if you learn the basic way to automatically correct an image. Automatic correction isn't as good as hand-tuning tonal values, but it's an excellent place to start.

Use Automatic Correction Techniques

1. Open the file named **chairs.psd** from the **RF_Intro_Photoshop** folder. Activate the Levels dialog box. There's a good amount of tonal value all the way on the left (in the shadows), and all the way on the right (in the highlights). Although it's an acceptable image, there is room for improvement.

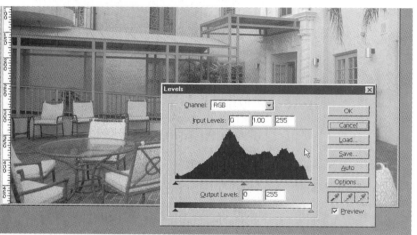

2. Move the slider in the middle of the histogram to the right. The midtones of the image darken considerably. If an image is overly bright, shifting the midtones to the right can bring out details that weren't initially apparent.

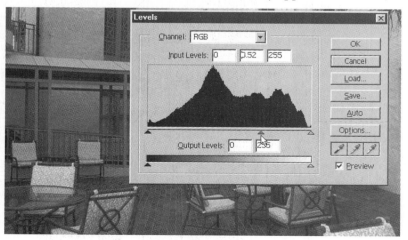

3. Move the midtones slider to the left of center; the image brightens in the midtones. For images that are too dark, adjusting the midtones can result in a more balanced image.

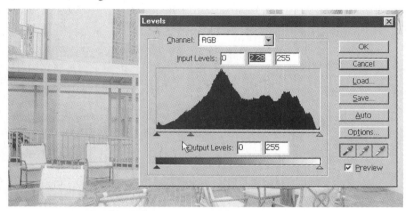

4. Release the slider. Hold down the Option/Alt key, and the Cancel button turns into the Reset button. Click the Reset button, and the image returns to its original state.

5. Now try something different. Instead of moving the midtones slider, move the shadow slider (the one on the left) to the right; then move the highlight slider (the one on the right) to the left. The image sharpens noticeably. This sharpening effect — created by compressing the tonal ranges into a smaller space — increases the *contrast* of the image.

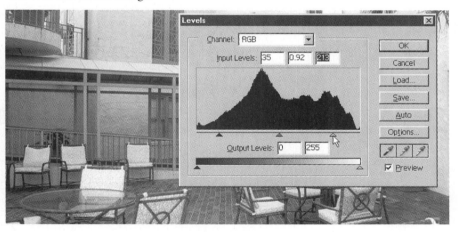

6. Click OK instead of resetting the image. Now activate the Levels dialog box again by pressing Command/Control-L. The histogram is different; there are fewer tones and they're spread over the entire range. The reduced tonal range image is much sharper and has more contrast — but it doesn't contain nearly the depth of tones as the original.

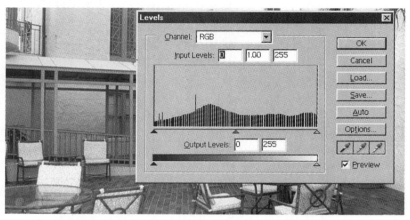

7. You can see this for yourself in the following comparison. The image with the reduced tonal values is on the left, and the original image — with the details in the window frame intact — is on the right.

8. For now, you can take the guesswork out of correcting your images by using Photoshop's Auto Correct functions. From the File menu, select Revert to re-open the original image — before you started modifying the tonal ranges. From the Image menu, select Adjustments>Auto Color.

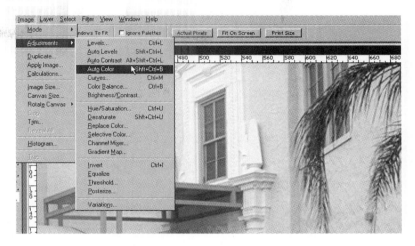

9. Try undoing the menu command (Command/Control-Z) and applying Auto Levels and Auto Contrast. When you're done experimenting, close the file without saving your changes.

If you want, you can try opening a few of the many images found in the **RF_Intro_ Photoshop** folder and looking at their tonal ranges, and examining the effect of Auto Correct and Auto Levels adjustments.

Auto Color is best used for color images; Auto Levels for black and white images. You're free to apply automatic contrast adjustments in the event an image doesn't look as sharp as you think it should; but often times other methods of correcting images — such as sharpening techniques and blur filters — produce much better results than simply compressing the tonal values in an attempt to reveal details.

It is a good idea to move slowly when it comes to correcting color and tonal values in your images, at least until you become comfortable with using the various tools, techniques, and options available in the Photoshop program. Auto-correcting an image usually won't hurt anything; so feel free to experiment, and then inspect the results before you commit the changes to a saved file.

Chapter Summary

In this chapter, you had the opportunity to gain a better understanding of the relationship and dynamics of size, resolution, and color depth, and how they affect the way images display and print. The ability for Photoshop to work with and save images in different color modes allows the designer to use one program to create, alter, and export images in a variety of formats. Whether the image will be used in print production, as a transmitted presentation, or on a Web site, Photoshop can accomplish the tasks. By knowing how colors react, and the limitations of converting one color mode to another, the designer can maintain the highest quality of color in an image.

Images that you will manage in Photoshop may come from a variety of sources and be exported or saved to a number of file types. As you create documents, it is important to know the relationship between resolution and lines per inch for halftone creation. It is equally valuable to know how much resolution should be included in various images prepared for Web application. As you work with a variety of images and different color spaces, you will discover the importance of achieving consistent results.

NOTES

2 The Photoshop Environment

Chapter Objectives:

In this Chapter, you will learn how to move around in the Photoshop working environment, and become familiar with the program's many tools, palettes, menus, toolbars, and dialog boxes. Familiarity and comfort with the Photoshop workspace is a critical step in learning to harness the power of the program. In Chapter 2, you will:

- Learn to manage palettes, menus, and tools.

- Begin to learn keyboard equivalents, which can dramatically improve your efficiency.

- Explore the Photoshop Toolbox, and develop a basic understanding of which tools are used to perform specific tasks.

- Learn about the tool Options bar, which provides tool-specific settings for flexibility and extensive control over how tools function.

- Learn to efficiently navigate around a Photoshop document while you're working.

Projects to be Completed:

- Gulls Poster (A)

- Fallsbridge Menu Cover (B)

- Jazz Postcard (C)

- USA Poster (D)

The Photoshop Environment

In this chapter, we explore the Photoshop working environment — a combination of palettes, toolboxes, option dialogs, windows, and interface elements that comprise the area where you work.

To start Photoshop, you can double-click the application icon, its alias icon (Macintosh) or shortcut (Windows); or you can double-click a Photoshop document icon.

The Workspace

When you start Photoshop, the program briefly displays the title (or splash) screen. Once it's loaded (it may take a few seconds), you'll see the Photoshop environment. In this example, we took the liberty of loading an image. This is what would happen if you double-clicked a file icon, as opposed to double-clicking the application icon, to launch the program.

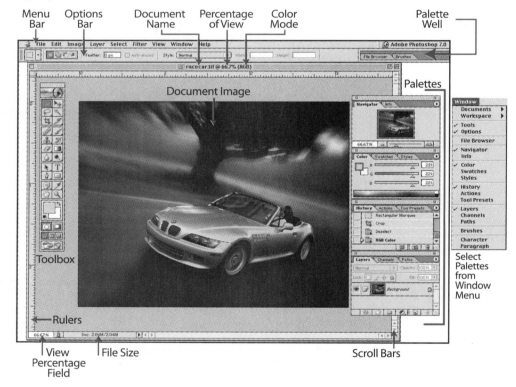

Let's take a few minutes to review the main components of the working environment:

- **Menu Bar.** This bar shows the names of the menus from which you can choose.
- **Toolbox.** This box shows the tools to use for graphic modifications.
- **Document Name.** This area shows the name of the document in use, its file format, view size, color mode, and information about the channels.
- **Color Mode.** This area shows the document's current color mode.
- **Palette Well.** This feature is new to Photoshop 7, and provides a common docking location for your palettes. Once you've dragged a palette (or palette group) onto the Well, a single click displays the palette directly underneath its name tab.
- **Rulers.** These measurement aids are toggled with the Show/Hide Rulers command from the View menu or by pressing Command/Control-R. The units into which they're divided are determined from one of the Preferences categories.
- **Scroll Bars.** Standard in many applications, these navigation aids allow you to scroll the screen up/down/sideways to view the different parts of the image.
- **Color Palette.** This palette enables you to select colors from a variety of color modes and from several color bars.
- **Swatches Palette.** This palette provides a preloaded set of color swatches from which to select; you can load and save custom swatch palettes.
- **Brushes Palette.** This palette allows you to select and adjust brushes.
- **Layers Palette.** This palette is used to manage layers.
- **Channels Palette.** This palette contains controls for viewing individual color components of the image (i.e., the red, green, or blue data), and controls for masking different parts of the image.
- **Paths Palette.** This palette enables creation and adjustment of paths within an image.
- **Navigator Palette.** This palette allows you to move the viewing area to different parts of the image.
- **Info Palette.** This palette provides RGB and CMYK color information, X/Y coordinates of the cursor, and the width and height of a selection within an image.
- **Options Palette.** This palette allows you to adjust settings for different Photoshop tools.
- **Actions Palette.** This palette offers automation features. Several pre-defined actions already exist in the palette, and you can create custom actions by using the palette's recording functions.
- **History Palette.** While you're working, the History palette tracks each command, function, or process you employ. You can use the palette to jump back to a previous state, delete steps, or record a series of processes into an action.

The Photoshop working environment can be customized to suit your specific needs. In fact, you can save different setups — including palette locations, palette availability, palette arrangement, and other display attributes.

Whenever you use Photoshop, the program remembers the settings from your previous session. This means that if you already used the program (or someone else used the machine before you did), settings might not be as you expect — or as they're shown in these exercises.

This list is by no means complete; there are many other dialogs, palettes, and tools that aren't immediately visible when you start the application. You'll work with all of the Photoshop tools as you complete the exercises and projects in this book.

If the file size on the Status bar is clicked and held, a print preview box appears, showing where on the page the image will print at the current print settings. Command/Control-clicking the file size information shows print tiling information; Option/Alt-clicking displays information about the size, resolution, and color depth of the image. Clicking the arrow to the right of the file size allows you to select what is displayed in the window: document size, dimensions, profile, scratch sizes, efficiency, timing, or the tool currently in use.

Although Photoshop might seem intimidating at first, you don't need to know every available command, tool, and technique before you start using the program. Your knowledge of the program will grow as you use it. Even the most experienced users learn a new feature or technique when they work on new projects; the same will undoubtedly be true for you.

Customize the Photoshop Environment

1. Start Photoshop. To ensure the screen images in this exercise match what you see on your monitor, select Workspace>Reset Palette Locations from the Window menu. Then, from the Edit menu, select Preferences>Display & Cursors. Set Painting Cursors to Brush Size, and Other Cursors to Precise. Click OK when you're done.

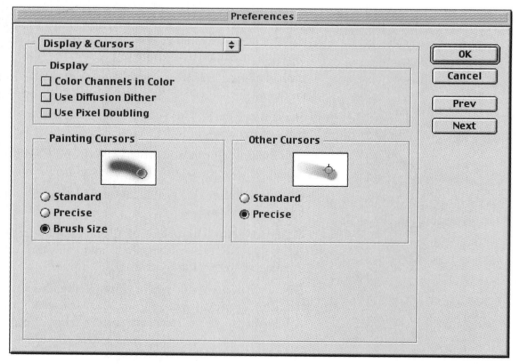

If your monitor is very cluttered, it might be hard to see the palette you're looking for. If the selection is checked on the Window menu, try toggling the display off and on again — that way you can see it when it appears.

2. Palettes may be moved on screen by dragging the bar at the top of the palette. Click and hold the bar at the top of the Layers/Channels/Paths palette, and drag it around. You find the palettes are "magnetic" — if they get close to one another, they stick together. They also stick to the edges of your monitor. This makes it easy to organize them.

3. Click on the Window menu to see a list of palettes. Those with checkmarks are already active; palettes that don't have the checkmark aren't currently showing/active.

4. If it is not active, select Info from the Window menu to show the Info palette. If the palette group is not visible, the entire palette group reappears on screen with the chosen tab activated.

5. From the Window menu, select Info to remove the checkmark; the entire group disappears.

6. Palettes may be separated from, or moved between, palette groups by dragging a tab from one group to another. Click a tab on any palette, and drag it onto the work area or to another palette group.

7. You can also dock palettes vertically. To do so, select the tab you want to dock, and drag it to the bottom of the group where you want to dock it. It appears at the bottom of the group. It stays there until you drag it onto the work area or onto the group itself.

8. If you frequently use certain palettes and want to keep your screen free of clutter, you can drag the palettes to the Palette Well in the upper-right corner of the monitor. Click on their tabs and drag them to the Palette Well. To access any palette in the Well, click its tab. You can drag them out of the Well using the same technique in reverse.

9. Palettes may also be docked to the Palette Well through their pop-up menus (found under the arrow icon at the upper-right corner of each palette).

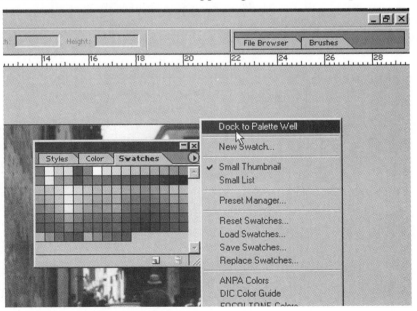

Docking frequently used palettes to the Palette Well reduces clutter and increases efficiency.

10. To make certain the palettes on our monitors look alike, let's reset them to Photoshop's defaults. From the Window menu, select Workspace>Reset Palette Locations. Also note you can save a custom workspace for later recall. Set up your screen the way you prefer, and then select Window>Workspace>Save Workspace. You are asked to name your custom workspace. It's now available from the workspace list. This allows for customization based on task or operator preference.

Create a New Document

1. From the File menu, select New. The New dialog box appears. Select Letter from the Preset Sizes pop-up menu, and change the Resolution to 300 pixels/inch. Set the Mode to RGB Color, and select White from the Contents section.

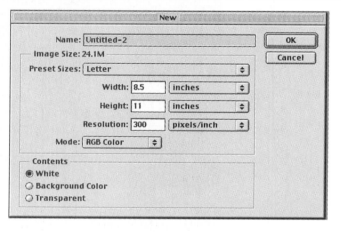

2. The New dialog box has three sections. The Name section allows you to enter a name for your document. In the Name box, type "first_image". Image Size controls the dimensions, image resolution, and color mode of the document. The width and height of the image can be set in pixels, inches, centimeters, points, picas, or columns by clicking the pop-up list. Each dimension has arrows that allow you to increase or decrease the value. A new feature in Photoshop 7 provides a selection of preset sizes as shown.

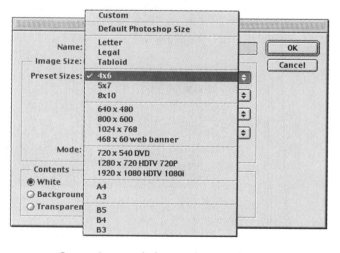

Preset sizes can help speed up production.

3. Set the measurement units to inches. Enter "4" for Width and "3" for Height. Press the Tab key after entering each value to advance to the next field.

4. Click the pop-up list next to the Width setting. Select the picas setting. Notice the 4 changed to 24; there are 6 picas to an inch, and Photoshop automatically made this calculation for you.

5. Change the units back to inches; the values change again. For our first image, set the Width and Height dimensions to inches.

6. If the dimension units are set to anything except pixels, the Resolution setting also changes the image size. Type "300" in the Resolution field; then type "50" in the Resolution field. Notice how the image file size changed with each new resolution setting.

7. The units pop-up list next to the Resolution setting allows the resolution to be interpreted as either pixels/inch or pixels/cm (centimeter).

8. Changing units of measurement does not affect file size; it merely changes the default size at which certain applications (including page-layout programs such as Adobe FrameMaker, Adobe InDesign, Adobe PageMaker, and QuarkXPress) initially display the image when it is imported. For this image, set the Resolution to 72 and units of measurement to pixels/inch.

9. The last Image Size section is Mode. Even though Photoshop can work in eight different color modes (which we'll discuss later in the book), only five modes are available when creating a new document. For now, set the Mode to RGB.

10. The final section in the New dialog box is Contents. This option sets the initial background of your file. The choices are White, Background Color, and Transparent. Make certain the White radio button is selected, and click OK.

11. This is your first Photoshop document; keep it open for the next exercise.

Before we save the document, let's return to the Preferences menu. It's a good idea to save files with the appropriate file extensions. If you're working on a Windows-based system, the extension is saved automatically (even if you don't see it); on a Macintosh, the extensions are not automatically saved, but you should consider using them to ensure quick and accurate file selection.

Set Preferences for Saving Files

1. Continue working in the open document. Select Preferences>File Handling from the Edit menu.

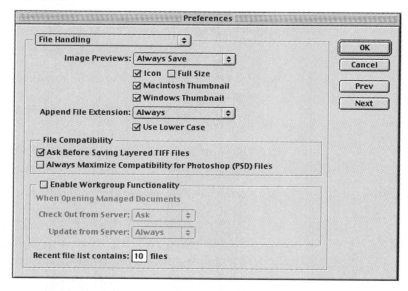

2. If you're on a Macintosh, check the Always option for the Append File Extension setting.

3. Click OK. This may seem to be a small detail, but it means that Photoshop always selects the correct file extension for you — it's one less setting you have to make.

4. You may choose to turn off the Always Maximize Compatibility for Photoshop (PSD) Files check box. Leaving this box checked results in larger file sizes, as Photoshop saves a *flattened file* (all layers merged into a single layer) as well as the layered file.

Save the Document

1. Continue working in the open document. Select Save As from the File menu.

2. Click the Format/Save As box to see the list of formats from which to choose. Scroll down to the bottom and highlight TIFF (Tagged Image File Format).

Just when you thought you understood the meaning of the term "navigate", another use for the word arises: navigating around files and folders from within the Save (or Open) dialog box. This usage refers to moving up and down through the folders on your hard drive. Don't let these multiple uses confuse you — navigate always refers to moving around in some manner.

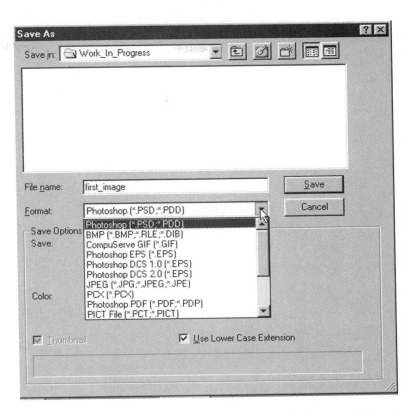

3. Navigate to your **Work_In_Progress** folder. Save the image as "first_image", and click Save. Notice that Photoshop automatically attaches the .tif file extension.

4. The document is being saved as a TIFF file, which causes an extra dialog box to appear. Image Compression options allow you to make the file size considerably smaller. Although not all programs support compression, most offer this support. For our purposes, select LZW for Image Compression, and Macintosh for the Byte Order.

Even if you're working on a Windows-based system, the Macintosh/LZW format is perfectly acceptable and fully compliant with other Windows applications. It's best if you get into the habit of using as few different formats as possible, and this one works perfectly well for both Macintosh and Windows platforms.

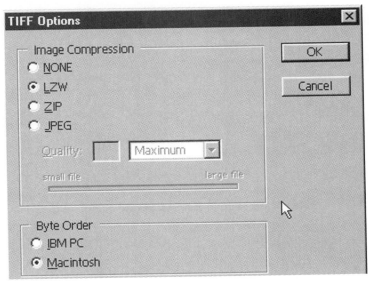

5. Click OK to complete the process.

Navigating

In almost all cases — with very few exceptions — you need to move around an image while you're working on it. One example of navigation is zooming into a specific area of a picture so you can fix a problem; another is the need to zoom out so you can see the entire image at once. Sometimes you'll want to use every available inch of your monitor; other times you might want Photoshop on half your monitor and Illustrator (or another application) on the remainder. It all depends on what you're doing at any particular moment.

Each of these scenarios — and many others — requires the ability to efficiently navigate, as well as take full advantage of the various document-viewing modes.

Move Around an Image

In recent years, the term navigation has become associated with Web pages and other interactive formats — where the user clicks buttons, text elements, or graphic objects to move to different sections of a site (or presentation). In this book, we use the term to denote moving around a Photoshop document.

1. From the File menu, select Open. Navigate to the **RF_Intro_Photoshop** folder, and open the file named **strand_keywest.psd**. It's a photograph of a famous old movie theatre in downtown Key West, Florida.

2. Activate the Navigator palette (Window>Navigator). On the palette is a small slider that can be used to change the viewing percentage. Slide it all the way to the left. You zoom all the way out of the image. Notice the small red rectangle on the preview in the palette. It represents how much of the image you see. Now move the slider to the right. You zoom into the image and the red rectangle shrinks accordingly.

3. You can also type a fixed percentage into the field on the lower left of the palette. Click in the field, delete the current percentage, and enter "300". The Hand tool should be active at this point (if not, select it from the Toolbox). Place it on the image, and try pushing the picture around the monitor. Notice that the red rectangle in the Navigator palette moves at the same time.

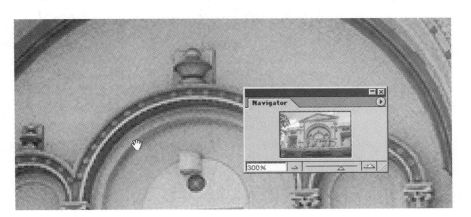

4. Press Command/Control-0 (zero). The image resizes to fill the available space. Watch the Navigator palette or the Title bar to see the current view percentage.

5. Press the "F" key. The first time you press it, Photoshop takes over the entire monitor — neither other menus, nor the desktop, are visible. Press it again, and the image appears on a black background. This is the preferred view for color retouching and painting assignments because it's the least distracting. To return to regular view, press the "F" key one more time.

6. When you're done experimenting with moving and resizing the view, close the file without saving it.

Keyboard Navigation

As you learn Photoshop, you'll find there are many different ways to perform similar tasks. For example, you can select the Zoom tool by clicking on it in the Toolbox or by pressing the "Z" key. In addition, you can zoom by:

- Selecting Zoom In or Zoom Out from the View menu.
- Pressing Command/Control-plus (+) or Command/Control-minus (-).
- Pressing Command/Control-Spacebar or Option/Alt-Spacebar to temporarily toggle the Zoom tool + or -.
- Changing the view percentage in the lower-left corner of the window.
- Changing the scale factor on the Navigator palette.

All of these options work; but for novice Photoshop users, it is easiest to concentrate on a few shortcuts that work for the widest variety of tasks. You will gradually learn the rest of the shortcuts as you become more familiar with the program.

From the list above, the two best zoom choices are Command/Control-Spacebar and the Navigator palette. When dialog boxes are open, the items in the Toolbox are not available; the character sequence Command/Control-Spacebar temporarily activates the Zoom tool from nearly any dialog box, as well as when working on the document with another tool. The Navigator palette combines the functionality of both the Zoom and Hand tools in a visual format; using this palette allows you to quickly and easily navigate your document.

We've already listed several keyboard commands in the material covered so far. Here are a few additional useful keyboard combinations available in Photoshop:

- **Option Key (Macintosh) or Alt Key (Windows).** This key, used with any painting tool, temporarily toggles the Eyedropper tool.
- **Shift Key.** This key, when used while dragging any painting or effects tool, constrains tool movement to horizontal, vertical, or diagonal (45 degree) lines.
- **"D" Key.** This key returns the swatch colors to their default setting of black and white.
- **"X" Key.** This key swaps the foreground and background colors.
- **Delete Key (Macintosh) or Backspace Key (Windows)**. This key fills a selection with the background color when in a background layer or a channel.
- **Option-Delete (Macintosh) or Alt-Backspace (Windows)**. These keys fill a selection with the current foreground color.
- **Option/Alt Keys**. Pressing these keys while in many dialog boxes changes the Cancel button to Reset, allowing you to reset the dialog box to its default values without starting over.
- **Command/Control-0 (Zero)**. This key combination makes your image fit your screen
- **Command/Control-Option/Alt-0 (Zero)**. This shows your image at 100%.
- **Spacebar**. This key activates the Hand tool.

Remember, nearly every tool in Photoshop has a keyboard equivalent. If you're not certain of the shortcut for a particular tool, move the cursor over the tool in the Toolbox, and hold it there for a few seconds. A help box appears, showing the name of the tool and its shortcut (in parenthesis).

The Photoshop Toolbox

Most of the work you do in Photoshop requires the use of tools — which are found in the Toolbox. To select a tool, either click on its icon in the Toolbox, or press the associated key. You can see the keyboard equivalents in this illustration.

Although each space on the Toolbox displays a single icon, tools can also be components in a set of related tools.

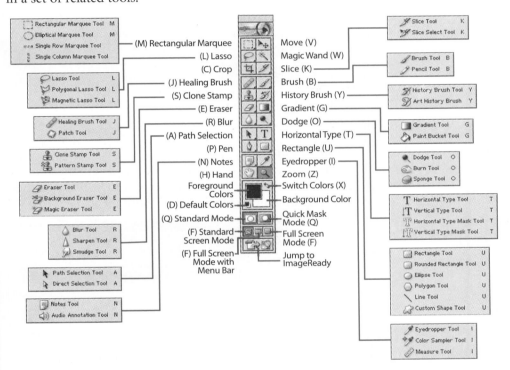

To select an alternate tool (one that's not currently visible in the Toolbox), click the tool, hold down the mouse button, and drag to the tool you need. When you release the mouse button, the new tool is selected. You can also cycle through certain groups of similar tools using the keyboard command for that tool group. For example, pressing the "L" key moves through the three different lasso tools (which you'll learn about in the chapter on Selections).

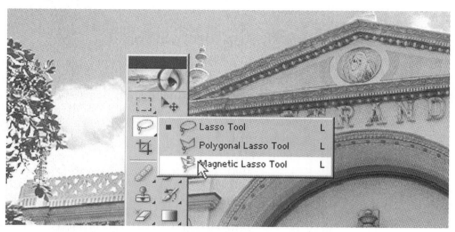

Many tools are part of a set; to access an alternate tool, click and drag to select the desired icon/tool.

Tool Options

Most tools have specific options associated with them; if you're using a selection tool, the tolerance or shape of the selection area can be set, as well as certain other attributes. These options are shown on a bar above the image.

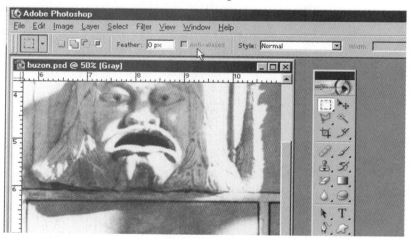

If you're using the Shapes tool, the options offer settings related directly to creating shapes, as opposed to those associated with selecting portions of an image.

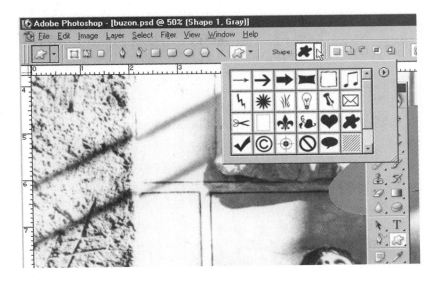

Selection Tools

The first four tools in the Toolbox, the Type Mask tool, and the Vertical Type Mask tool (with an outlined capital "T") are used for isolating and repositioning specific areas of an image without affecting the rest of the picture. Here is an overview of other tools in the Toolbox:

- **Marquee Tools.** These tools allow you to select areas of the image within its boundaries. A marquee may be elliptical, rectangular, or a single row of pixels.

- **Move Tool.** This tool allows you to move a selection or layer within the boundaries of the Document window.

- **Lasso, Polygonal Lasso, and Magnetic Lasso Tools.** These tools allow you to draw freehand marquees, capturing an image area within its boundary. The Lasso is used to draw a freehand marquee that encircles parts of the image; the Polygonal Lasso tool uses straight lines created by point-to-point clicking; the Magnetic Lasso tool traces an edge on the basis of the color of the pixels and the tolerances you set for the tool.

- **Magic Wand.** This tool allows you to capture contiguous or noncontiguous pixels that are similar to the initial pixel upon which you clicked. The range of pixels selected is determined by the Tolerance setting on the Magic Wand Options bar.

- **Crop Tool.** This tool allows you to permanently cut off (crop) parts of an image.

- **Slice and Slice Select Tools.** These tools allow you to create user-defined slices of an image for creation of Web graphics.

Painting Tools

The next set of tools is defined as painting tools. Painting tools add or remove pixels from images. They're similar to their physical counterparts and include paint brushes, sponges, airbrush tools, pencils, pens, patching tools, and tools that can remove imperfections from photos. There's even a tool that removes paint after it has been placed on the page; it moves the pixels back to a previous time, before you performed the action that needs to be fixed. Here is a brief description of the painting tools; you'll use them all before the end of the book:

- **Paintbrush Tool.** This tool allows you to apply color to an image. The width of the stroke is determined by the brush selected from the Brushes toolbar. The paint engine in Photoshop 7 is completely revamped and creates much more organic and painterly effects.

- **Pencil Tool**. The Pencil tool creates hard-edged lines. Generally, this tool is useful only when working with bitmapped images, which are hard-edged by nature.

- **Healing Brush and Patch Tools.** These tools behave in a manner very similar to the Stamp tool. They are new tools in Photoshop 7. They use complex calculations to adjust the color and texture of added pixels to match the existing pixels that surround them. These features make cloning in a gradient easier than ever before, and work well when retouching skin tones.

- **Clone Stamp and Pattern Stamp Tools.** These tools overprint part of an image to another area within the same image or into another image. The Clone Stamp tool duplicates one part of the image to the other from a reference point on the image; each stroke paints more of the image. The Pattern Stamp tool uses the rectangular selection marquee to select part of the image as a pattern. The Pattern Maker filter then defines the pattern. It paints over designated parts of the image with that repetitive pattern.

- **History Brush Tool.** This tool repaints parts of an image to any selected state or snapshot in the History palette. The desired state is selected by turning on the History Brush source at the far left of each listed state or snapshot. The Art History Brush paints with stylized strokes to any selected state or snapshot in the History palette.

- **Eraser Tools.** These three tools are stacked under the Eraser icon. The Eraser tool enables you to paint with any of the other painting tools by selecting a brush size and erasing a saved state on the History palette. The Background Eraser tool erases areas over which it is dragged to create transparency. The Magic Eraser tool converts solid colors to transparency with a single click.

- **Gradient and Paint Bucket Tools.** The Gradient tool creates linear, radial, angular, and reflected gradients — smooth blends between shades of a single color, between two colors, or as a mixture of several colors and transparent areas. Linear gradients are smooth gradations in tone in a straight line. The reflected gradient produces a mirror-image linear gradient with each side of the image representing half of the total width. Radial and diamond gradients begin at a center point and radiate in concentric circles or diamonds from one color to another. The angular gradient creates shades in a counterclockwise sweep around the beginning point of a blended area. Photoshop comes with a set of gradients; you can also create and save custom sets of gradients. The Paint Bucket tool fills areas of similar color with the foreground color or a pattern. By adjusting the tolerance, you can determine how close the color of the image pixels needs to be in order to be affected by the tool.

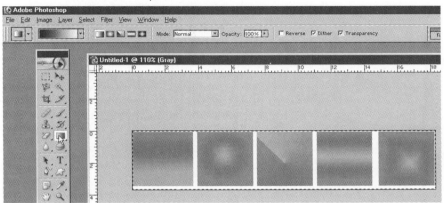

The last two tool sets in this section of the Toolbox are used to apply effects to specific areas of an image. They can blur or sharpen parts of an image, simulate the effects of a damp sponge (essentially reducing or increasing the color saturation, or intensity, of the image), and dodge (lighten) and burn (darken) areas. You'll have an opportunity to work with all of the tools as we move forward.

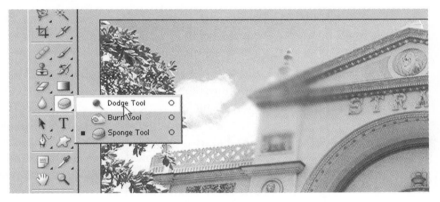

Path Tools

If you've ever worked with Adobe Illustrator, or another program designed to create vector art, you will find the path tools are relatively familiar:

- **Path (Component) Selection and Direct Selection Tools**. These tools are used to manipulate individual paths. The path is chosen with the Path Component Selection tool; individual elements, such as anchor points and segments, may be selected and manipulated using the Direct Selection tool.

- **Type Tools**. These tools are used to create type filled with the foreground color (by default) or any other color you select. Type is created on a special type layer that is labeled on the Layers palette with a "T". This is "live" type and may be edited at any time. When the Type tool is active, the Vertical Type tool and Type Mask tool are available from the Options toolbar; type may be set vertically, or a type shape may be created directly with the Type Mask tool on a normal image layer.

- **Pen Tools**. The Pen tools pop-up menu contains seven tools for selecting, creating, and editing paths. Paths may be created directly in Photoshop or pasted from the clipboard from Adobe Illustrator. The standard Pen tool creates paths using Bézier curves. The Freeform Pen tool allows you to draw a path as if you were drawing the path on paper, while you draw completely "freehand" with the Freeform tool. Add Anchor Point and Delete Anchor Point tools are self-explanatory — they either add or delete points on a path. The Convert Anchor Point tool changes corner points to smooth points and smooth points to corner points.

- **Shape Tools**. These tools include the Rectangle, Rounded Rectangle, Ellipse, Polygon, Line, and Custom Shape tools. While these tools are mostly self-explanatory, note that the Line tool draws straight lines in an image, with or without arrowheads, and can also be used as a measuring device. Photoshop ships with a number of custom shapes. You may also create custom shapes, and add or edit shape libraries.

Tools That Provide Information

This set of tools is designed to provide information about your images. They also provide the ability to place written notes and audio annotations (so other team members can understand your design processes), and tools that can both show you the color values in a specific spot on an image, and assign that color to the background or foreground swatches. Here is an overview of the information tools:

- **Notes and Audio Annotated Notes Tools.** These tools allow you to attach comments to an image. This can be particularly useful during an editing cycle. The notes are automatically saved with the document.

- **Eyedropper and Color Sampler Tools.** These tools are used to select and monitor color for adjusting an image. The Eyedropper tool allows you to select foreground and background colors, either from a color palette or directly from an image. You can sample the color of a single pixel, or average the color of an area 3 pixels × 3 pixels or 5 pixels × 5 pixels. Simply clicking on the image changes the foreground color used for painting. You can change the background color by holding down the Option/Alt key while clicking on the color sample. The Color Sampler tool allows you to place up to 4 sample markers that can then be monitored from the Info palette. Delete a sample by holding down the Option/Alt key while clicking on the color sample. The pop-up menu for this item also includes the Measure tool, with which you can obtain information about the size of elements within an image, much the same as using a ruler.

Use the Eyedropper Tool

1. From the File menu, choose Open, and navigate to the **RF_Intro_Photoshop** folder. Select the file named **sailboat_beach.tif**.

2. Select the Eyedropper tool from the Toolbox.

3. Drag the Eyedropper tool across the image. Observe how the foreground color swatch near the bottom of the Toolbox changes as you move through the different colors in the image.

4. Release the mouse button when you see a color you like on the foreground color swatch. The foreground color changes to that color.

5. Change the background color swatch by holding down the Option/Alt key as you drag again. Stop when you find a color you like for the background.

6. Use the Marquee tool to select a portion of the photo. Press the Delete key. The deleted portion is filled with the background color. Press Command/Control-Z to undo this deletion. Press Command/Control-D to deselect all.

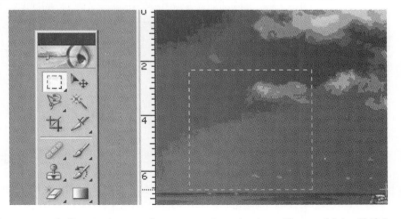

The Marquee tool allows you to make rectangular selections; if you add the Shift key while dragging the cursor on an image, the shape is constrained to a perfect square.

7. Select the Eraser tool from the Toolbox. Drag the Eraser tool across the photo several times. Observe how the Eraser paints the background color in its path.

8. Now click on the Eraser tool, and select the Background Eraser from the pop-up menu. Drag it across the image. This time, the background turns transparent.

9. Finally, select the Magic Eraser tool from the Eraser pop-up menu. Set the Tolerance to 16. Click anywhere in the sky. It selects all contiguous colors within its assigned tolerance and turns the background transparent.

10. Select Revert from the File menu, and leave the file open for the next exercise.

Tools That Affect Views

The last set of tools changes the way an image is displayed on your monitor:

- **Hand Tool.** This tool allows you to move the image around within the Document window.

- **Zoom Tool.** This tool is represented by an icon that resembles a magnifying glass. This tool enlarges the area of the screen where you click, allowing you to see fine details within the image. When you click and drag, you can draw a marquee box that isolates and magnifies a specific area of your page. To reduce the image, you can press the Option/Alt key while using the tool.

Use Other Information Tools

1. Select the Zoom tool by clicking on the white magnifying glass near the bottom of the Toolbox. Click the tool on the image several times. The view gets larger on the screen. If you zoom in more closely, you can see the individual pixels on the screen. This technique is similar to using the Navigator palette as we did earlier.

2. Drag the magnifying glass to zoom in closely on an area in the image.

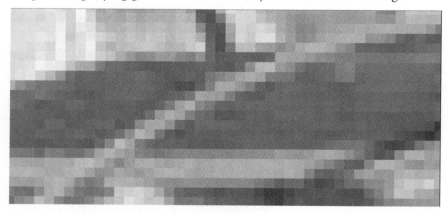

3. Notice the percentage listed in the lower-left corner of the Image window. This is the current image view percentage in pixels; 100% means there is 1 pixel displayed on screen for each pixel in the image; 200% means that each image pixel is displayed by 4 screen pixels (2×2), and so on. Click in this box, enter the value "400", and press the Return/Enter key. The image view changes to reflect the new scale percentage.

Command/Control-plus (+) zooms into the image; Command/Control-minus (-) zooms out. Command/Control-0 (zero) fits the image into the available space.

4. Hold down the Option/Alt key. The plus (+) sign inside the magnifying glass turns into a minus (-) sign. Now click the image with the Zoom tool, and notice the view zooms out, making the image smaller. Double-click the Zoom tool (not the image), and the image returns to 100%.

5. Double-click on the Hand tool in the Toolbox. The image displays as large as possible on the screen.

6. Close the document without saving.

Other Toolbox Controls

The bottom of the Toolbox palette holds a few additional controls:

- The color swatches, which you have already used, display the current foreground and background colors.

- Clicking the foreground or background swatch activates Photoshop's Color Picker. It allows you to directly enter color information according to one of several color modes.

- Clicking on the tiny black-and-white swatches in the lower-left corner of the palette, or pressing the "D" key on the keyboard resets the foreground and background colors to their defaults — black and white. At the upper right of the swatches is a small curve with arrows on both ends; this is the Switch Colors icon. Click this icon or press the "X" key on the keyboard to swap foreground and background colors.

- The two rectangles inscribed with circles set the painting mode. Regular mode, the icon on the left, is the default for painting. The icon on the right, Quick Mask, allows you to create a marquee selection using painting tools rather than the marquee tools. The "Q" icon allows toggling between the modes.

- The next three buttons at the bottom of the Toolbox are window controls. They change the way Photoshop displays the image on your monitor. The left icon can display multiple images, each in its own window; this is Photoshop's default mode. The middle icon displays a full-screen image on a neutral gray background. The last icon in this section also displays a full-screen image, but on a black background with no visible menus. The "F" icon allows toggling among the modes.

- The final button is Jump to ImageReady, for use with Web images.

Chapter Summary

Photoshop's working environment is designed to provide control of your artwork and to present feedback as you prepare documents. Paying attention to details, such as making the effort to establish preferences that reflect the way you work, pays timesaving dividends during the production cycle. It is also the best way to prevent errors from creeping into your workflow as you use documents created in Photoshop in other applications.

Getting to know your tools is an important part of mastering any craft. As you develop skills throughout this book, you will come to know which tools are most efficient for each task; in time, you will automatically select the appropriate tool. You will use tools to effectively gather information as you create images, select elements upon which to apply special effects, and modify portions of images to achieve a desired result.

3 *Selection Techniques*

Chapter Objectives:

As you work through this chapter, you will learn the importance of solid selection skills. You'll come to understand how Photoshop's various selection tools can be used to isolate and protect specific portions of an image, and how to develop complex selections. As you gain more experience, you will know which selection tool should be used to generate the best results in the most efficient manner. In Chapter 3, you will:

- Learn the basics of selection techniques, and how they all share certain attributes.

- Find out how anti-aliasing is used to create smooth edges on your selections.

- Explore the lasso, marquee, and Magic Wand tools, and learn about the types of selections they produce.

- Discover how to modify your selections.

- Experiment with transformation tools that can duplicate, scale, rotate, flip, and distort selections.

- Find out how to save and load selections for later use, or for use in another document.

Projects to be Completed:

- Gulls Poster (A)

- Fallsbridge Menu Cover (B)

- Jazz Postcard (C)

- USA Poster (D)

Photoshop techniques and functions can either be applied globally (to an entire image) or locally (to a selected portion of the image).

When combining images, changing backgrounds, replacing colors, or performing other image-editing tasks, selection techniques are only part of the equation; layers, channels, masks, and other functions also come into play. Knowing how to quickly and effectively make complex selections, however, is arguably the most important skill you can develop.

Selection Techniques

Photoshop includes many tools that can be used to modify an entire image; a blur filter can be applied to the whole picture, or the intensity of a yellow cast can be reduced globally using the Curves control. In many cases, however, you will want to limit changes to specific portions of an image.

If you wished to change a model's sweater from red to blue, you would first make a careful selection of the pixels that comprise the sweater portion of the image, and then change the hue (color) of only those selected pixels. In another example, a photograph of a model home was taken on an overcast day, but you feel the image would be much more effective with a blue sky. To make this modification, you would select the pixels that make up the sky, and use the File>Paste Into command to replace the area with a bright blue sky.

The motorcycle in the left image was selected using a variety of tools. The selection was then inversed, so the sky became the selected area instead of the motorcycle; this protected the cycle while we changed the background to the one you see on the right.

Without a doubt, one of the most important Photoshop skills you can develop is the ability to make accurate selections. If you understand selections and how they work, you will be well on your way to mastering the use of many Photoshop functions.

The conventional airbrush artist uses a clear plastic masking material called *frisket* to cover areas of the artwork that shouldn't be altered. Photoshop selections are simply an electronic version of this physical technique; areas outside the selection area are protected from change — exactly as they would be if they were covered with plastic.

A selected area is highlighted by a blinking marquee, often called *marching ants.* When you apply paint tools, filters, or other controls, they only affect pixels within the selected area.

The terms "select" and "selection" are also used when discussing which buttons in dialog boxes and Option menus to choose. In the present context, "selection" refers to any technique that allows modification of parts of an image while protecting the rest of the image from change.

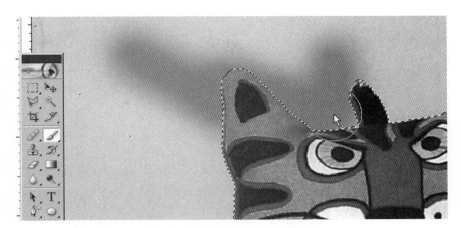

In this example, you can see that the cat's head is protected, while the background area is colored by the paintbrush.

Selections can be made using selection tools or by activating layers that contain individual components of the image in Photoshop. There are many different ways to use the selection tools on specific pixels in an image. We'll explore several methods in this chapter.

Common Selection Tool Attributes

Although each of the tools works in a slightly different manner, the end results are the same — one or more selected areas. Each of the tools also shares certain common traits, which are the same regardless of which tool you're using to create a selection. These commonalities can be seen in the Options palette toolbar.

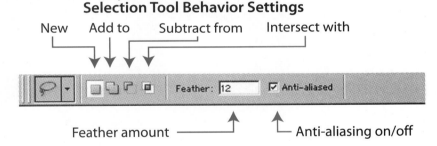

As you work with the selection tools, you'll get a chance to use all of these common options; for now it will help to briefly describe them:

Profile Mismatch Errors: When you're opening an image, you may get an error message that says that the embedded color profile contained in the image doesn't match the one you're currently using. If this happens, refer back to the Getting Started section to learn how to disable the warning. Color profiles will be discussed in Chapter 10.

- **Selection Tool Behavior Settings**. These four icons determine what happens when you use one of the selection tools. "New" is the first button; it creates a new selection. "Add to" is the second button; it adds to existing selections. "Subtract from" is the third button; it removes portions of an existing selection. "Intersect with" is the last button; it results in a selection that is the intersection of existing and new selection areas.

In this example, we selected a rectangular area, and then created an oval selection using the Intersect with selection behavior. The resulting selection is the area where the two overlapped.

- **Feather Amount**. Feathering is a technique that softens the edges of a selection. If feathering is set to 0 (zero), selections have hard edges; as you increase the feathering amount, the edges become increasingly fuzzy. In this example, we created 3 selections and deleted the contents. In the first circle, the feathering was set to 0 pixels; in the second, it was set to 20 pixels; in the third, it was set to 50 pixels. You can see the effect quite clearly.

All three of these circular selections are the same size; you can see that feathering softens the edge of each selection from the outside in.

- **Anti-Aliasing**. Anti-aliasing helps to blend the edge of a selection into the surrounding pixels. In the following example, the selection on the left was done without anti-aliasing; you can see that the edges of the circle are jagged (undesirable effect). On the right, the edges of the circle appear much smoother (desirable effect). They slowly blend into the colors of the background. Both selections were filled with gray to make them more visible.

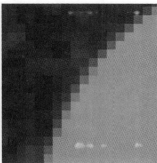

The circle on the left exhibits a jagged edge; the one on the right (details of which can be seen in the second image) uses anti-aliasing, which smoothly blends the edge into the surrounding pixels.

When you're using the Rectangular Marquee tool, you don't have access to anti-aliasing; the check box is turned off and dimmed. The tool creates straight-sided selections that don't benefit from the technique.

Basic Selection Tools

There is a wide variety of techniques that can be used to select regions of an image; so many, in fact, that it's best to start with basic tools and move on to more complex selection methods once we have a solid understanding of how they work.

There are several categories of selection tools:

- **Marquee Tools**. Marquee tools are used to select rectangular or oval areas.
- **Lasso Tools**. Lasso tools are used to select irregular areas.
- **Magic Wand Tool**. This tool is used to select areas containing similar colors or tones.

You'll get a chance to work with each of the selection tools as we move forward.

The Marquee Tools

There are four Marquee Selection tools. To see them all, click the Marquee tool (on the upper-left corner of the Toolbox) and hold the mouse button down for a moment.

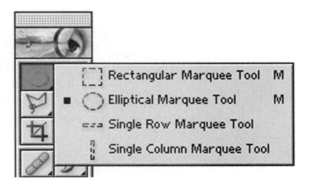

The Rectangular Marquee tool creates rectangular or square selections (normally with square corners, but certain attributes, such as feathering, can soften them). The Elliptical Marquee tool, on the other hand, selects oval or circular areas.

To select an area with one of the tools, click the tool on the edge of the area you want, and drag the mouse. Any pixels contained within the boundaries of the shape are selected, and display the "marching ants". It doesn't matter if you drag up, down, or to the left or right. The selection begins where you first click, and ends where you release the mouse button. Both the Rectangular and Elliptical Marquee tools work the same way.

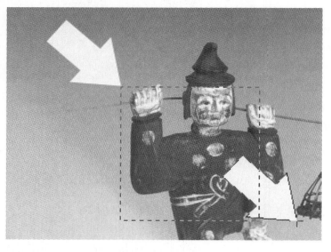

In this example, we clicked on the upper left and dragged down to the lower right. We could have started on the lower right and dragged up and left to select the same area.

In addition to the common options attributes (New, Add, Subtract, Intersect, Feathering, and Anti-aliasing), you can control other aspects of the Rectangular and Elliptical Marquee tools. For example, you can set a Fixed aspect ratio (such as 3:1, or 5:4) of a selection, or fix the size of the selection itself.

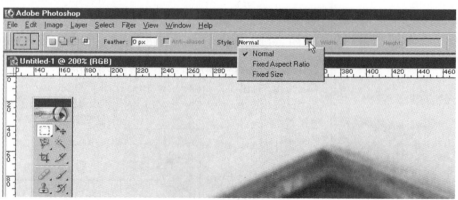

At first, selection tools may seem difficult to use, but as you become more familiar with how they work — and how you can control their behavior — making complex selections becomes second nature.

Use the Rectangular Marquee Tool

1. Open the file **oranges.tif** from the **RF_Intro_Photoshop** folder. Press the "D" key to return the background and foreground colors to their defaults (black and white).

2. Press the "F" key once. The image fills the screen, surrounded by a neutral gray background.

3. Click the Rectangular Marquee tool on the Toolbox, or press the "M" key (for marquee). If pressing the "M" key selects the Elliptical Marquee tool, either change it on the Toolbar or press the Shift-M keys.

4. Drag the tool diagonally over the image to form a rectangle, and then release the mouse button. A selection rectangle of "marching ants" appears.

5. Sometimes you'll need a square selection rather than a rectangular selection. Press Command/Control-D to deselect the current selection. Draw another rectangular selection; but this time, hold down the Shift key while making the selection. The shape is constrained to a square.

6. Keep the image open and the selection intact for the next exercise.

Add to and Subtract from Selections

1. In the open image, make a new selection, and then click the "Add to" selection button on the Options toolbar. Draw several more selections. Each one is added to the selection you previously made.

2. Click the "New" selection button, and draw a new selection. Notice that the previous selections were deselected. Now hold down the Shift key and make another selection. Instead of constraining your selection to a square, the second rectangle is added to the first selection. The Shift key adds to a selection when another selection already exists within the image.

3. Begin another selection; but this time, press the Shift key after you begin making your selection. The first selection disappears, and another square is drawn.

4. Let's add a square to an existing selection. Press the Shift key, and then start a new selection; release the Shift key, and then press the Shift key again while drawing the selection. The first Shift adds to the selection; the second Shift constrains the selection.

5. Add another rectangle to the current selection by pressing the Shift key before beginning the selection; this time, make certain that your new selection overlaps part of the existing marquee border. The two selections merge into one.

Two of the marquee tools automatically select a single row (or column) of pixels. These tools are particularly useful for cleaning up the edges of a rectangular image, such as a dialog box screen shot.

Selections can be constrained to equilateral shapes (squares, circles) by holding the Shift key while dragging the selection tool. If you press Shift before you drag, however, you add the new selection to any active selection.

6. Now press the Option/Alt key, and draw a selection that overlaps one corner of your existing selection. When you release the mouse button, the overlapped portion of the selection is deselected — the Option/Alt key subtracts from an existing selection. You could also use the "Subtract from" selection button.

7. Now click the fourth button, the "Intersect with selection" button. Draw a new selection that overlaps part of the existing marquee border. You see that the only area selected is where both selections overlap.

8. Press Command/Control-D to deselect. Close the file without saving.

The Elliptical Marquee tool works the same way as the Rectangular Marquee tool; you click, drag, and release the mouse button to make your selections. The only difference is that the Elliptical Marquee tool is used to select circular or oval areas of the image.

This example shows a number of circular selections that were feathered and used to display flowers on a Dutch patio.

The Lasso Tools

Not all selections are rectangular or elliptical. To handle other shapes, you can use the lasso tools. Rather than a restricted rectangular or elliptical shape, the lasso tools offer a free-form, "follow-the-cursor-anywhere" mode. When you release the mouse button, the selection joins the last point to the first point, enclosing the selection.

Regular Lasso Tool

If you select the Lasso tool and drag the cursor across the page, a freehand line trails the cursor. When the mouse button is released, the line becomes a selection marquee. Looking closely at a selection shows how it follows pixel boundaries.

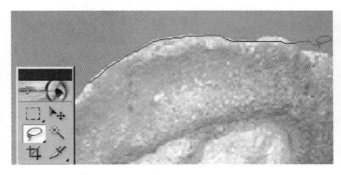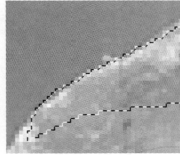

When drawing the selection, the line is solid. When the mouse button
is released, the line becomes a "marching ants" selection marquee.

The Lasso tool selects entire regions. If you release the mouse button before you're finished selecting the area you want, the point at which you started dragging and the point at which you stopped automatically connect.

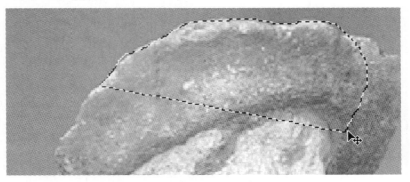

This doesn't really present a problem, however, because you can always add more of the image to the selection area.

Polygonal Lasso Tool
The Polygonal Lasso tool allows you to click from point to point in a series of straight-line segments. The dashed line stretches like a rubber band, allowing straight-edged selections. To close the polygon, either double-click on your current position, or single-click on the starting point of the selection.

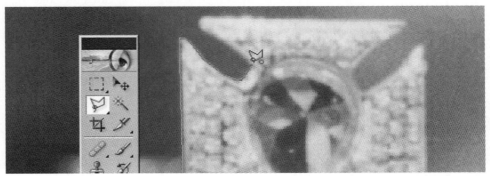

This tool can be tricky to use — but very effective when the selection area you're trying to create follows geometric lines.

Use the Polygonal Lasso Tool

1. Open the file **tall_buildings.tif** from the **RF_Intro_Photoshop** folder.

2. Analyze the photograph. We have clean lines, so this is an ideal project for the Polygonal Lasso tool. Press Shift-L until the Polygonal Lasso tool is active.

3. You need to select the buildings; click at the intersection of the building and the margin of the photo. Then click at each intersection of straight lines, including the edges of the page. Double-click to finish the selection.

4. Save the file as a Photoshop document (.psd) to your **Work_In_Progress** folder as "tall_buildings.psd". Close the file.

Magnetic Lasso Tool

Trying to accurately outline a selection with the Lasso tool can be a tedious process, especially if you are using a mouse instead of a graphic tablet and stylus. It's rather like drawing with a bar of soap. The Magnetic Lasso's built-in intelligence makes the process considerably easier — it automatically finds the edge for you.

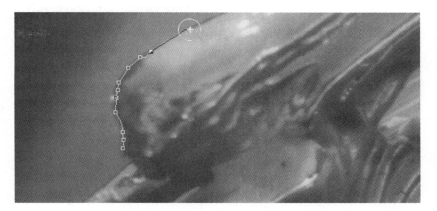

There are several settings that affect the behavior of the Magnetic Lasso tool. As usual, they're found in the tool's Options toolbar:

- The Width setting determines the distance at which the tool senses an edge.
- Edge Contrast controls the tool's sensitivity to color change. To make a precise edge between two relatively subtle shades, decrease the Width setting (use a lower percentage of Edge Contrast). When edges are clearly defined, you can use a larger Width setting and higher percentages of Edge Contrast.
- The Frequency setting determines the number of anchor points placed along the selection edge. Higher numbers increase the complexity of the selection.

When you're using the lasso tools to define a selection, you should first analyze the image to determine which is the best tool to use. This exercise provides you with some experience using the Magnetic Lasso tool.

Use the Magnetic Lasso Tool

1. Open the file named **florence_hotel.psd** from the **RF_Intro_Photoshop** folder. Select the magnifying glass (the Zoom tool) and zoom in to the window on the upper right of the image.

2. Select the Magnetic Lasso tool. Using the appropriate fields in the Options bar, make the following changes to the tool's behavior: set the Feather to 0 pixels; uncheck Anti-aliased; set the Width to 30 px; set the Edge Contrast to 10%, and set the Frequency to 20.

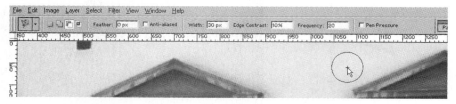

3. If you can't see the width of the tool (a round circle on the image), go to the Edit menu and select Preferences>General; make sure to check Brush Size for Painting Cursors, and Precise for Other Cursors. These settings ensure that you can see the size of the brush instead of the tool icon — which is totally unsuited for real work. This exercise is far more effective when you can see the brush size.

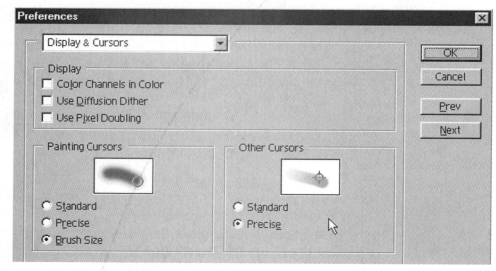

Even though the Magnetic Lasso tool automatically places anchor points as you drag the tool around an object, you can manually add points by clicking the mouse as you go. Remember, the higher the Frequency setting, the more points the tool generates.

4. Use the mouse to begin tracing the edge of the upper-right window. It is not necessary to be extremely careful. You will find the tool does not work very well; it's likely that the selection isn't exactly following the edge of the window.

The Bracket keys ([and]) can be used to reduce or enlarge the size of any brush, regardless of the tool you're using. In this example, they're being used to change the Width setting for the Magnetic Lasso tool.

5. Discard the selection you just made using Command/Control-D. Zoom in closer to the image, and use the Left Bracket key ([) to reduce the width of the tool to 8 pixels. If you continue to hold the key, the number keeps shrinking; if you go too far, use the Right Bracket key (]) to make it larger.

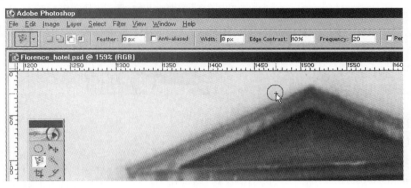

6. If you change a few of the other settings, the accuracy of the tool can be dramatically improved. Try an Edge Contrast setting of 6%, and a Frequency setting of 50.

7. Run the tool around the upper frame of the window with these new settings. You'll probably find that they produce a much better selection. Remember — run around the edge, but don't be overly careful. That's the beauty of the tool — it can be used to quickly establish a complex selection. You can always use other tools to refine the selection once you have created the basic outline.

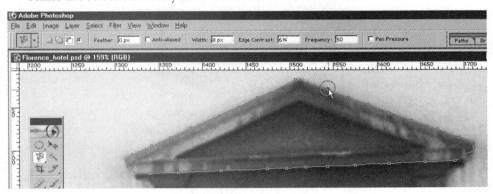

When you come full-circle to the point where you started, the tool icon appears, and the selection is complete.

8. Keep the file open and continue to experiment with the Magnetic Lasso tool and the other selection tools in your arsenal. Try refining your selections using combinations of selection tools and behaviors. Making accurate selections will occupy a lot of your time as a Photoshop professional; you can't get enough practice. When you're done, close the file without saving changes.

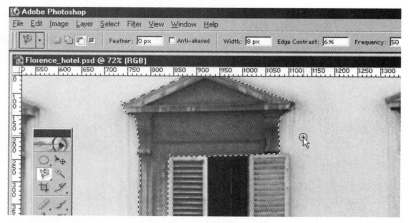

By holding down the Option/Alt key after starting a selection with either of the lasso tools, you can access freehand lines with the Polygonal Lasso tool, or straight lines with the regular Lasso tool.

Although there are many experienced users who feel the lasso tools aren't an effective way to create selections, we feel they're underused and underestimated. This is partially because there are many other ways to make selections; but it's also because most people don't work with the lasso tools long enough to develop expertise with them. You should try to become comfortable with as many selection methods as possible. One technique will never be applicable to all assignments.

The Magic Wand Tool

The Magic Wand allows you to select areas containing similar colors or shades. The Tolerance setting allows you to control the sensitivity of the Magic Wand — whether it selects pixels with identical color values, or pixels within a wide range of similar colors. This exercise should provide a good understanding for how the tool works.

Use the Magic Wand

1. Open the file **capital.tif** from your **RF_Intro_Photoshop** folder. This photo looks a bit drab, so we're going to select the sky area and change the image to a bright sunny day. Select the Magic Wand tool. The Options bar changes to reflect attributes specific to the Magic Wand tool. Set the Tolerance to 12.

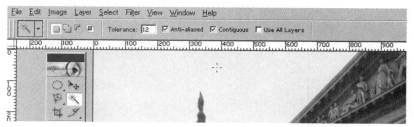

2. Click on the sky. Almost nothing happens (very few pixels are selected) because the tool's sensitivity to color change is so low. Only pixels within 12 shades of each other are selected. The image contains thousands of different colors; limiting the Tolerance to such a small range creates a minute selection.

3. Use Command/Control-D to cancel the current (small) selection. Check to see if the New selection button is active. If not, select it before the next step.

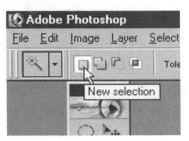

If you use the Add to Selection option with the Magic Wand tool, you can click several times in different areas to increase the number of selected pixels. It's best to get as close as possible with the Tolerance setting, however, and then refine the overall selection.

4. In the Options toolbar, set the Wand's Tolerance to 24 and click the sky again. If only 1 or 2 pixels are selected, click around until you've selected almost the entire sky.

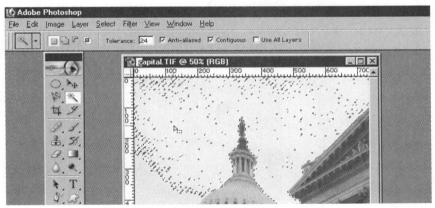

5. Use Command/Control-D again to deselect. Change the Tolerance to 36 and click the sky again. This setting is much closer to what we need.

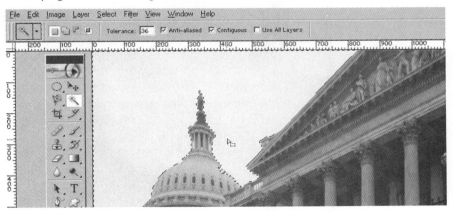

6. It's still not perfect; zoom into the rotunda and change to the regular Lasso tool. Use the Add and Subtract selection buttons where necessary, and refine your selection.

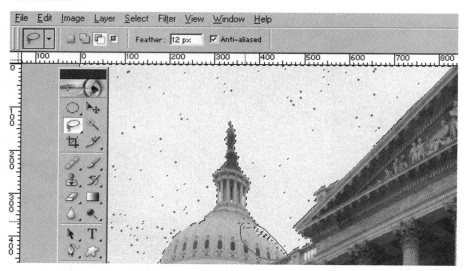

7. Keep working to refine the selection; it may require some patience to get it right.

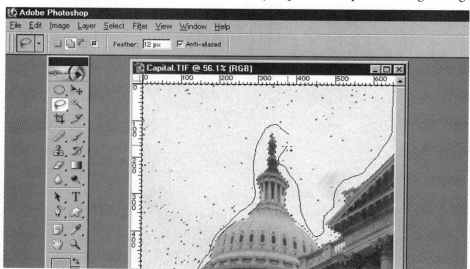

8. Open the file **clouds.psd** from **the RF_Intro_Photoshop** folder. Press Command/Control-A to select all and Command/Control-C to copy the image to the clipboard. Click on the capital document to activate it, and then choose Edit>Paste Into to place the clouds in the selection. Use the Move tool to position the clouds to your liking.

Use Shift-Command/Control-V for the Paste Into command.

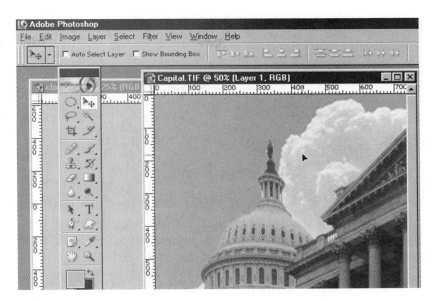

9. When you are satisfied with your new image, save the file to your **Work_In_Progress** folder as "capital.psd", changing the file Format to Photoshop. If it's not as perfect as you would like, go back to the beginning, load the original images, and try to improve the final results.

Manipulating Selections

As we continue to work through various Photoshop techniques such as layers, masks, type elements, and other features, creating and managing selections will continue to be a factor. In this section, you're going to try a few more selection techniques, experiment with changing the contents of selections, and learn to store and recall selections.

Transforming Selections

Transform tools can be used to duplicate, rotate, scale, flip, distort, and even apply realistic perspective effects to selections. The Transform tools are found in the Edit menu.

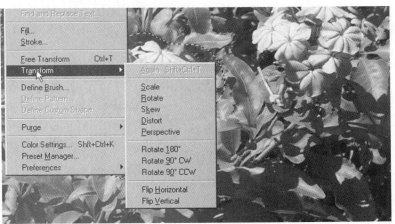

Most transformations are self-explanatory:

- Scale allows you to change the size of a selection.
- Rotate is used to spin a selection. The menu includes a number of preset rotations that are set to 180 degrees, 90 degrees clockwise, and 90 degrees counterclockwise.
- Skew and Distort provide ways to stretch and pull a selection into a different shape.
- Perspective is the visual phenomenon that causes railroad tracks to eventually meet on the horizon — even though the distance between them remains constant. This transformation technique can be used to simulate that effect.
- Flipping a selection on its horizontal or vertical axis turns it over, either top-to-bottom (horizontal) or left-to-right (vertical). If you copy a selection and then flip it, you can create mirror images.

In the following exercises, you'll have an opportunity to apply transformations to selections.

Transform Selections

1. Open **plumbago.jpg** from the **RF_Intro_Photoshop** folder. Select the Lasso tool, set the Feather amount to 12 pixels, and draw a rough selection border around the blue flower. Make sure the selection is slightly larger than the object.

2. From the Select menu, choose Modify>Contract, and try shrinking the selection by 10 or 12 pixels. Don't allow the selection marquee to get too much smaller than the flower. You may have to experiment a bit to get it right.

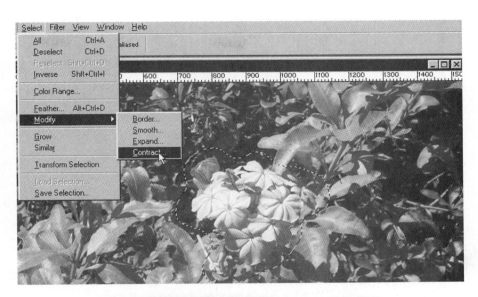

Adding the Shift key to the Option/Alt-drag technique constrains the movement of the clone. If you want to create a copy of a selection directly to the right, left, above, below, or at a 45-degree angle to the original, hold down the Shift key while you're dragging.

3. Select the Move tool, and hold down the Option/Alt key. Click on the selection and drag it to the left. This technique creates a clone (copy) of the selection.

4. In nature, no two flowers look exactly alike. From the Edit menu, select Transform>Flip Horizontal. The cloned selection turns over.

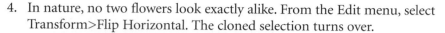

The feathered edge of the selection helps the clone realistically blend into the background.

5. Use the Option/Alt-drag technique to make another copy of the flowers, moving it to the lower-right side of the image. Select Edit>Transform>Scale; control handles appear. Hold down the Shift key, grab the handle on the upper-left side of the box, and drag in toward the center of the flower. It shrinks. Reduce it to half its original size.

6. Look at the Options toolbar. As long as you don't press Return/Enter — which commits the transformation and lays the selection down onto the image — you can edit and modify the rotation angle of the object, its size, and its exact position on the page. Take special note of the Reference Point icon — it allows you to determine whether measurements or transformations occur from the center of an object (the default position), or one of its corners or sides.

You can repeat any transformation using the Edit>Transform Again command.

The box that appears around a selection when you choose a Transformation command is called the bounding box.

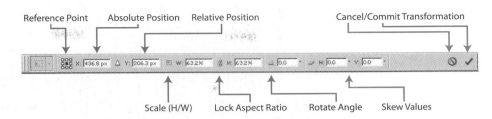

Reference Point   Absolute Position   Relative Position   Cancel/Commit Transformation

Scale (H/W)   Lock Aspect Ratio   Rotate Angle   Skew Values

The Edit>Free Transform command allows you to spin, scale, skew, or distort a selection at the same time.

7. Press Return/Enter, or click the Commit Transformation button (the checkmark on the far-right side of the Options toolbar) to accept — or commit — the scale.

8. Continue experimenting with the various transformations — keep making copies of the flowers and flip, rotate, and skew the results. When you're done experimenting, close the file without saving.

When you're performing a transformation, the Options toolbar doesn't limit you to a single function. If you're scaling an object, as you did in the previous exercise, you can also rotate, skew, or reposition a selection at the same time. Simply enter the appropriate values in the desired fields and Photoshop applies them all at once. In the next exercise, you're going to learn how to automatically add a stroke to a selection and how to fill areas of an image; both present excellent methods of isolating and highlighting specific details of your artwork.

Fill and Stroke Selection Areas

1. Open the file named **stilthouse.psd** from the **RF_Intro_Photoshop** folder. Save it into your **Work_In_Progress** folder. Click the default color swatch option in the main Toolbar to make black the foreground color and white the background color.

2. Select the Rectangular Marquee tool, and make sure the Feather amount is set to 0. Create a rectangular marquee that surrounds the structure.

3. Select Stroke from the Edit menu. In the Stroke dialog box, enter 6 for the Width of the stroke, and Center for the Location. Keep everything else the same in the dialog box, and click OK to create the stroke.

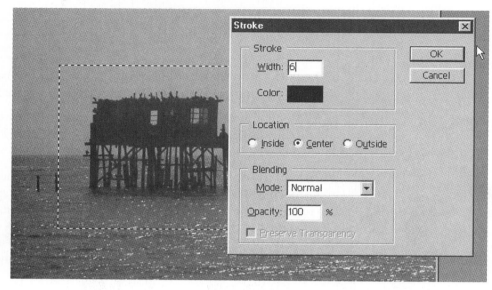

4. Press Shift-Command/Control-I. This is the Inverse command; it turns the selection inside out. What was selected (the stilt house) is now deselected, and the area around it becomes selected.

5. You're going to keep the stilt house in its original condition and fade the background surrounding the stroked frame you just created. Select Fill from the Edit menu. Select Background Color from the Use drop-down menu, and change the Opacity value to 50%. This fills the selected area with white — but instead of filling it completely, the opacity value allows the image to show through.

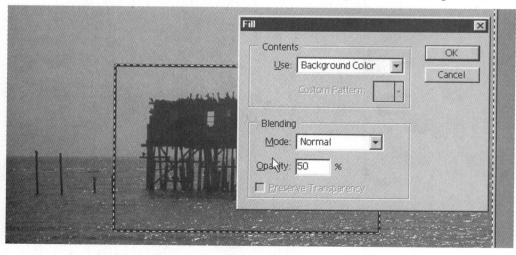

When you choose the Center option and the width is set to an odd number of pixels, the larger number of pixels (i.e., 2 pixels, in the case of a 3-pixel stroke) are placed inside the selection border because Photoshop can't divide a pixel in half.

6. Click OK. Press Command/Control-D to deselect the image. Save it and close the file when you're done.

The Center option you applied to the stroke split the frame in half; the fill affected the outside pixels, and the inside pixels retained their original black color.

When you Shift-click with the Magic Wand tool, a "+" sign appears below the Magic Wand icon to remind you that you are adding to the selection.

The same technique that you used in the previous exercise can be used to create vignettes — an effect that's very popular and commonly used in a variety of imaging and image compositing applications. To achieve this effect, we simply took a picture of the Empire State Building in New York City, created a rectangular selection with a 30-pixel feather, inverted it, and filled the area with 100% black. We can generate the same effect by using Command/Control-Delete to fill the area with the foreground color.

Grow and Similar commands use the Tolerance value set in the Magic Wand Options toolbar. Repeated application of these commands expands your selection incrementally, depending on this value.

Preserving Selection Information

Imagine that you just completed a rather complex selection. What happens to your selection if you need to work on another job, or it's time go home? Photoshop's Select menu includes tools for saving and loading the selections you have created.

When selections are made, they can be saved — any number of selections can be saved in a given image. The entire selection may be saved, or a new selection can add to, subtract from, or intersect with an existing selection.

Selections are saved as channels and/or masks, which are essentially the same thing. We will explore their use in more depth in a later chapter of this book. For now, let's focus on the mechanics of creating, saving, and loading selections.

Save and Load Selections

If you press the Shift key before beginning a selection, you add to an existing selection. Press the Shift key after you begin a selection to constrain the selection to a square. Press the Shift key before drawing, then release and press it again to add a square to a selection.

1. Open the document **stone_crabs.psd** from your **RF_Intro_Photoshop** folder. Save it into your **Work_In_Progress** folder.

2. Select the Magnetic Lasso tool. Set the Width to 10 pixels, the Edge Contrast to 6%, and the Frequency to 51.

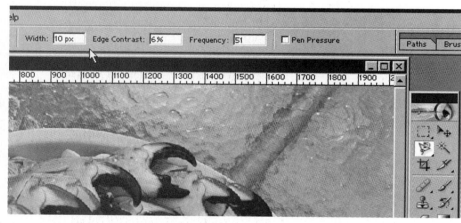

3. This setting should make it fairly easy to select the platter. Run the tool around the outside edge of the plate. If necessary, use the Add to selection and Subtract from selection buttons to refine the shape.

4. Choose Save Selection from the Select menu. Selections are saved as channels —
   something you'll learn more about in the next chapter. For now, simply name the
   channel "whole_platter" and click OK to accept the name.

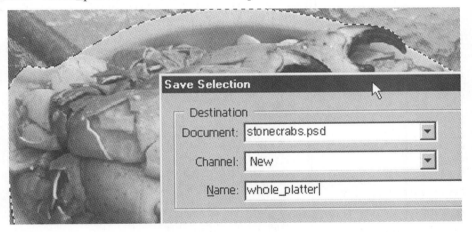

Notice that you can save channels into other documents using the pop-up Document menu.

5. Now create a selection for the small plate of butter. When you're done, save the
   selection as "small_plate".

6. Save the file. Even if you close it now, the saved selections remain intact. Try it: close the file, and open it again. Choose Load Selection from the Select menu, and pick the whole_platter selection from the pop-up menu. Click the Invert check box. This automatically loads the selection, and then turns it inside out — just as you did when you created the stilt house frame.

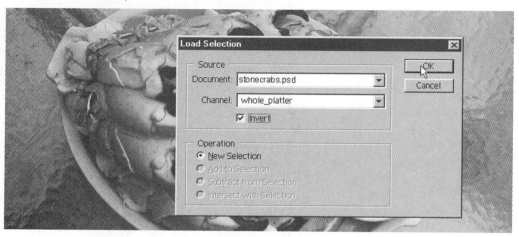

7. Select Fill from the Edit menu, and fill the area surrounding the platter with 60% Black.

8. Invert the selection again using Shift-Command/Control-I. Choose Load Selection from the Select menu, and this time, subtract the small_plate selection from the image (check the Subtract from selection button).

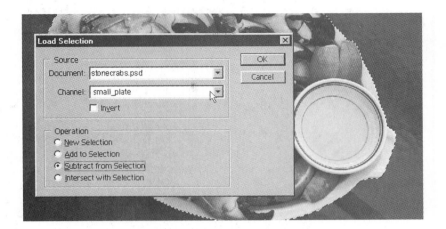

9. When you click OK, you'll see that the butter dish isn't selected, but the rest of the platter is. Save and close the file.

10. From the **RF_Intro_Photoshop** folder, open the file named **crabpainting.psd**. Take a look at it. We used the same file you were just working with to create this graphic, which was originally designed for a restaurant advertisement. We used the same selections, and simply added some lighting effects and a few filters. It is important to remember that we could only have done this with the use of selections. When you're done reviewing the graphic, close the file without saving it.

When you start to learn about retouching, color correction, and other more advanced imaging functions, you'll be able to use these various selection techniques to carefully and effectively isolate, transform, protect, and modify complex selections.

Chapter Summary

In this chapter, you learned the importance of Photoshop's selection tools. You learned that all selection tools have common attributes, including feathering and anti-aliasing.

You learned to use the Rectangular and Elliptical Marquee tools. You worked with the regular, Magnetic, and Polygonal Lasso tools. You used the Magic Wand tool and the Paste Into command to replace a dull sky with an alternative image from another document. You learned how to use the Transform functions to scale, rotate, flip, and distort a selection. Lastly, you created, saved, and loaded selections using the Save Selection commands, and you viewed the results of using complex selections to create professional-looking artwork from a simple scanned image.

4 Working with Layers

Chapter Objectives:

In this chapter, you're going to begin learning about how to use layers — one of Photoshop's most powerful and useful functions. Although layers can substantially increase the size of your files, and require considerable system resources, they are critically important when you're developing complex and structured images. In Chapter 4, you will:

- Learn how layers are essentially discrete images, which are stacked on top of each other in the Layers palette.

- Explore the Layers palette and its associated icons, options, and menus.

- Learn to create, hide, lock, link, and rearrange layers.

- Work with layers and layer techniques to develop professional and realistic composite images.

- Become familiar with layer styles — a rich assortment of effects that are applied to objects on a layer without actually making permanent changes to the objects themselves.

- Learn the use of shape layers — one of the three options associated with the shape tools, and one that makes use of clipping masks.

- Understand how to strategically approach projects that call for the use of layers, and how to optimize their application.

Projects to be Completed:

- **Gulls Poster (A)**

- Fallsbridge Menu Cover (B)

- Jazz Postcard (C)

- USA Poster (D)

Working with Layers

Among Photoshop's most powerful functions, layers are used to composite images and to apply special effects and color correction settings without making permanent changes to the image. They are very important for developing structured, multi-component projects such as navigation bars or informational graphics destined for use on the Web. Sites can have dozens of buttons, text layers, graphics, and background images; using layers and layer sets allow you to efficiently organize and manage a large number of components.

As your Photoshop skills develop, the projects you work on become more complex, and you increasingly seek to master the program, you'll find many ways to apply layers in your day-to-day design activities.

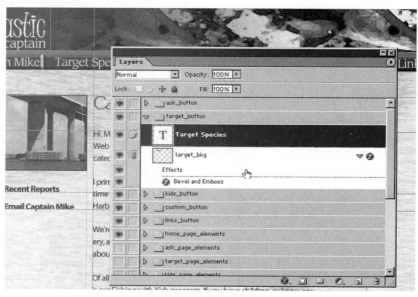

Layers are stacked directly on top of each other, and — depending on the visibility and transparency settings — you can see through them. You can also drag them to different positions in the layer stack.

Layers are essentially discrete images that are stacked on top of each other to form the final image. Layers can be transparent or partially transparent; they can contain text elements, vector objects, photographs, or any other types of components you can create with Photoshop. Unlike channels, layers can contain colors, and special layers are available that can be used as fills, masks, shapes, color correction adjustments, and much more. Blending modes, which we'll cover later, provide extensive control over how tones, colors, and objects interact between layers.

Blending modes provide a great deal of control over how images on different layers interact. For example, you can use color pixels based on the darkness of an underlying layer, or create colors based on combined values from multiple layers. Since Blending modes are also available for painting tools, we felt it was better to address them in a chapter dedicated to the topic.

TIFF files can now contain layers — but it's a good idea to completely flatten a document (or a copy of a document) prior to saving it as a TIFF. You can also flatten the document while you're saving it — which eliminates a step and can save some time.

Think of layers as individual pieces of acetate stacked on top of one another; you can see through them, rearrange them, hide them, lock them, and apply special effects to them.

Layers can only be contained in certain file types. The first — and most common — is the native Photoshop format (.psd). Other file types can also support layers — most notably TIFF files — but it's a good idea to keep your original layered files in Photoshop format and create a flattened copy for distribution. These formats would either be TIFF or EPS for print projects, and GIF or JPEG for use on the Web.

Layering is a powerful technique that allows flexibility in the design and modification of an image, but if you're not careful, layers can quickly consume system resources. It's a good idea to carefully plan your documents before you use layers; they can dramatically increase the size of an image, and require additional memory, disk space, and scratch space.

Layers remain intact until you *flatten* them. The process of flattening combines objects on separate layers into a single layer.

Layers, unlike channels, can contain colors. They are actually entire images that are lying on top of, or underneath, other images. Layers can be transparent; this means you may cut the background out of one image and place it on top of another, allowing part of the lower image to show through.

Photoshop's layers allow you to create versatile artwork. You could, for example, create a standard advertisement with an image and logo, and then add several layers of text. You could colorize the logo or background according to the current marketing plan. Whatever text, logo, and background are needed for a particular publication, all the pieces could reside in a single-layered file.

The Layers Palette

Layers are controlled from the Layers palette. In most cases, everything you'll need to do with layers can be accomplished from here, although there are alternative ways to add layers, apply layer styles, and modify layers. For now, we're going to work with the Layers palette — and show you the other ways of applying layer techniques from the Options menu.

Layer sets are folders within the Layers palette that are very useful for storing related components — such as buttons for a Web site or a collection of related icons. You cannot "nest" sets — a set can only contain layers, not other layer sets.

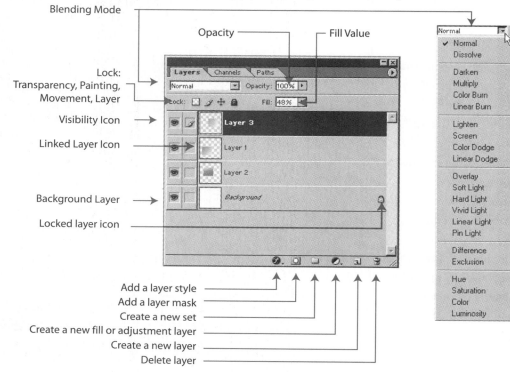

Blending Mode

Opacity

Fill Value

Lock: Transparency, Painting, Movement, Layer

Visibility Icon

Linked Layer Icon

Background Layer

Locked layer icon

Add a layer style
Add a layer mask
Create a new set
Create a new fill or adjustment layer
Create a new layer
Delete layer

Multilayer Documents

From this point forward, you'll do extensive work with layers — not only in this chapter, but in most of the remaining chapters as well. Let's work with a multilayer document.

Work with Layers

1. Open the document **banana_split.psd** from your **RF_Intro_Photoshop** folder. Note that it already has a Background layer and two type layers.

2. We're going to add the company's logo to this image. From the File menu, choose Place, and select **ice_cream_shoppe.eps** from the **RF_Intro_Photoshop** folder. Drag it to the lower-left corner of the image, and when it is positioned to your taste, press Enter/Return to complete the placement process .

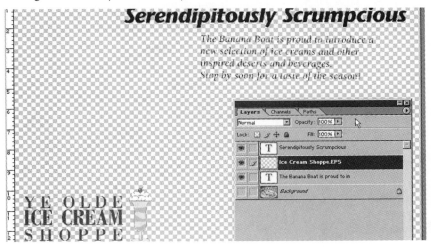

3. A new transparent layer is added to the image. Note that the layer is created with the same name as the placed image, **ice_cream_shoppe.eps**. At this point, the Background layer, the type layers, and the ice_cream_shoppe.eps layer are visible. The type and image areas are all transparent. Hide the Background layer by clicking the visibility icon. Now you can see how transparent layers actually look.

4. Let's make the body copy easier to read by lightening the background. Certain types of layer commands cannot be applied to the Background layer — including opacity changes and fills. To convert the background to a normal layer, double-click its name in the Layers palette and assign a name to it. In this case, name it "photograph". Click OK to apply the change.

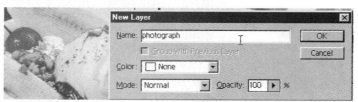

5. Draw a rectangular marquee around the text box. From the Image menu, select Adjustments>Brightness/Contrast. Set the Brightness to +30 and the Contrast to -60. The photograph in the background fades. The type, however, remains unchanged because the active selected layer is the only one that's affected by painting tools, filters, or other actions.

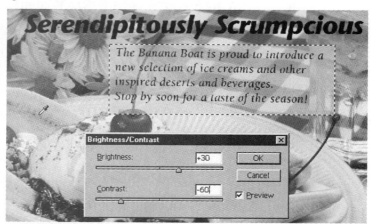

6. Save the file to your **Work_In_Progress** folder, and then close the file.

Photo Composites with Layers

The real strength of layers lies in the compositing of photographs. You may want to composite multiple images, and then — once you think the job is finished — decide that you need to radically change a background or other element. Without layers, you'd have to start all over again.

Create a Composite

1. Open the image **picnic.tif** from the **RF_Intro_Photoshop** folder. Press the "D" key to reset the foreground and background colors.

2. Double-click the Background layer, and click OK when the dialog box appears. This changes the Background layer to Layer 0 — a normal layer that can contain transparent areas.

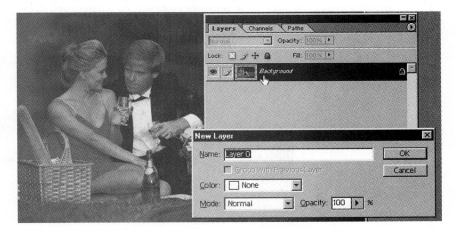

3. Use the Rectangular Marquee tool to select the people in the image. Be sure to allow some extra room around the couple. From the Select menu, choose Modify>Smooth, and set the Sample Radius to 10 pixels. Click OK. This rounds and softens the corners of the selection.

4. From the Select menu, choose Feather, and set the Feather Radius to 10 pixels. Click OK. From the Select menu, choose Inverse to turn your selection inside out. Press the Delete key to create a border that fades to transparent. Press Command/Control-D to deactivate (deselect) the selection.

5. Click the New Layer icon at the bottom of the Layers palette to create a new layer called Layer 1. Drag this layer below Layer 0.

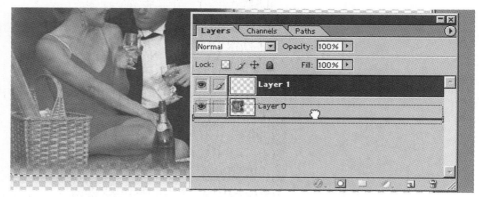

6. Press the "X" key to exchange the foreground and background colors, and press Option/Alt-Delete to fill the layer with white. Now you can change the color of the vignette background at any time without redoing this part of the image.

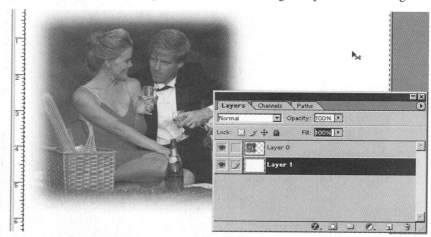

7. Open the image **bubbly.psd** from your **RF_Intro_Photoshop** folder. Choose Load Selection from the Select menu, and load the bubbling bottle selection. Press Command/Control-C to copy the selection to the clipboard.

8. Close the **bubbly.psd** file. Press Command/Control-V to paste the bottle into the picnic image. A new layer is automatically created to hold the contents of the clipboard. Drag the layer to the top of the layer list.

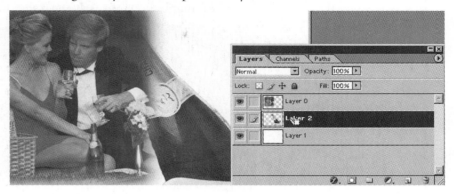

9. Activate Layer 2, the champagne bottle layer, and use the Move tool to position the champagne bottle wherever you prefer.

10. Add a new layer, Layer 3, and fill it with White. Move the layer to the bottom of the Layers palette. Turn off Layer 1 (the white background layer).

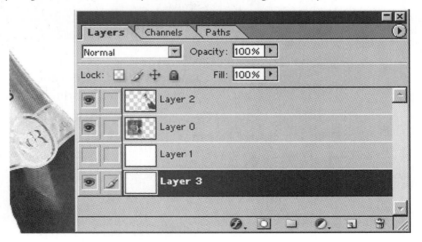

You'll have a chance to explore the use of filters in an upcoming chapter. In this exercise, you have the opportunity to preview the kinds of effects you can create with filters.

11. On this layer, we're going to create a texture that resembles handmade paper. From the Filter menu, choose Noise>Add Noise. Move the slider until the figure reads 115, or type "115" into the dialog box. Select a Distribution of Gaussian. Make sure the Monochromatic check box isn't checked. Click OK.

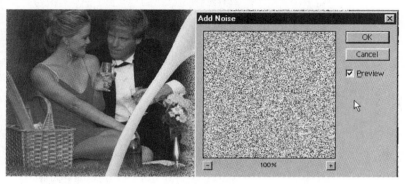

12. From the Filter menu, select Blur>Gaussian Blur. Enter "1.0" for the Pixel Radius. Click OK.

13. Now choose Pixelate>Facet from the Filter menu. Run the filter a second time by pressing Command/Control-F, or choosing it again from the Filters menu. (It will be at the top of the list after you run it.)

14. Next choose Filter>Stylize>Emboss, and set the Angle to 45°, Height to 2 pixels, and Amount to 60%. Click OK.

15. Select Layer 1 and experiment with changing the Opacity slider for the layer. This allows the paper texture to show through — but only partially. Set the Opacity to 48%. You now have a single file with two decidedly different appearances. Save the file as "picnic_ad.psd" to your **Work_In_Progress** folder.

Now that we have a master document, we can save copies for different uses.

16. Select File>Save As. Check Save As a Copy. Uncheck the Layers box — this automatically flattens the layers in the copy. Save the file as a TIFF image called "picnic_ad_1.tif" to your **Work_In_Progress** folder.

17. Change the Opacity of Layer 1 to 100% to hide the texture. Save As a Copy again to save a flattened TIFF version with a white background. Call the image "picnic_ad_2.tif" and save it to your **Work_In_Progress** folder. The flattened versions of this file could be cropped and placed into your page-layout program, while the original image can be saved for further adjustments.

18. Close the file without saving.

In this example, you used layer transparency to change the intensity of a level. You can also fill a layer with a color and adjust the density percentage of that fill; both are commonly used effects.

The Opacity and Fill options that are available on the Layers palette affect the entire selected level — and can't be used to change the opacity or fill of a selection/portion of a level. When you're making changes to an entire level, however, Opacity and Fill options are very effective because their values aren't permanent. You can move the sliders at any time (as long as you haven't flattened the layer) and modify an effect.

Layer Styles

In addition to managing the appearance of two-dimensional images, Photoshop enables us to add dimension to both complete images and parts of images using its powerful Layer Styles feature. Layer styles are easy to apply, they are editable, and they are reversible. As with all other Photoshop features, the image's resolution and ultimate use must be taken into consideration before applying these effects.

The effects may be applied to images or type, and multiple effects may be applied to the same layer. If the same effect is applied more than once to the same layer, the results may not be what you anticipated — but can easily be reversed/removed.

Drop Shadows

The effect most often used is the drop shadow, which provides substantial depth and realism to an image. Shadows can be combined with other effects to heighten interest or to enhance realism. Be careful to avoid overusing these effects, which reduces their value to each image.

This exercise makes use of ATC fonts — specifically ATC MapleUltra. If you haven't installed the fonts, refer back to the Getting Started section at the beginning of the book; you'll find installation instructions for both Macintosh and Windows platforms.

Apply a Drop Shadow

1. Open **bull_rider.psd** from the **RF_Intro_Photoshop** folder. It contains two layers: one for the background photograph, and one for the type.

2. Select the Measure tool from the Toolbox. Draw a line that parallels the shadow being cast by the raging bull. Watch the tool Options bar at the top of the window, and you'll find it's around a 22° angle.

3. Select the type layer and apply Layer>Layer Style>Drop Shadow. Set Blend Mode to Multiply, Opacity to 60%, Angle to 22°, Distance to 25 pixels, Spread to 0, Size to 10 pixels, and click the Use Global Light check box. Click OK.

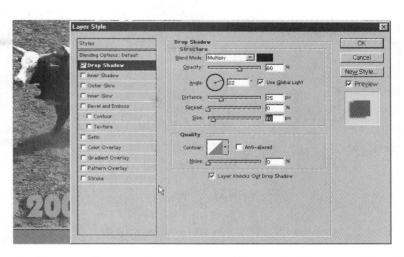

4. Save the file to your **Work_In_Progress** folder as "bull_rider.psd", and leave it open for the next exercise.

Bevel and Emboss Features

Beveled and embossed elements can be used as part of a photograph to very subtly alter the overall effect of the original, or they may be individual elements, constructed for a specific purpose. More and more people are building Web pages with flashy buttons, and the Bevel and Emboss features can be used very effectively for this purpose.

Add Inner Glow

1. In the open **bull_rider.psd** file, note that the words look stark and out of place. Let's soften them a bit. Select the type layer, then select Layer>Layer Style>Inner Glow. Choose a light tan from the glove on the cowboy's left hand. In the Structure section of the Layer Style dialog box, set Blend Mode to Dissolve, Opacity to 70%, and Noise to 10%. In the Elements section, set Technique to Softer, Source to Center, Choke to 0%, and Size to 5 pixels. In the Quality section, set Range to 50%, and Jitter to 0%.

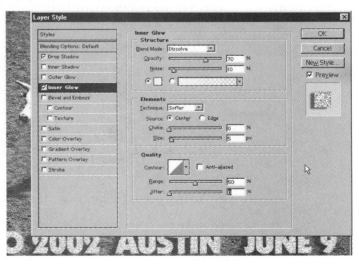

Notice the type layer has acquired a new symbol, telling you that a layer effect has been applied.

2. Take a look at the Layers palette. You can see that the type layer is now displaying an icon indicating that styles have been applied to the layer. You can click the small triangle to expand the list (since there's more than one applied style).

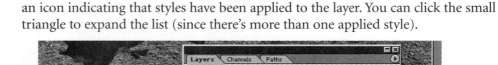

3. Save the file to your **Work_In_Progress** folder as "ride_em.psd". Close the file.

The Use Global Light check box enables you to determine a shadow angle for the entire image and use it consistently. When you check Use Global Light at the time you set an angle, it becomes the default for that image.

Create Multimedia Buttons

1. Create a new RGB file with a Width of 72 pixels, a Height of 21 pixels, at a Resolution of 72 pixels/inch (ppi). From the Contents section of the New dialog box, make the background Transparent. Name the file "forward.psd".

One of the best aspects of layer styles is that they are applied to the layer, and not to the object on the layer.

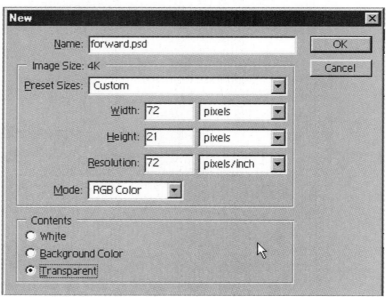

2. Set the foreground color to Red, and fill the layer.

3. From the Layer menu, select Layer Style>Bevel and Emboss. In the Structure section, set Style to Inner Bevel, Technique to Chisel Hard, Depth to 100%, Direction to Up, Size to 4 pixels, and Soften to 2 pixels. Accept the defaults in the Shading section, and click OK.

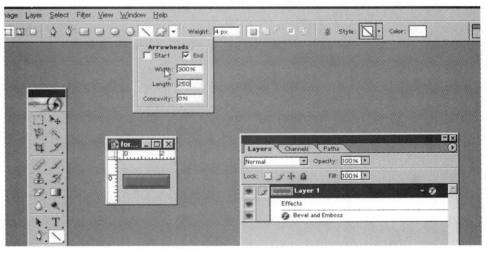

4. Create a new layer. Press the "X" key to exchange the foreground and background colors, making the foreground color white.

5. Select the Shape tool from the Toolbox, pick the Line tool from the Options bar (at the top of the window) and set its Weight to 4 pt. Select the End Arrowhead and set its shape to a Width of 300%, Length of 250%, and Concavity of 0%.

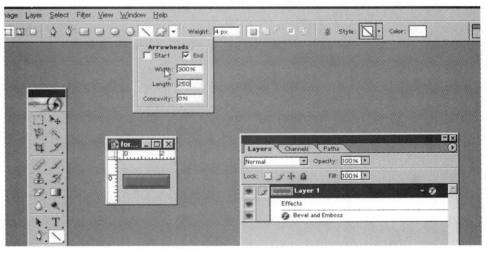

6. Draw an arrow in the center of the button. (Press the Shift key to constrain the line to horizontal.) A new layer is automatically created for the shape.

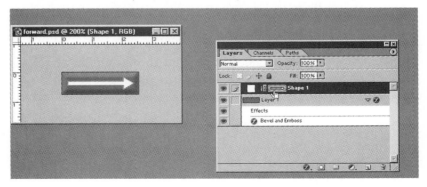

7. To create the illusion that the arrow is cut into the button, Select Layer>Layer Style>Bevel and Emboss. In the Structure section, set Layer Style to Inner Bevel, Technique to Smooth, Depth to 100%, Direction to Down, Size to 3 pixels, and Soften to 1 pixel. Leave the Shading section at its defaults. Click OK.

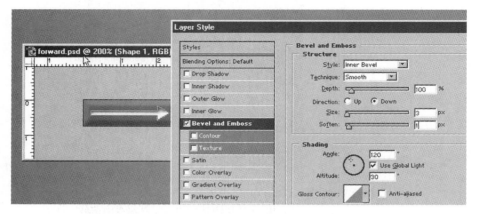

When creating shadow effects, pay attention to the details of the photograph you're working on. Shadows created by shadow effects should flow in the same direction and be the same approximate density as shadows in the photograph. When that doesn't happen, the image looks artificial.

8. Save the file to your **Work_In_Progress** folder as "forward_up.psd".

9. Now let's create the depressed, or "down" state of this button. Go to Layer 1, and change the Bevel and Emboss effect. Click the Down radio button, and then click OK.

10. On the Shape 1 layer, we're going to move the shadow that is currently inside the arrow to the bottom of the arrow. In the Shading area of the dialog box, click the Gloss Contour icon.

11. In the Contour Editor, reverse the Contour Map by dragging the Input point to 98% and the Output point to 0%. Click OK.

12. Save the button as "forward_down.psd" to your **Work_In_Progress** folder. Close the file.

In most Web and interactive design projects, there are actually two, three, and sometimes four versions of a button. These different versions are created to accommodate the different "states" that a button might be in at a given moment in time. These states include:

- **Up.** This is the default state for a button, and represents an idle state; no one has touched it or moved the pointer over its position on the page.

- **Over.** This state exists when the user moves the pointer over the button, but still hasn't clicked the mouse.

- **Down.** This state occurs when the user clicks the button.

These three states are the most common, and designers generally build one set of buttons for each of the states. When they're put together in a Web page, HTML or JavaScript code executes what's called a *rollover*, and the buttons appear to change based upon the user's actions.

Effects should be used to enhance an image; they should not be used simply for the sake of using the effect. When they are used sparingly, layer styles make images look more dynamic. If overused, they can overwhelm the design.

Shape Layers

The shape tools can be used to create three types of objects.

The first is a shape layer that contains a clipping mask in the shape of the object. The result is a vector object, isolated on its own layer, which offers the advantages of higher output resolution, the ability to apply styles to the shape, and all the other benefits of layers.

The shape tools can also be used to generate normal paths, such as those created with the Pen tool, and normal raster objects filled with pixels. The Paths and Fill Pixels options are placed on the current drawing layer; if you have the Shape Layers option turned on in the tool's Option bar, then new layers (containing clipping masks) are created every time you draw a new shape or clone an existing one using the Option/Alt-drag command.

To change the type of shape that's created when you use the tool, use one of the three mode buttons on the left side of the shapes Options bar.

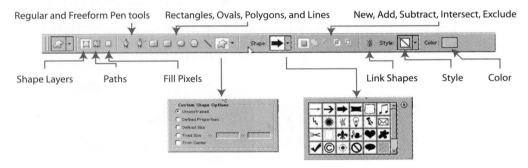

Let's use a shape layer with a photograph to experiment with one way they can be put to use.

Work with a Shape Layer

Shape layers aren't the only way the shape tools can be used; they can also create pen paths and regular raster objects.

1. Open the file **wimbledon_tennis.psd** from your **RF_Intro_Photoshop** folder.

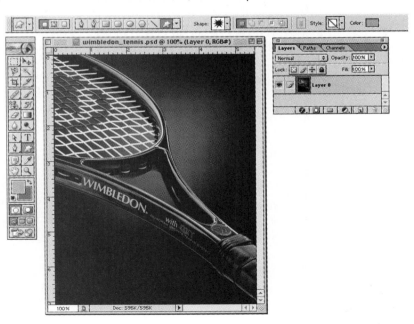

2. Change the foreground color to the color of the type on the racquet by clicking on the type with the Eyedropper tool to sample the color.

3. Select the Custom Shape tool (it may be hiding under the Rectangle tool), and set it for a starburst shape.

4. Select the Create New Shape Layer option from the Options toolbar. Draw a large starburst, and position it low and to the left as shown.

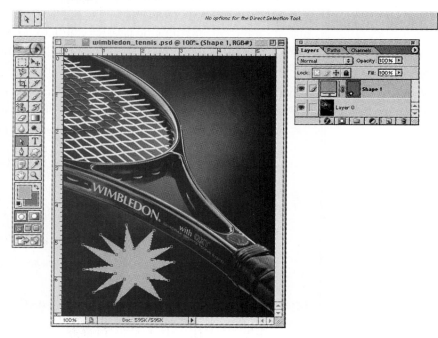

5. Click the Direct Selection tool from the Toolbox and adjust some of the anchor points to randomize the starburst.

6. Change the foreground color to Red using the Swatches palette.

7. Select the Type tool and type "$199" inside the starburst shape.

8. Double-click the shape layer to add a layer style. Set the parameters as shown in the following dialog box.

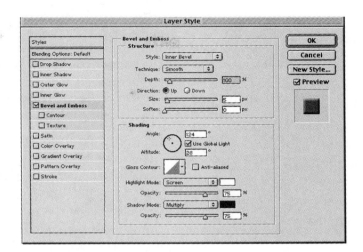

9. Drag the layer style to the type layer. A duplicate style is added.

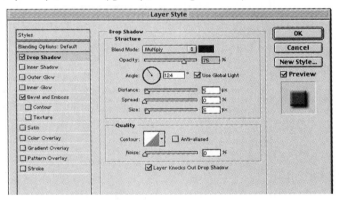

10. Double-click the style layer and add a drop shadow to the type as shown.

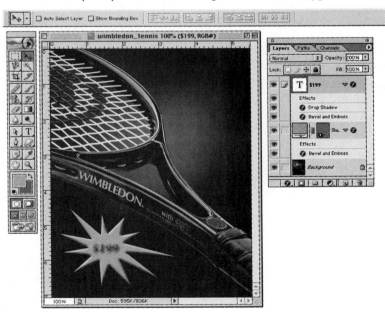

11. Close the file without saving.

A shape layer is in vector format, so it has hard edges. Elements in shape layers can be adjusted using the Selection tool and the Direct Selection tool. In order to save and print the vector data, the file must be saved as an EPS file with the appropriate settings.

Strategies for Using Layers

Some considerations in planning a composite or photo manipulation involving layers are discussed below. The answers to the following questions determine how many layers you will use, how many layers you will maintain at one time, and how many layers you will keep. To avoid costly delays at the end of a project, it is important to answer as many of these questions as possible before you begin your work.

- What is your largest final use for this image? Before you begin, you should be certain that all of your source images are suitable for the final size of the piece you're working on, and all images that will be composited are of compatible resolution. Otherwise, you may degrade image quality by excessive scaling.

- Will you keep the individual parts of a composite or layer group available in a separate file for later changes? Once you have worked on a composite, you could flatten the image to save space; this is common practice with an image that is going to be used only once. You may, however, want to save the original image in Photoshop format and save a copy in a printable, flattened format. This provides the ability to make modifications and use the image in a variety of printed or online pieces. This is especially true in Photoshop 7, where you can edit text in a special text layer, include vector information generated by the drawing tools, or edit layer effects, such as drop shadows. You may even want to maintain several different files. You might want one with all the layers you generated to allow for alterations, one simplified PSD or EPS to allow printing to PostScript-savvy printers, and one flattened file for printing to non-PostScript devices or placement in a page-layout application

Layers consume a lot of RAM. Carefully plan your documents and combine layers as needed to conserve system resources.

- How much scratch disk space and memory do you have available? The more RAM and free disk space you have, the more layers you can use. Photoshop sometimes requests as much as five times the size of the file in scratch disk space, regardless of how much RAM is available. Many users have an entire hard drive set aside as Photoshop's scratch disk. Many high-end Photoshop users are not satisfied unless they are at the cutting edge in both RAM and hard drive technology as well as system speed. The money spent on these systems is soon recovered in time saved and/or the ability to work in a "job-efficient" if not "system-efficient" manner. Photoshop 7 allows you to specify up to four separate drives for scratch disk space. Be aware, however, that some filters run entirely in RAM. If enough RAM is not available, the filter won't run.

- How much long-term storage space do you have available? Sometimes you'll find that even though you have enough immediate resources — RAM and scratch disk space — you don't have enough storage space to archive all of your files. In this situation, you may choose to flatten the image once it is finished to conserve hard drive space. If it is imperative that you keep all layers intact, you can separate the layers into individual flattened documents with the layer transparency and masks saved as channels, and the documents saved as JPEG or compressed TIFF files. When you need them, simply reassemble the layers into the original file. Be aware that using the JPEG file format can cause a loss of image quality. Also, to do this with editable text and effects layers, you must first render or transform the layers to a non-editable state. With the proliferation of relatively inexpensive CD burners, this problem is easily solved.

- How much time do you have available? The less time you have available, the more important it is to choose the fastest method to create an image. Working in layers is not always the quickest way to complete an immediate, simple project.

Chapter Summary

In this chapter, you worked extensively with layers. You created them, managed them, and used them to achieve a variety of effects, including compositing multiple images, adding depth and shape to drawing objects, and creating Web objects. You'll have additional opportunities to work with layers as we move forward. Masking, clipping, and other functions also involve the use of layers, but are best understood in their own context.

Complete Project A: Gulls Poster

5 Channels and Masks

Chapter Objectives:

This chapter introduces you to the concepts of channels and masks, and builds on your knowledge of creating complex selections. All Photoshop documents have channels containing color information; here you'll learn to add additional channels for special applications and effects. You will also begin working with masks, which allow only certain portions of an image to show through. In Chapter 5, you will:

- Learn about channels: what they are, how they are used, and how to manage them.

- Become comfortable creating standard masks, and learn how they're used to hide or display specific areas of an image.

- Discover how to apply Gradient masks, and how variable density in a channel affects your images.

- Discover how to use Channels to create the illusion of depth in your images (3-D).

- Discover how Adjustment Layer masks allow adjustments to be made on selected portions of an image.

Projects to be Completed:

- Gulls Poster (A)
- Fallsbridge Menu Cover (B)
- Jazz Postcard (C)
- USA Poster (D)

Channels and Masks

Making selections can be a complex and sometimes difficult task. As you learn more about selections and how they affect the interaction between various tools, filters, techniques, and the image itself, you will gain an appreciation for well-developed selection skills and the artistic control they can offer you.

When a new Photoshop document is created, or when you open a scanned image file, the image information is arranged in specialized components known as *channels*.

Channels

Imagine a light table covered with piles of film. Each pile contains one, three, or four pieces of film. Each piece of film contains a component of an image. Black-and-white images have only one channel — the black one — and therefore would have one piece of film. An RGB image has three channels — one each for the red, green, and blue components. A CMYK image has four channels — one each for cyan, magenta, yellow, and black components. In addition to individual channels, Photoshop's Channels palette displays a composite image; it looks like a channel, but it's labeled RGB or CMYK, depending upon what color mode is being used for that particular image.

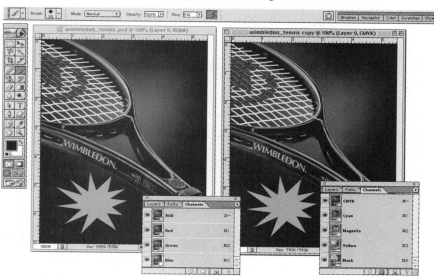

The channels in these images can be viewed independently by turning the appropriate visibility icons on or off. On the left, the RGB image shows three channels plus the composite, while on the right you can see four channels plus the composite.

Alpha Channels

An Alpha channel is a special type of channel that stores selections. If you make a selection, choose Select>Save Selection, and assign a name to the selection, an alpha channel is created with that same name. You can then use the alpha channel to create a mask in your image. Any alpha channel can be loaded as a Quick Mask by turning its visibility eyeball on at the same time as the composite channel. A *mask* is an area that shows or hides specific areas of the image. You can create up to 24 channels (color and alpha) in one Photoshop document.

As a professional designer, you're going to be working with two primary distribution methods. The first is print media, which, in almost all cases, requires CMYK or grayscale images. The second is distribution on the Web (or other digital models, such as CD-ROMs). The Web requires RGB images, either in JPEG or GIF format. Print media requires much higher resolution than that needed for the Web, and therefore results in much larger files.

Think of a mask as a hole in a piece of black cardboard; the only part of the underlying image that shows through is that section directly underneath the hole. This image shows the channel named feather_frame.

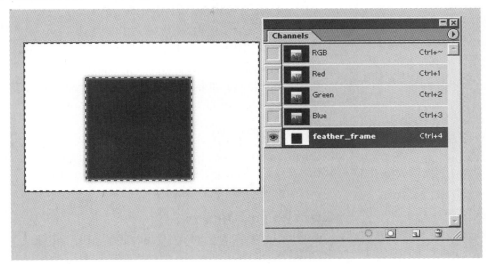

It's a soft-edged channel that was created by saving a feathered rectangular selection. The second image shows the effect of the channel when applied to an image of the East River in New York City.

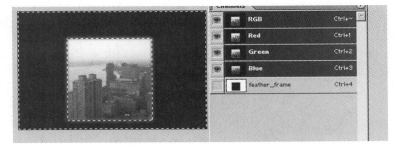

Channels can be used to record selections. The selection might be a complex tracing of shapes to isolate them from the rest of the image. This selection/channel could have a hard edge or may include a feather value to allow changes to blend with unchanged areas. The advantage of using channels is that they record what is selected (white), what isn't selected or is masked (black), and what is partially selected (the gray areas) in direct proportion to the gray value.

Managing Channels

Depending on your particular workflow, you may need multiple alpha channels in your image (you can have up to 24). When you've finished developing an image and you're getting ready to output the file, you should save a copy (in the appropriate format) with all alpha channels and paths removed. Many printing devices produce unpredictable results when asked to print a TIFF that contains channels or paths.

Profile Mismatch Errors: When you're opening an image, you may get an error message that says that the embedded color profile contained in the image doesn't match the one you're currently using. If this happens, refer back to the Getting Started section to learn how to disable the warning. Color profiles will be discussed in Chapter 10.

All images use channels to record color information; but how do we know how much red, green, and blue should appear in each pixel to create the illusion of a red truck in a green meadow? Designers and production specialists manipulate the grayscale of each channel to adjust color. They also use channels as a tool to create shadows, smoothly composite images, and apply effects such as embossed type and 3-D highlights and shadows.

Channels serve 2 simple purposes. First, they act as a grayscale print of each primary color. When overlaid on screen (RGB color mode), white areas in the Red channel, for instance, display red; black areas display no red. (CMYK color mode is the reverse of this.) An amount of 25% shows as 75% gray, while 60% shows as 40% gray.

Gradient Masks

Using Gradient masks is vital in image compositing. Gradient masks allow smooth blends at the edges of images, help soften or fade one image into another, or simulate the reflection of one object onto the surface of another.

Channels and Density

The ability to record density or grayscale values provides great power and flexibility during the development process, enabling users to control how much (light) or how little (dark) an applied effect has on different parts of an image. A channel containing a gradient from light to dark has the effect of gradually protecting or hiding pixels in the image that appear where the gradient channel darkens. Density masks are used to create professional compositing, filter effects, and fades for cast shadows and reflections.

A good way to learn this concept is to complete the following exercise that uses a Gradient mask.

Use Gradient Masks

1. Open **pokey.tif** from your **RF_Intro_Photoshop** folder. Press the "D" key to reset the foreground and background colors to their defaults. From the Image menu, select Canvas Size. Anchor the image to the upper-middle box, and crop the canvas to a Height of 3.125 in. When the warning box appears, press Return/Enter to proceed.

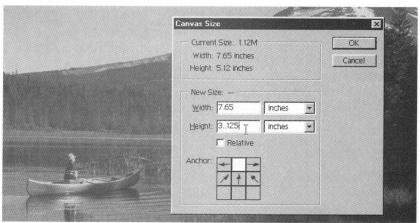

2. Return to the Image menu and select Canvas Size again. Double the Height to 6.25 in., and anchor the image to the upper-middle box.

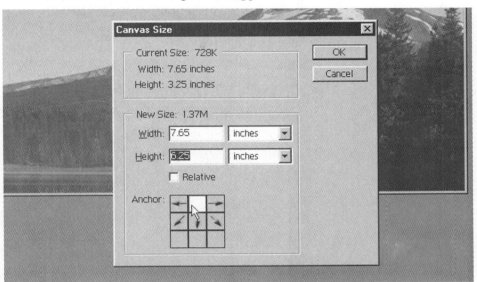

3. Using the Magic Wand tool, select the white area at the bottom of the image. Make sure the Tolerance setting isn't any greater than 25. In the Channels palette, click the Save Selection as Channel icon to convert the current selection into a new alpha channel. Double-click the channel and rename it "Gradient".

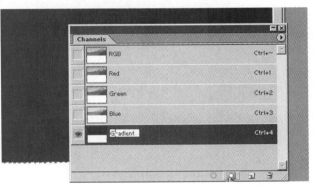

4. Working in the Gradient channel, click the Linear Gradient tool, and set it to Foreground to Background. Make certain that White is the foreground color and Black is the background color, and that the tool's Opacity is set to 100%. Press the Shift key, and drag the gradient from the bottom to the top of the white region of the mask.

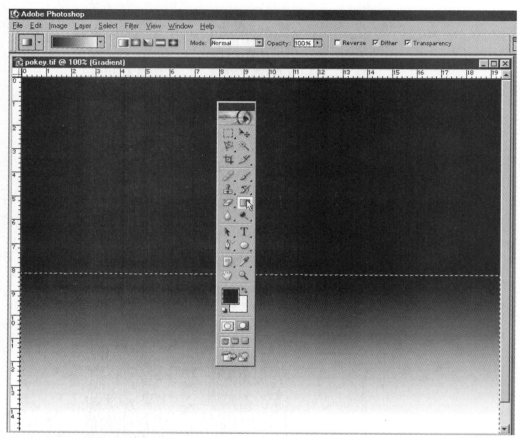

5. Return to the RGB channel. From the Select menu, choose Inverse to select the top scene. Press Command/Control-C, then Command/Control-V to paste a copy of the scene into a new layer. From the Edit menu, choose Transform>Flip Vertical, and reposition the selection at the bottom of the image.

6. Load the Gradient Selection mask (Command/Control-click on the Gradient channel). Press the Delete key, which deletes pixels that are not protected by the mask (the white area). The result is a smooth fade-out that fades in the same direction that the mask lightens. These pixels are less protected from being deleted.

7. Save the file as "pokey_reflected.psd" to your **Work_In_Progress** folder, and then close the file.

Creating Depth Where None Exists

Light defines how we see in the real (non-digital) world. The surface of an object absorbs, reflects, and redirects light according to its shape, adding dimension to the object. High points reflect a lot of light — sometimes eliminating detail. These areas are called *specular highlights*. Normally, lighted areas, called *highlights*, create the illusion of raising items off the surface. Indentations and low areas cast shadows.

In the digital world, the direction, hardness, and tonal values of highlights and shadows affect how a 3-D illusion appears. For an image to appear raised from the surface, shadows are generally placed at the bottom and right sides of the shape or selection. To create the illusion of being depressed into the surface, highlights are used in those positions. The edge thickness and fuzziness determines how far the object appears to be from the surface. Thicker and fuzzier shadows make the shape very depressed or embossed, while harder, narrow edges create only the slightest hint of dimension. Consider the colors of both the object and the surface. In real life, shadows and highlights contain a tint of the predominant color(s); they aren't just shades of gray.

This next exercise demonstrates how to visually raise a two-dimensional object from a flat surface. To do this, we're going to learn how to create two types of special alpha channels — one which simulates highlights, and the other to create the shadows.

Create Highlight and Shadow Masks

1. Open **rough_stone.tif** from the **RF_Intro_Photoshop** folder. It's a basic stucco background.

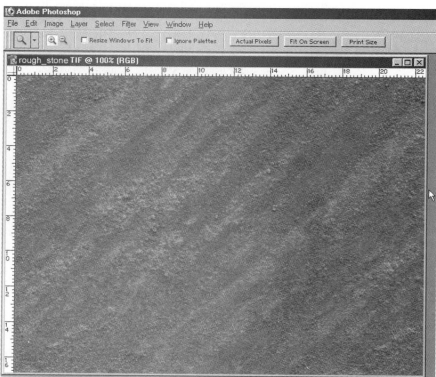

2. Make certain the Layers and Channels palettes are showing. From the File menu, select Place. Select **tropical_interiors.eps** from the **RF_Intro_Photoshop** folder. Click Place to place it directly onto a new layer. Resize the image, holding down the Shift key to maintain the aspect ratio, and position it as shown. When you're satisfied that it roughly matches this visual, press Command/Control-Return/Enter.

3. In the Layers palette, Command/Control-click the new layer; the contents of the layer are selected. In the Channels palette, click the Save Selection as Channel button. This turns a selection of the placed graphic into a channel. Double-click its name in the Channels palette, and name it "Type Inside".

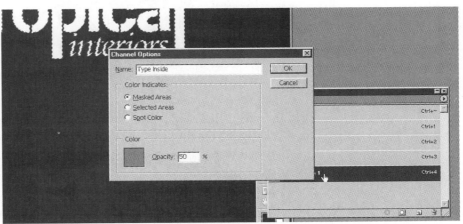

4. Copy the channel by dragging it to the New Channel icon. Double-click this channel and rename it "Type Outside".

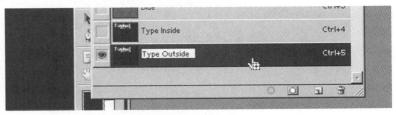

5. With the selection still active, choose Modify>Expand from the Select menu. Enter "3 pixels" and click OK. This expands the selection by 3 pixels in every direction.

6. Press the "D" key followed by the "X" key to select and then exchange the default colors, making the foreground color black. Now press the Delete key to clear the extra regions of the mask. This expanded outline of the type contains the space for the shadows and highlights we're going to create.

7. Duplicate the Type Outside mask by dragging it to the New Channel icon, and name it "Blur Mask". At this point, you should have three additional channels (a total of six in addition to the composite RGB channel).

8. With the Blur Mask channel active, press Command/Control-D to deselect it. Choose Blur>Gaussian Blur from the Filter menu. Use a Radius of 2.5 pixels to soften the edges of the mask.

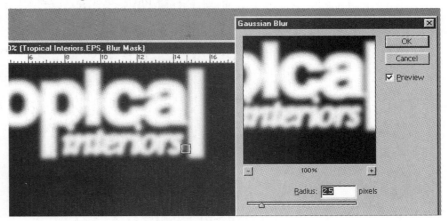

9. Duplicate the Blur Mask channel; name it "Highlights". Choose Stylize>Emboss from the Filter menu. Set the Angle to 45°, Height to 3 pixels, and Amount to 100%. Click OK when these settings are complete.

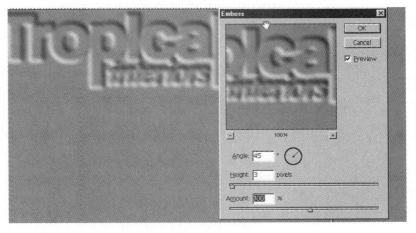

10. Duplicate the Highlights channel. Rename the new channel "Shadows".

11. Activate the Highlights channel by clicking it once. Press Command/Control-L to activate the Levels dialog box. Select the Set Black Point Eyedropper tool.

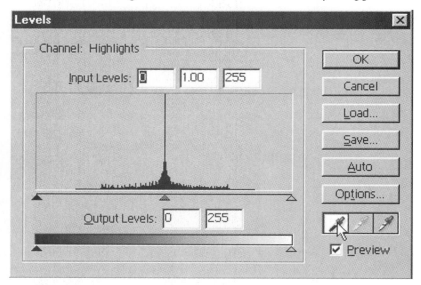

12. With the Set Black Point Eyedropper tool, click anywhere on the gray image area. This sets 50% gray as the darkest tone in the image, resulting in all of those areas turning black. The upper-left edges of the type objects retain their tonal values, thus creating the Highlight mask. Click OK.

A Gaussian Blur used in conjunction with a Density mask causes strange artifacts to develop.

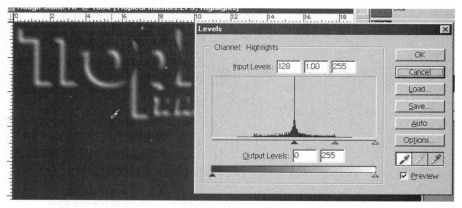

13. Activate the Shadows channel. From the Image menu, select Adjustments>Invert, or press Command/Control-I to create a negative mask. What was light is now dark and vice versa.

14. Press Command/Control-L to repeat the Level adjustment executed in Step 12 (set the black point by clicking on a gray area of the image). Since the image was inverted before selecting the black point, the highlights are reversed — we now have a Shadow mask. Click OK.

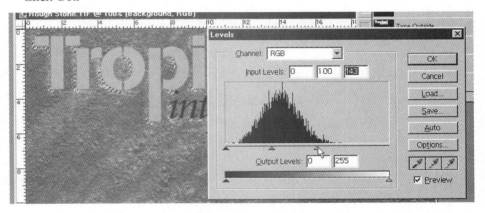

15. Make sure the Background layer is active. If it's not, the next steps won't work. Activating the Background layer also activates the RGB composite channel.

16. Now we'll use these channels as selections to highlight and shadow the pixels in the actual color image. In the Channels palette, Command/Control-click the Highlight mask to load it as a selection. Press Command/Control-L to open the Levels dialog box. Lighten the shadow tones in the Highlight selection area by sliding the white (right) Input Levels slider to achieve a white point of 143. Click OK.

17. Load the Shadow mask channel. In the Levels dialog box, set the black (left) Input Levels slider to achieve a black point of 88. This darkens the selection to create the shadows. Click OK, and then deselect.

18. Save the file as "3d_text.psd" to your **Work_In_Progress** folder, and close it.

Practicing Complex Techniques

With minor modifications, this same basic technique can create a range of different effects. Once you're familiar with the concept of creating Highlight and Shadow masks, it's a good idea to practice the technique until you can easily repeat it.

Highlights, shadows, and midtones comprise the tonal range of an image. So-called "specular highlights" are outside normal tone calculations — they are ignored when determining the brightest point in an image. An example of this might be the sparkle of a diamond.

Sometimes, it helps to list the steps of a complex technique in the order of execution. To create Highlight and Shadow masks, you would:

- Load or create the background.
- Place or create the artwork.
- Create and save the "inside" mask.
- Duplicate and expand.
- Blur and Emboss.
- Duplicate twice — name one channel "Highlights" and the other "Shadows".
- Set the black point of Highlights to 50% gray with the Levels command.
- Invert the tone map of Shadows, and set the black point to 50% gray.
- In the composite image, load/lighten Highlights, then load/darken Shadows.

Many variations are possible with this technique. For example, on a high-resolution file, the embossed channel can be made tighter (with smaller, more defined edges). The technique can be used to sharpen edges by loading the inside mask into the blur channel and filling it with 50% gray. You can also use the channels to add noise and other effects.

Layer Masks

The relationship between channels, masks, adjustment layers, and selections is one of the most important in the Photoshop program; how these features work together provides image-makers with very sophisticated creative control.

Layer masks and Adjustment Layer masks are special kinds of channels. Adjustment Layer masks allow you to make adjustments on selected portions of an image. Each has unique characteristics, but both are in fact channels and can be edited in the same manner.

In the following exercise, we're going to create a poster that features a theatrical production of "12 Angry Men" — with both male and female students as the actors. To more accurately reflect the social mix, the play has been renamed to "12 Angry Jurors".

Use Layer Masks

1. Create a new document with a Width of 16 inches and a Height of 11.5 inches. Use the RGB Color Mode, and choose a Transparent background. The Resolution should be 150 ppi (pixels per inch). Name the file "playbill.psd" and save it into your **Work_In_Progress** folder.

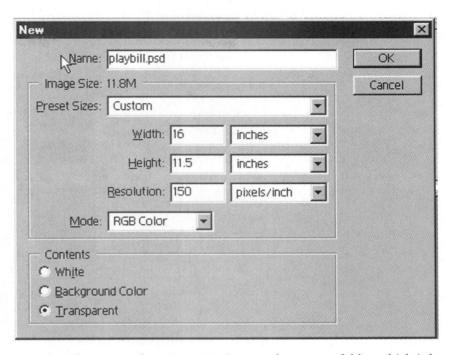

2. From the File menu, select Open. Navigate to the **Jurors** folder, which is located inside the **RF_Intro_Photoshop** folder. Select all of the files at once, and then click the Open button.

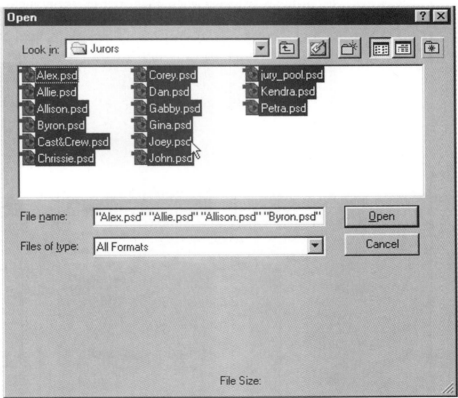

3. From the Window menu, select Documents>Tile. This arranges the open documents so you can see them all at the same time. For a project like this, it's a good idea to use this option. Press the Tab key to temporarily turn off the toolbars.

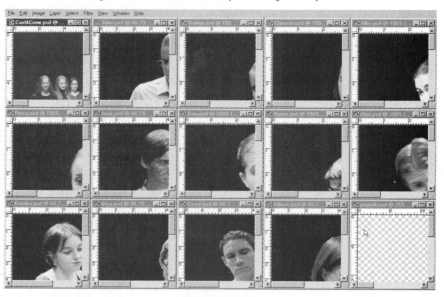

4. Turn on the toolbars and palettes again by pressing the Tab key. Now you're going to import each of the open images into the **playbill.psd** file. Simply click the first image and drag it onto the transparent **playbill.psd** document. The cursor changes into an arrow displaying a plus (+) sign, indicating the image is being added to the document.

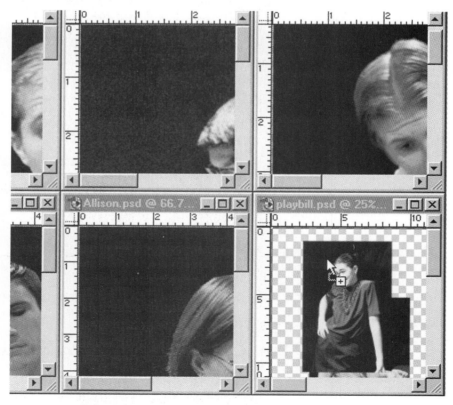

You can create composite images by dragging a layer from one file into another file. It works the same way as dragging the image itself onto an open document; it automatically creates a new layer to accommodate the imported image.

5. Once the first image appears in the **playbill.psd** file, close the image. Move onto the next image, drag it to the **playbill.psd** file, and then close the image. Move all the images into the document, and then press the "F" key to fill the monitor with the image. If it's not already visible, activate the Layers palette (Window>Layers). You'll see that for every image you added, Photoshop added a layer.

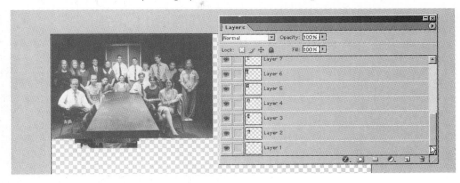

6. Select the Move tool from the Toolbox and drag the images around. Find the image containing the entire cast, and move it to the center of the image. Rename the layer "cast_photo".

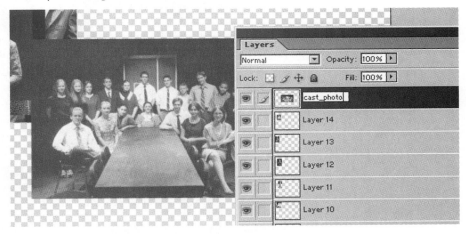

7. Move the cast_photo layer to just above Layer 1. This places it beneath the individual images of the cast members.

8. Select the first layer at the top of the stack. Use the Move tool to position the image outside of the cast_photo image. Select the next layer down, and repeat the process until you've arranged all of the individual juror images around the photo of the entire cast. Since each image is rectangular, some obscure those underneath — but that's OK for now. When you're pleased with the balance, save the file.

9. With the Move tool still selected, look at the Options palette at the top of the window. One of the check boxes turns on the Auto Select Layer option. Check it. This automatically selects any layer containing an individual juror when you click on one of the faces (or any of the juror pixels).

10. Activate the Brushes palette — it's probably in the Palette Well at the upper right of your monitor. Click the Brush Tip Shape button, and create a round brush with a Diameter of 100 pixels, and a Hardness setting of 0%.

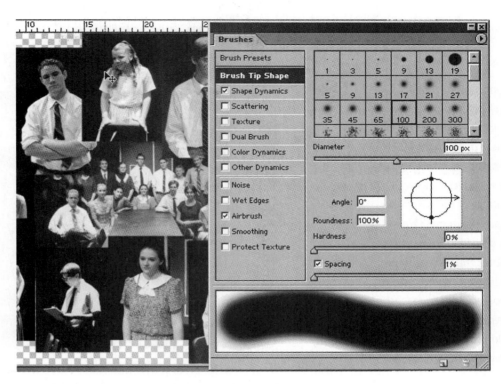

11. Pick one of the jurors, and click the Add Layer Mask icon on the Layers palette. It's the small hollow circle.

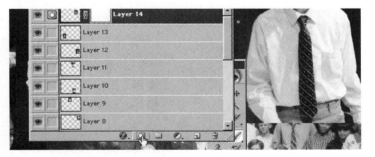

Command/Control-clicking an alpha channel loads the channel as a selection. Activating the channel and clicking the selection icon at the bottom of the palette loads the active channel as a selection. Remember that a selection must be active (marching ants) to protect areas from painting. Painting is allowed only in selected areas when a selection is active.

12. Make sure the foreground color is set to Black and the background color is set to White. Paint a mask around the edge of the juror so the image doesn't obscure the ones beneath it. The point is to create a soft-edged mask to help blend the images together.

13. Select the next juror, and add a Layer mask to that layer as well. Continue painting the masks on each layer, blending the images together. Remember, first select the layer with the Move tool, then add a Layer mask, then pick the paintbrush, and paint the mask. It's OK if the transparent background shows through — you'll fix that in a minute.

Note the box between the image icon and the visibility eyeball icon. When a layer with a Layer mask is active, an icon of either a paintbrush or a mask is visible in the box. If you click back and forth between the mask and the image icon, you can see the change. This indicates which portion of the layer is active. You can paint on the mask to modify it, or you can make changes on the paint layer. Inadvertently painting on the paint layer can potentially cause problems; always be aware of where you are working. When a paintbrush seems to work incorrectly, or not at all, you are probably on the paint layer, and that is what's causing your problem.

Each channel adds to the size and complexity of the file. Channels that are no longer needed should be eliminated to reduce the size and complexity of the image.

14. When you've completed creating all the Layer masks (there should be one for every layer except Layer 1), select Layer 1 and fill it with Black. Take a look at the results, and adjust the masks and layer positions as necessary. Save and close the file when you're done.

15. We created a sample of what the poster could look like with a little bit of extra work — such as the addition of some type and layer styles. You can see the sample by opening the file named **playbill_final.jpg** from your **RF_Intro_Photoshop** folder.

Using Quick Mask Mode

Quick Mask mode allows you to turn any selection into a mask while your image is active, without having to access the Channels palette. In order to save a selection made or modified in Quick Mask mode, you can either revert back to regular (marching ants) mode, or copy the Quick Mask channel in the Channels palette while it is active. A Quick Mask channel appears in the Channels palette if you have the channel open; but the channel is automatically deleted when you finish working with the mask. You can use the Quick Mask mode to alter a selection area; once you have made the selection you want, you can then save it as a standard alpha channel selection when you exit Quick Mask mode. You can also start a Quick Mask by loading an alpha channel selection.

Make a Quick Mask

1. Open the file **trike.psd** from the **RF_Intro_Photoshop** folder. This custom vehicle was built from the front end of an automobile grafted to a motorcycle frame. Unfortunately the background is less than perfect. Let's apply a Zoom effect that is common in custom motorcycle publications.

2. Press the "Q" key to enter Quick Mask mode, or click the Quick Mask Mode button at the bottom of the Toolbar.

3. Choose a medium-size soft-edge brush from the Brushes palette. Press the "D" key to ensure that black is the foreground color. Paint over the vehicle; it's not necessary to be extremely precise.

Red is the default display color for masks because it simulates Rubilith — a transparent red acetate sheet that was used to mask images in the days before computers were used in print and design environments.

4. The Quick Mask Mode button allows you to modify the mask with almost any standard filter or tool. The masked area is shown as transparent red. (This default color may be changed at any time by double-clicking the Quick Mask channel and accessing the Color Picker by clicking the colored square.)

5. When you've finished painting, click the Standard Mode button, or press the "Q" key on the keyboard. Notice that by painting around the mask, you've created a selection; you used a soft-edge brush, so the selection also has a soft edge. Painting (or using any tool or filter) on a Quick Mask affects only the selection; it does not affect the image.

6. Press Command/Control-C then Command/Control-V to copy and paste the selected area to a new layer. Turn off the Background layer visibility eyeball to see the soft edge of your new layer.

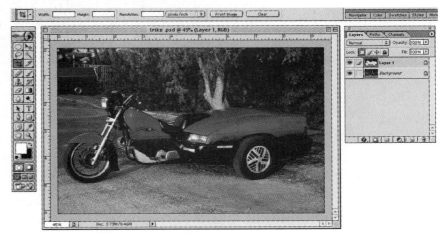

7. From the Filter menu, select Blur>Radial Blur. Set the amount to 45, and Check the Zoom and Good radio buttons. Be sure to move the Blur Center slightly to the left to align the Zoom effect.

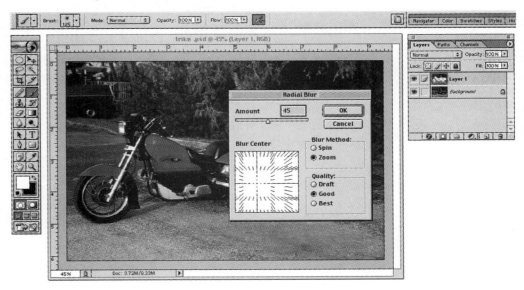

8. In the final image, the vehicle explodes from the page. Any touch up work can easily be done with a Layer mask on the Blur layer to blend the effect with the static shot of the vehicle.

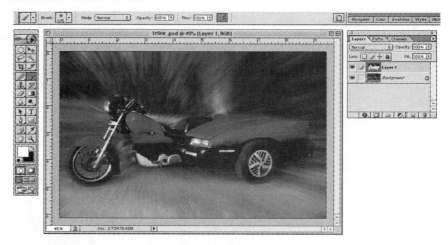

9. Save and close the file.

Quick Mask Options

Double-clicking the Quick Mask Mode button displays the Options dialog box. Choosing Masked Areas (the default) causes the Quick Mask to behave as you've already seen: painting with white reduces the mask and adds to the selection; painting with black adds to the mask, shrinking the selection. Choosing Selected Areas causes the Quick Mask to behave exactly opposite from what we've seen: painting with black reduces the mask and adds to the selection; painting with white adds to the mask, shrinking the selection. It's the same as inverting a selection.

Chapter Summary

In this chapter, you worked with and explored the differences between color channels and alpha channels. You experimented with alpha channels and with the Quick Mask mode. You gained an understanding of how channels work, and found you can mask portions of a layer to protect them while working on another element of the layer. Using channels, you created an image with a layered and shadowed effect. You learned to use channels to create highlights and shadows, and know how to apply effects that are similar to layer styles, but offer far more flexibility and control.

6 *Painting Tools*

Chapter Objectives:

Photoshop's painting tools enable designers to enhance images in many ways. The newly redesigned paint engine provides increased functionality, flexibility, and control over the behavior of the painting tools. In addition, the new healing and patching tools provide improved methods of repairing and retouching images. In Chapter 6, you will:

- Learn about the Brushes palette and how to select the shape, size, and style of your brushes.

- Discover how to use the Pencil tool to create line art.

- Explore the use of the Paintbrush tool, and learn to apply soft edges and colors to your artwork.

- Discover how to apply airbrush settings to almost any of the painting tools.

- Learn how to use the painting tool options, including pen pressure, pen tilt, and the stylus wheel.

- Apply fills to your images using the Gradient Fill and Paint Bucket tools.

- Discover how to selectively delete portions of an image using several different eraser tools.

- Learn how to copy pixels using the Clone Stamp tool, and how to repair images using the Healing brush.

Projects to be Completed:

- Gulls Poster (A)

- Fallsbridge Menu Cover (B)

- Jazz Postcard (C)

- USA Poster (D)

Painting Tools

Photoshop 7 introduces a totally revamped paint engine that allows more control and a much more organic feel for those who use the software to create painterly effects from scratch. The new paint engine's sophisticated tools also offer more control for those who work on photographs. The available options and controls are quite extensive. We will begin to explore them in this chapter.

Each painting tool has an Options Bar that allows control over the way the tool interacts with the image. Most settings are unique to the specific tool being used, but the tools have some settings in common. Among the common paint options are Brush, Blending Mode, Opacity, and Flow.

This image shows the Options bar for the Clone Stamp tool. Painting tools each have specific options, but all offer a Brush pop-up menu, Blending Modes, Opacity, and Flow controls.

Readers who have had some experience with earlier versions of the Photoshop program will notice several items right away. The place on the Toolbar previously allocated to the Airbrush tool now shows an icon of a band-aid; the band-aid represents the Healing brush. If you look at the Options bar, you will see an airbrush icon. This icon is on the Options bar because in Photoshop 7, almost any brush can be an airbrush. This capability allows users to apply airbrush effects while cloning, erasing, burning and dodging, and using the Blur and Sharpen brushes — providing an additional level of control to the designer.

All of the regular painting tools provide the ability to set a Blending mode. A Blending mode combines image information according to mathematical rules. In addition, all painting tools have an Opacity slider on the Options toolbar. The Opacity slider allows adjustment of the transparency of the color, pattern, or effect being applied to the image. When opacity is less than 100%, repeated applications of color are required to make the paint more opaque. For example, if the Paintbrush tool is set to 25% opacity, the first stroke combines 25% of the foreground color and 75% of the image. If the area is stroked again with the same color (after releasing and then again depressing the mouse button), a bit more of the image is obscured by paint. If the brush is applied enough times, the image is entirely obscured. When the Airbrush option is chosen, the user can set the flow rate as well as the opacity.

The Brushes Palette Returns

In earlier versions of Photoshop, brushes were chosen from the Brushes palette. In recent years, this palette was absent from the program; brushes were chosen from the Options toolbar. Photoshop 7 marks the return of the Brushes palette. In this ambitious remake of the paint engine, the Brushes palette is a necessity due to the myriad options and shapes, as well as the ability to customize any brush with a variety of controls. Brushes can vary in size, shape, angle, spacing, hardness, and pattern. Any brush can be modified via a list of customizable style controls.

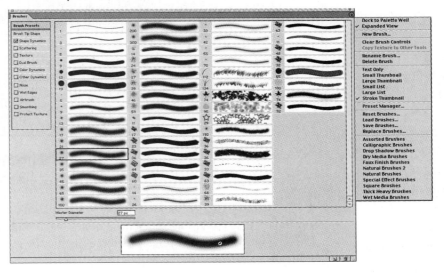

Stroke Thumbnail view of the Brushes palette.

Note that the brushes in the upper-left row appear hard-edged, while those below them have soft, fading edges. Brushes lower in the list are patterned. Generally speaking, "hard" brushes are not actually hard, except as compared to "soft" brushes. Hard brushes have very small, softened, or *anti-aliased* edges; soft brushes have wide, soft edges to blend colors smoothly into the underlying image. Each brush has a number under its tip-shape icon with the number representing the width of the brush measured in pixels.

The pop-up menu of the Brushes palette lists the additional brush libraries that ship with Photoshop. Brushes can be edited and added to the Brushes palette by clicking the triangle at the top of the pop-up Brushes palette, and then selecting New Brush.

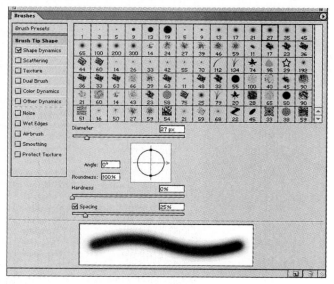

Clicking the Brush Tip Shape button in the Brushes palette opens a dialog box with many options. There is a list of style check boxes (each with its own set of controls accessed by clicking on the style name), icons representing the currently loaded tip shapes, and several controls to further modify any of them:

- **Diameter.** Diameter indicates the width of the brush (at its widest horizontal point), measured in pixels.

- **Hardness.** This setting designates how hard or soft the edges of the brush are. Even if Hardness is set to 100% (the default for Photoshop's hard-edged brushes), the edges are still softened slightly to create an anti-aliased brush. Conversely, even when a brush is softened to 0% Hardness, the center of the brush is still solid.

- **Spacing.** The Spacing setting represents how often a brush stroke repeats. The percentage listed is a percentage of the width of a brush. For example, a round, 20-pixel brush with a 200% Spacing would draw a series of dots 20 pixels in diameter, with 40 pixels between the start of the first dot and the start of the second dot. Most of Photoshop's default (hard) brushes have a Spacing of 25%, which appears as a continual flow; others may vary, depending on their attributes. Unchecking the Spacing check box causes the spacing to vary according to the speed of the mouse. The faster the line is drawn, the more space between the dots.

- **Roundness.** Changing the Roundness value creates an elliptical brush, which can then be set at any angle. Both the Angle and Roundness may be set by keying in the degree of rotation and percent of roundness, or by manipulating the graphic in the center of the dialog box.

Other things you should know about brushes:

- You can save or load sets of custom-created brushes, or append one set of brushes to another, by clicking the black triangle in the upper-right corner of the Brushes palette to activate the drop-down menu. Use this menu to reset the Brushes palette to the default (original installation) settings.

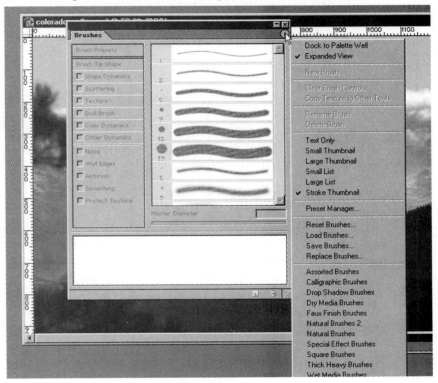

- Photoshop allows definition of irregularly shaped brushes; select any area of the image using the selection tools, and choose the Edit>Define Brush command.

- Brush shape, color, and other dynamic attributes allow you to fade brush strokes from foreground to background, from foreground to transparent, or to fade the weight of the line. Using these three settings, you can achieve almost unlimited effects while painting.

- Increased support for graphics tablets, such as those by Wacom, allow users to control the paint stroke via pen pressure, pen tilt, and stylus wheel. These can be set under the Control sub-menu for each applicable brush style. The Fade control is found here as well and allows the user to set a number of steps over which the stroke fades out.

Use the Brushes Palette

1. Create a new 240 ppi RGB document, 500 pixels wide by 500 pixels high with a White background. Select the Paintbrush tool, and be sure the Brushes palette is open. Press the "D" key to reset the default foreground and background colors.

Elliptical brushes are good for creating calligraphic lettering. A set of calligraphic brushes ships with Photoshop and can be loaded or appended to the existing list.

2. Select Brush Presets from the Brushes palette, and scroll down to the brush that resembles a single blade of grass. Paint back and forth with this brush. You are making what looks like dune grass. Imagine how it would look with greens or browns in place of the default colors of black and white. Try changing your foreground and background colors and using the brush again.

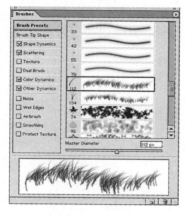 

3. Move the Diameter slider to the right or left to increase or decrease the size of the brush. Notice that the Preview window in the lower part of the dialog box dynamically changes as you move the slider. A brush may be sized from 1 to 999 pixels (the maximum size of the preview, however, is about 50 pixels).

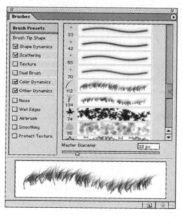 

4. Select a brush with soft edges. Move the Hardness slider back and forth, and watch the brush edges change in the New Brush window.

5. Select Brush Tip Shape. Drag the dots at the top and bottom of the graphic in the lower center of the dialog box and watch the shape of the brush change; drag the arrow to vary the angle of the brush.

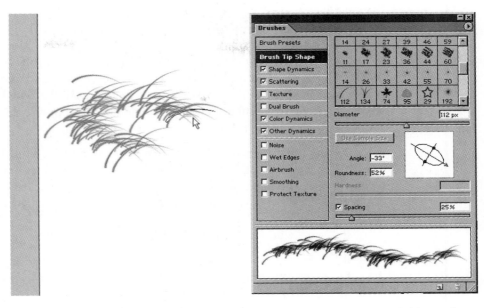

6. Note that you can also enter values directly into the appropriate fields on the palette. Experiment with different settings using both fields and sliders until you get a feel for how changes affect the brush.

7. Click the pop-up menu button and select New Brush to save your changes. Note how the new brush is added to the Brushes palette.

8. If you wish, return to the default set of brushes. Click Brush Presets, then select Reset Brushes from the drop-down menu that appears from the black triangle in the upper-right corner of the Brushes palette. Click OK to reset the brushes to their original condition.

9. Close the file without saving your changes.

Take some time to experiment with the Brushes palette. It represents a complete make-over of the program's paint engine. Up until now, Photoshop has not been known for its painting capabilities; now many artists can remain in the Photoshop environment to finish their artwork instead of using other paint programs in conjunction with Photoshop.

The Pencil Tool

The Pencil tool is unique among the painting tools. It is ideally suited for use with bitmap (black-and-white) images, or for creating hard outlines using horizontal or vertical strokes. This is because the Pencil tool has no anti-aliasing attribute; as such, it is rarely used with photographic images.

The Pencil tool draws the foreground color — if it's set to white, and the background is also white, you won't be able to see what you're drawing.

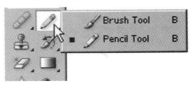

Use the Pencil Tool

1. Create a new 240 ppi RGB document, 5 in. wide by 5 in. high with a White background. Select the Pencil tool from the Toolbox. It may be hidden under the Paintbrush tool; if so, press Shift-B until the Pencil tool is revealed, or click on the Paintbrush tool, and hold down the mouse button until you can select the Pencil tool.

2. The Pencil tool, while extremely useful for editing bitmapped images, is rarely used with photographic images. Open the Brushes palette and take a look at the brushes. Notice how hard they are. The Pencil tool is never anti-aliased.

3. Select the 45-pixel brush in the Brushes palette.

4. Choose a blue color from the Swatches palette.

5. Draw a few lines. They display edges known as *jaggies* — a stair step effect that can sometimes detract from the quality of your images. When editing bitmaps, however, the Pencil tool is invaluable.

6. Leave the image open for the next exercise.

The Paintbrush Tool

Unlike the Pencil tool, the Paintbrush tool is always anti-aliased. Even hard-edged brushes have anti-aliasing built in. The softer brushes allow for a smooth, blended application of color. You can achieve interesting effects working with textured brushes.

Use the Paintbrush Tool

1. In the open file, select the Paintbrush tool (press Shift-B) and note how the brush changes in the palette. Choose a green color to make it easy to distinguish the Paintbrush marks from your Pencil marks. Make sure the Opacity is set to 100%.

2. Paint a few strokes. Notice how much smoother the lines are as compared to the Pencil tool lines. Experiment with the Hardness slider to see how the edges change. To access the Hardness slider, click the Brush Tip Shape button in the Brushes palette.

3. On the Options bar, move the Opacity slider down to 25%.

4. Without releasing the mouse button, paint with the Paintbrush tool, crossing over areas already painted.

5. Notice that no matter how many times you paint over a particular area, the paint remains at 25% opacity, allowing 75% of the image to show through. Release the mouse button, then paint over the area again. Now the areas where paint overlaps become more opaque.

Photoshop ships with a number of brush sets that are located in the Photoshop>Presets> Brushes folder. You can load them from the Brushes palette pop-up menu.

Reset Brushes...
Load Brushes...
Save Brushes...
Replace Brushes...

Assorted Brushes
Calligraphic Brushes
Drop Shadow Brushes
Dry Media Brushes
Faux Finish Brushes
Natural Brushes 2
Natural Brushes
Special Effect Brushes
Square Brushes
Thick Heavy Brushes
Wet Media Brushes

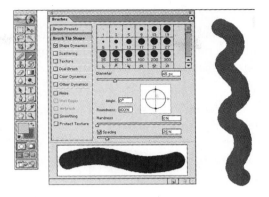

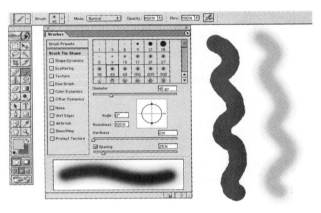

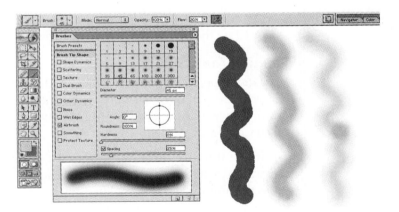

In the examples above, the same 45-pixel brush was used to paint all 3 strokes: Number 1 set as a pencil, Number 2 set as a normal brush, and Number 3 set as an airbrush with a 20% flow rate. Note the area on Number 3 where the brush was held still as the paint continued to flow.

6. Return the Opacity slider to the 100% setting, and check the Wet Edges check box.

7. Change the foreground color to Red, use the same brush, and paint again. The center of the stroke is partially transparent, while the paint pools up on the sides creating a watercolor wash effect.

8. Deselect the Wet Edges option. Leave the image open for the next exercise.

The Airbrush has a Flow Rate slider that makes it behave similar to its real-world counterpart.

The Airbrush Tool

In past versions of the program, the Airbrush was a separate tool. Now, most brushes may be set to operate as airbrushes. All you would need to do is click the Airbrush icon on the Options toolbar, set a flow rate in the box next to it, and you'd be ready to go.

The Airbrush tool produces an even softer edge than the Paintbrush tool, unless the flow rate is set to a high value and a harder-edged brush is selected; then the results resemble those from the Paintbrush tool. The difference is that without lifting the mouse button, painting repeatedly over a given area gradually makes it more opaque. This results in a more natural painting style, making it especially useful for photo retouching.

Use the Airbrush

1. In the open image, select the Airbrush option.

2. Adjust the Flow Rate slider to 20%.

3. Select the same 45-pixel soft brush and a bright blue color.

4. Hold down the mouse button over the image without moving the mouse and watch what happens. The longer you hold down the mouse button, the larger and more opaque the spot becomes.

5. Release the mouse button. Change the Flow Rate setting to 90% and try it again. The end result is the same, but it happens a lot faster because the pressure is higher. Airbrush opacity relies upon pressure rather than a distinct opacity setting, so overlaying strokes result in a more opaque color. The speed with which the paint becomes opaque depends upon the Flow Rate value.

6. Close the file without saving changes.

Painting Tool Options

Increased support for graphics tablets, such as those from Wacom, allow control based on pen pressure, pen tilt, and stylus wheel. These controls are dynamic, responding to the drawing style of the artist. They can be found on many of the brush styles under a button called Control.

The image you're going to use for the next exercise was shot with a Cannon D30 digital camera and a 300mm lens. Even with the long lens, the camera was too close for the subject's comfort, and she wouldn't stay in one place long enough for precise composition. Even though the photographic image is an interesting one, the possibility of enhancing it becomes more enjoyable using Photoshop 7. The process of getting from the original photograph to the basic watercolor is a long and complex one. We don't have time for the entire process here, but the final steps to finish the project provide an excellent example of the practical use of painting tools and brushes.

Explore a Finished Piece

1. Open **turkey.psd** from the **RF_Intro_Photoshop** folder.

2. In the Layers palette, turn on the visibility icons one at a time to see the evolution of the image. Some layers might obscure the image — hide those layers.

3. Experiment with the Grass and Dune Grass brushes from the Presets menu, using the Eyedropper tool to choose colors from within the image to maintain color harmony.

4. Notice the use of a Layer mask to allow the sharp area to come through in the Grass/Mask layer.

5. At times, various blur (Motion & Gaussian) effects were used to make the brush strokes fit into the image. The Watercolor filter was used lightly to keep the emphasis on the focal point of the image. The additional birds were made from the main subject, and then blurred and degraded to become compositional elements.

6. Close the file when you're done. Don't save the changes you've made.

You may wish to revisit this file from time to time as your skill level grows and recreate it for yourself. There is no better way to learn than to experiment with the software.

Working with Fills

Photoshop's two fill tools, the Paint Bucket tool and the Gradient Fill tool, are used to fill defined areas with a predefined color, pattern, or gradient. Unlike the tools we have previously discussed, they do not employ a brush. The areas to be filled may be defined by a Tolerance setting alone, or they may be further defined by a selection.

The Gradient Fill Tool

The Gradient Fill tool is used to fill large areas with color. Five types of gradients may be created: linear, radial (circular), angle, reflected, and diamond.

A standard gradient blends the foreground to the background color. Gradients, however, may also be constructed to blend foreground to transparent, or to blend several colors. A number of gradients and gradient libraries ship ready-to-use with Photoshop.

To apply a gradient, the tool is drawn across the area over which the blend is applied. The gradient fills either a selected area or the entire image.

Use the Gradient Fill Tool

1. Create a blank RGB canvas with a White background that is 5 in. wide by 5 in. high with a Resolution of 240 ppi. First, let's create a linear gradient fill. Select the Gradient Fill tool (it may be hidden under the Paint Bucket tool), and click the Linear button on the Options bar. We're going to make a simple gradient using the default colors with black as the foreground and white as the background.

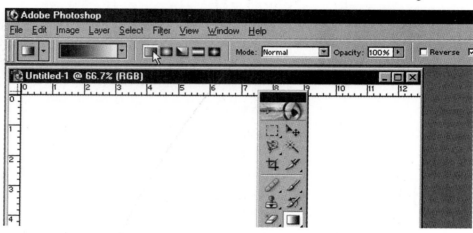

2. Click on the left side of the image and drag the cursor across the image, leaving about an inch on each side. If you hold down the Shift key while dragging, the fill is constrained to 45°.

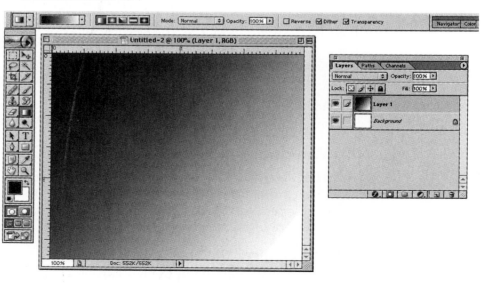

3. The image is filled with 100% of the selected color at the beginning of the fill, and changes to 100% white at the end of the fill. Note that the area outside the beginning of your gradient is filled with 100% foreground color, and the area outside the area of the fill is 100% white. The blend only occurs between the starting and ending points.

4. Experiment with the other gradient tools to get a feel for the gradient patterns they create. Try using the Reverse button on the Options toolbar to see what happens.

5. Return to the Linear Gradient tool and redo your first gradient. Yours should resemble the above example.

6. Save the file into your **Work_In_Progress** folder as "gradients.psd", and leave it open for the next exercise.

The Paint Bucket Tool

This tool creates similar results to using the Edit>Fill command, except that the Paint Bucket tool is limited to using either the foreground color or a defined pattern. Tolerance, defined on the Options toolbar, specifies how close in color adjacent pixels must be if they are to be filled with paint. Tolerance may be set from 0 to 255. Zero (0) fills only pixels identical in color to the pixel on which you click; 255 paints every pixel in the image or selected area.

Anti-aliasing may or may not be used, depending on the image you're modifying. When the Contiguous box is checked, only pixels within the prescribed tolerance that abut one another are colored. The fill may be applied to a single layer or to all layers.

Use the Paint Bucket Tool

1. Continue working in the open document from the previous exercise. Select the Paint Bucket tool. It may be hidden beneath the Gradient Fill tool. If so, press Shift-G to cycle the Paint Bucket tool to the front.

2. Set the Tolerance to 32. Press the "D" key to use the default colors.

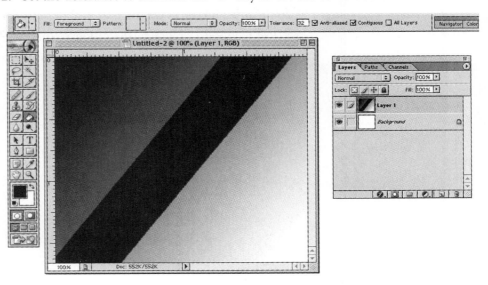

3. Click in the center of the gradient area.

4. Lower the Tolerance value to 10, and click again. A much smaller area is filled with color, as the lower tolerance selects fewer gray pixels on either side of the area where you clicked.

5. From the File menu, select Revert to change the image back to its original state. Leave the image open for the next exercise.

The Eraser Tools

It's always good to rid an image of unwanted elements. So far, you have used File>Revert on images, undone actions (Command/Control-Z), and used selections to delete unwanted parts of an image. The three eraser tools also allow you to delete portions of images; each performs distinct functions. As with Photoshop's other tools, it is important to know which eraser to use for which task.

The Eraser

The Eraser can behave the same as any of the brush painting tools (the Paintbrush, Airbrush, or Pencil tools), or it can be used as a simple square block. The type of tool it emulates is selected from the drop-down list on the Eraser Options palette. Except when the Block option is specified, you can assign a level of opacity to the eraser.

Instead of painting with the foreground color, the Eraser paints in one of three ways. If you are on a Background layer — a layer that contains no transparency — the Eraser paints with the background color. If you are on a layer that allows transparency, the eraser removes all image data, making the area transparent. Finally, if the Erase to History box is checked, the tool actually restores image data from the state you designate in the History palette. It is important to remember that the changes made by the Eraser are for the most part not editable; many tasks that appear to be candidates for erasure should probably be handled with Layer masks.

Use the Eraser

1. In the open image, select the Eraser, choose Brush Mode, and select a soft-edge brush of about 100 pixels. (A 100-pixel soft-edge brush is in the Brush Presets list.)

2. Set the brush Opacity to 100% and brush over the top layer in the document. The layer beneath becomes visible wherever you paint.

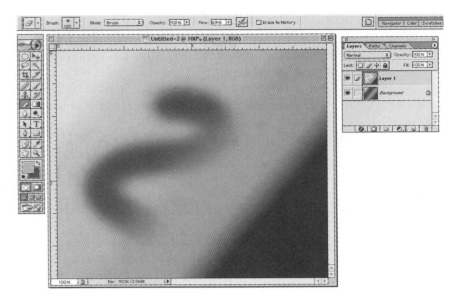

3. Turn off the visibility icon for the lower layer to see what the Eraser actually did to your file.

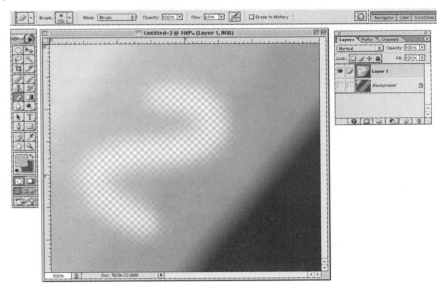

4. Close the file without saving.

The Background Eraser

The Background Eraser tool allows you to erase to transparency the pixels of any layer as you drag, while it protects edges and foreground colors. By choosing different Tolerance and Sampling settings, you can control the sharpness of the edges and the range of colors that are turned transparent. Background layers and layers with locked transparency are automatically changed to normal transparent layers.

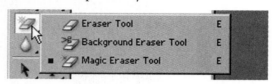

The Background Eraser is one of three tools designed to remove portions of an image.

When you click the Background Eraser on an image, a color sample is taken from the center of the brush. The portion of the brush that grabs the sample is called the *hot spot*; that color is deleted whenever it appears within the diameter of the brush. At the same time, the Background Eraser extracts color from the edges of foreground objects; when they are subsequently pasted into another image, there is no halo effect.

Use the Background Eraser

1. Open the image **mountain_child.tif** from your **RF_Intro_Photoshop** folder.

2. Press Shift-E to cycle to the Background Eraser tool (you may have to press it several times). Select a 65-pixel soft-edge brush. In the Options toolbar, set Limits to Discontiguous, Tolerance to 10%, and Sampling to Once. Using these settings, the Background Eraser selects only the first color in the hotspot. As you hold down the button and drag, only pixels sharing those color values (plus or minus 10%), are erased. We're using a Discontiguous Limit setting, so affected pixels don't need to be adjacent.

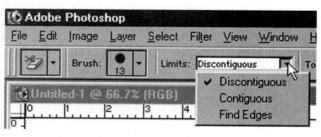

3. Click in the blue in the upper-left corner of the image. Holding down the mouse button, drag across the image. Only dark blue pixels are turned transparent.

4. Change the Limits option to Contiguous.

5. Keeping the center of the brush just above the mountains and the little boy's head, drag the brush across the image. Notice that the mountains and the little boy are untouched, while the sky is erased.

6. Select File>Revert, and leave the document open for the next exercise.

The Magic Eraser

The Magic Eraser tool has unique properties. With one click, you can erase an entire area of similar-colored pixels to the background color or to transparency, depending upon the nature of the layer. Pixels in layers with locked transparency are turned to the background color. Pixels in normal transparent layers are turned transparent.

As with the Background Eraser, the Magic Eraser tool's tolerance may be set, and pixel limits may be contiguous or discontiguous. You may erase pixels on all linked layers simultaneously, or only on single (non-linked) layers.

Use the Magic Eraser

1. With the document **mountain_child.tif** open, press Shift-E to cycle to the Magic Eraser tool.

2. Set the Tolerance to 10, Anti-aliased should be checked, Contiguous should be unchecked, and Opacity set to 100%. Since there is only one layer in the document, Use All Layers is irrelevant.

3. Click anywhere in the sky. A number of pixels are deleted.

4. Now increase the Tolerance to 30. Click in the upper-left corner. With the higher Tolerance setting, the boy's pack and much of his ball are deleted, as well as the sky.

5. Press Command/Control-Z to undo this change. Leave the Tolerance set to 30%, and check the Contiguous box. Click again in the top-left corner. A large portion of sky is deleted, but the pack and ball are left intact.

6. Close the document without saving.

The Clone Stamp and Healing Brush

One of the most useful tools available in Photoshop is the Clone Stamp tool. This tool permits cloning of information from elsewhere in the image or from another image.

The Clone Stamp tool copies image data from one area of the image (defined by Option/Alt-clicking on the area to be copied) or from another document. When you choose Aligned mode, pixels are copied relative to the position of the Option/Alt-click and the position at which you click the mouse to begin the clone. When the Aligned mode button is not selected, the reference is returned to the Option/Alt-clicked area at the exact position you originally clicked.

A new feature in Photoshop 7, the Healing brush is a remarkable example of imaging technology. It works much the same as the Clone Stamp in that you Option/Alt-click an area to establish a sample. The difference is that when you use it to paint, the new pixels are matched in color and texture to the surrounding area.

You cannot paint into an empty layer with the Healing brush. Creating a duplicate layer is one way around this limitation.

The Patch tool uses the same mathematical calculations as the Healing brush, but works a bit differently. Instead of Option/Alt-clicking, a lasso tool is used to draw a selection around an area, which is then dragged to an area of good pixels to start the healing process. The tool can be set to either Source or Destination, which determines whether the damaged area is dragged to a clean area to start the healing process, or the other way around. The Patch tool is a little counter-intuitive; experiment with it until you're comfortable with how it works.

Use the Clone Stamp

1. Open the image named **head_shot.psd** from the **RF_Intro_Photoshop** folder. Use the magnifying glass (Zoom tool) to zoom into the bottom of the image — you'll see that the model's thumb is clearly visible in the shot.

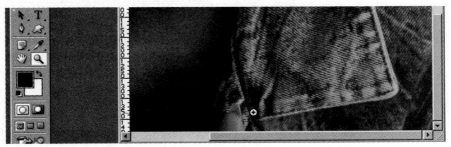

2. Select the Clone Stamp tool from the Toolbox. Use the Options toolbar and select Aligned (if it's not already active). From the Brush icon on the bar, select a soft, round 65-pixel brush.

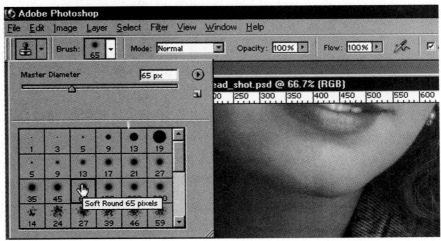

Be sure to select the Clone Stamp and not the Pattern Stamp tool.

3. Hold down the Option/Alt key, and click the seam of the jacket just above the thumb. This defines the *source area* — the part of the image from which to copy.

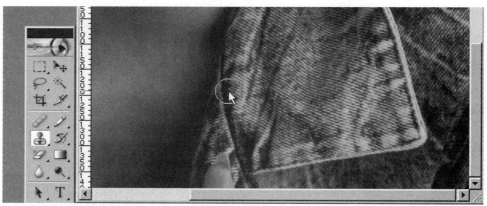

4. Create a new layer. Painting the repair on this layer protects the original — just in case something goes wrong.

5. With the new layer active, paint carefully to cover the thumb with jacket pixels. You aligned on the seam, so the detail looks convincing and the thumb is quickly removed.

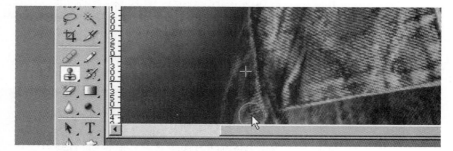

6. Leave the file open for the next exercise.

Use the Healing Brush

1. Press the "J" key to select the Healing brush.

2. Make a duplicate of the Background layer. The Healing brush needs pixels to match, and the duplicate layer provides a safety net for your original. Option/Alt-click on a smooth area of skin just beneath the eye. Paint over the small wrinkles just below the eye.

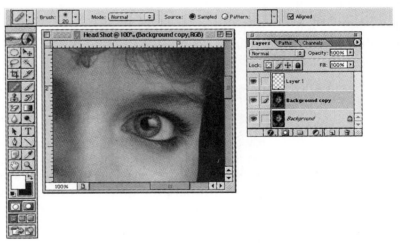

As you can see, the newly added pixels are (initially) not a good match. After a short pause, however, they are transformed to match the surrounding area, perfectly healing the wrinkles.

3. Press the Spacebar and use the Hand tool to move to the other eye.

4. Use the same brush to paint over those wrinkles. After the healing process is finished, select Fade Healing Brush from the Edit menu. This allows an additional level of control over the healing process. Often we want to soften wrinkles instead of removing them completely.

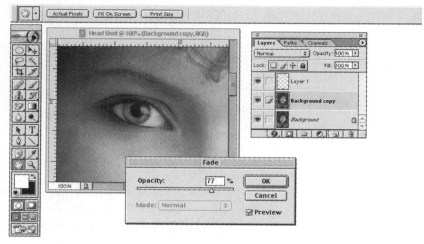

Due to changes in the Pattern Maker, which has been moved to the Filter menu, we will cover the Pattern Stamp in the chapter on filters.

5. Close the file without saving.

Learning to use the Healing brush and Clone Stamp tool takes time and practice. After gaining experience, you'll be able to apply them to the most complex retouching and repair projects and achieve perfect results.

Chapter Summary

Clearly, the Photoshop painting tools provide a variety of means to modify and create images. The new paint engine is a welcome addition for those who need a more organic feel for their work; it provides the rest of us with a multitude of new painting options. Each tool offers numerous ways to fill selected areas with color, to fill them with differing transparency, and to cause them to interact differently with underlying areas.

Free-Form Project #1

Assignment

You work at an advertising agency that is trying to impress Action Shoe Company, a new consumer-based client. The client typically runs ads that are 5 in. × 7 in. with a bleed off the bottom and the outside edge of the page. Action Shoe pays a premium for right-page positioning of these complicated advertisements.

Your assignment is to design an ad format that highlights the client's products — the shoes — displaying their use in settings that would appeal to the end-user.

To create a concept proof to show the client, you can determine which images you will feature and combine them with the company logo. Write a headline and a tagline to include with the images. If you want, you can obtain appropriate photographs from the Web; but if you do, be sure to credit the source. Alternately, you can use the photos and logo supplied.

Applying Your Skills

To design the ad, use the following functions, methods, and features:

- Create a new document of the correct dimensions.
- Open and crop one or more images.
- Create a product detail by selecting, cropping, and resizing an image.
- Combine images using layers.
- Use the Type tool or the Type Mask tool to create your headline and a tagline.
- Add the company's logo.
- Use a pattern, texture, or other filter-generated background; let the photo bleed, or use a flat color behind the images.
- Use the Extract filter to isolate silhouettes.
- Be sure to use the whole array of selection tools to create your selections and vignettes, and to work with different sized views to help you focus on the immediate task or the overall ad, as needed.

Specifications

- Execute the design on an 8.5-in. × 11-in. page.
- The finished ad size is 5 in. × 7 in.
- The resolution of the final image should be 300 ppi.
- The design should bleed on the right and bottom, allowing space for the magazine to use as trim. Use CMYK as the color mode.

Included Files

A collection of files is provided specifically for this assignment, including photographs and logos. These files are contained within the **RF_Free_Form** folder. You'll find this folder on the Resource CD-ROM.

Publisher's Comments

For this assignment it's important that you take some time to review ads in consumer publications and see how the professionals approach ad design. Since the ad will not contain much copy, the images must convey the message.

Don't let the design get cluttered. It's easy to enjoy the variety of tools and techniques that Photoshop makes available and lose sight of the purpose. Your goal is to sell product, not to build images. Keep it bold, keep the effect simple, and let the products speak for themselves.

Concept proofs are a vital part of the job. They provide the clients with the opportunity to see the possibilities you envision and select the approach they find the most appealing. Proofs also serve as guidelines while you're creating the final piece that meets your client's needs and preferences. In this case, the ad concept proof you create, if selected as the preferred approach, could serve as the model for a series of related ads about different products for the same client.

Review #1

Chapters 1 through 6

In Chapters 1– 6, you began your exploration of images, and learned how to use one image for multiple purposes. You started to navigate the Photoshop working environment, and you were introduced to the wide array of tools, palettes, menus, and options that are available to the designer. Selection techniques were presented, as well as masking skills, which allow you to single-out portions of your artwork for alteration, or guard it against modification. You were provided with detailed information on layers, and how they add depth and complexity to your work. Building on your knowledge of layers, you then learned how to apply channels and masks, which work in tandem with layers to develop sophisticated images. Finally, the painting tools were presented, providing a thorough overview of how the tools are used, and the effects they can produce. Through this series of discussions, exercises, and projects, you should:

- Understand how to manipulate images using Photoshop's painting and drawing tools.

- Be familiar with the various color modes, and know what mode should be applied to each type of deliverable.

- Be comfortable navigating around the Photoshop working environment.

- Know how to change the document view to enhance your selection technique.

- Be capable of making successful selections and image transformations using a variety of tools and techniques.

- Understand how to use layers, and navigate the Layers palette to apply layer styles to create special effects such as 3-D images.

- Be able to use channels and masks in conjunction with layers to develop detailed, complex artwork.

- Be familiar with the painting tools, how to select brushes from the Brushes palette, and set their size, shape, and style.

- Know how to delete, clone, and correct portions of your images using the eraser tools, Clone Stamp tool, and Healing brush.

7 Working with Type

Chapter Objectives:

Photoshop is known for it's state-of-the-art photo-retouching and graphic development capabilities. High-quality graphics alone, however, may not be enough to convey important messages to viewers. Designers must also be proficient in incorporating text elements. While Photoshop isn't considered a typesetting application, its type tools offer robust and powerful functionality. In Chapter 7, you will:

- Learn about the differences between raster and vector art.

- Expand your understanding of anti-aliasing, and how it softens the edges of your images.

- Explore the use of the Type tool, creating text elements and Type masks.

- Discover how to automatically create special type layers with the Type tool.

- Learn the difference between point text and text placed in text boxes, and how to effectively use both.

- Explore the Character and Paragraph palettes, and learn how they are used to modify and fine-tune text elements.

- Discover how to horizontally and vertically orient your text elements for maximum impact.

- Find out how to correctly output your text elements, anticipating and correcting problems before they occur.

Projects to be Completed:

- Gulls Poster (A)
- **Fallsbridge Menu Cover (B)**
- Jazz Postcard (C)
- USA Poster (D)

For assignments such as posters, banners, or other projects that contain a small amount of integral text, Photoshop can easily handle the entire job. If your project requires anything more than a minimal amount of text, however, it's probably more efficient to do the imaging work with Photoshop and add the text in an illustration or page-layout program.

Profile Mismatch Errors: When you're opening an image, you may get an error message that says that the embedded color profile contained in the image doesn't match the one you're currently using. If this happens, refer back to the Getting Started section to learn how to disable the warning. Color profiles will be discussed in Chapter 10.

Working with Type

In this chapter, you're going to learn how to add type elements to your documents — and how to effectively incorporate what many designers feel is the single most important component of their work. This sentiment is based on the concept that although a picture is worth a thousand words, the message might be open to interpretation without accompanying text.

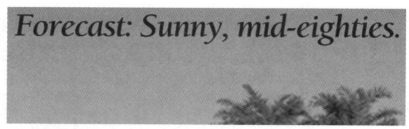

Before you begin working with Photoshop's type tools, let's discuss how the program handles type; text elements are fundamentally different than other components of an image. This difference is related to how type is defined by the program.

Raster and Vector Graphics

There are two types of graphics that you can create on your computer. The first type is called a *raster*, or *bitmap* graphic. Bitmap graphics are comprised of individual pixels, or bits. No matter how high the resolution of a specific image, if you look close enough, you'll see the pixels. Photoshop is primarily designed to create and edit raster images.

This detail of the palm tree shows the pixels that make up the image.

The second type of graphic element you can create is called a *vector* object. Vector objects aren't really made up of individual pixels. They're created using mathematical descriptions of paths (also called *strokes*) and the color or tones contained within those paths (called the *fill*). If you closely examine a vector object, you'll see that it's built from lines connected by points, often referred to as *anchor points*. Each point contains information about the curves or paths connected to it, and can be moved and/or reshaped.

Vector objects are constructed from paths, anchor points, and fills — not pixels.

When you create type in Photoshop, the result is a vector object. It can be edited in any way you choose — as long as you keep the file in native format. If you create a document that's meant to be used in another file (such as a page-layout program or as a Web application), you should save a copy of the document and keep the original intact. That way, if you need to make any changes to the text, the type remains intact — and editable. If you flatten the document, the type becomes rasterized and you lose the ability to make changes with the type tools.

Type elements reside on their own layers; if you flatten the layers, you lose the ability to highlight — and edit — the text.

Anti-Aliasing

Anti-aliasing is a technique used to soften the hard edges of type (and other objects) by creating a grayscale ramp along the edge. This visual trick makes bitmapped type appear to have a softer edge and helps eliminate pixelization. You can see the effects of anti-aliasing in the image that follows.

Photoshop allows you to specify no anti-aliasing, or you can use the anti-aliasing modes of Sharp, Crisp, Strong, or Smooth when type is rasterized. The effects of anti-aliasing are most apparent in the rounded letterforms.

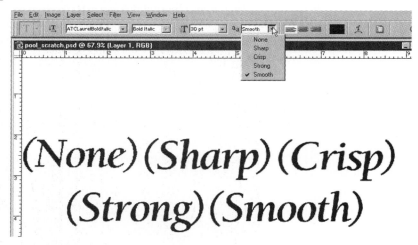

Type Tool

There are two types of objects you can create with the Type tool. The first is normal type: titles, descriptions, captions, and body text. The second object you can create is a Type mask, which acts like any other mask, allowing underlying images to show through. Type masks are particularly well suited to creating headlines and other graphic elements that require an image be contained within a text shape. The Type mask tool basically creates a selection as you type.

Both tools offer horizontal or vertical orientation; you can make type go across the page, or from top to bottom.

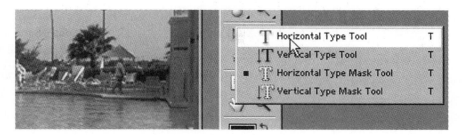

Type Layers

In most color modes (except Bitmap, Indexed Color, and Multichannel), every time you use the Type tool, a new type layer is created. Type layers behave the same as any other layer.

There are two ways to rasterize type — which converts it into a regular, bitmapped graphic:

- The first way is to flatten the layer, or merge it into the underlying layer. If a type layer is part of a set of linked layers, merging them rasterizes the type layer at the same time.

- The second way is to rasterize the type itself, or rasterize the entire layer containing the type. You can do this from the Layer>Rasterize menu.

Once type or a type layer is rasterized (or flattened/merged), the type is no longer a vector object.

You can apply layer effects to type layers from the Layer>Layer Style menu or by double-clicking the layer. Effects are applied to all type in the layer, so if you only want part of the type modified, you need to make it a separate type layer before making modifications.

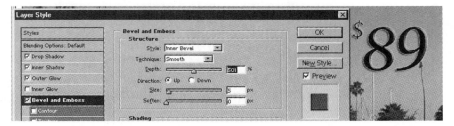

When a type layer has special effects applied to it, those effects are described in the Layers palette.

When you select the Type tool, Photoshop automatically creates a new layer, which is an editable text layer in vector format. As long as the file remains in native Photoshop format (.psd) and the layers have not been merged or flattened, that layer remains editable as text — even if special effects are applied.

New to Photoshop 7 is a spell check utility found under the Edit menu. This utility works in a similar manner to other spell checkers and is complete with multi-lingual capabilities.

The type options that are available in most page-layout programs are also available in Photoshop. You can assign specific fonts, leading, size, color, and alignment. Kerning, tracking, baseline shift, and other variables may also be applied.

Selecting the Type tool and clicking anywhere on the canvas activates the tool. The Type tool Options bar appears at the top of the page.

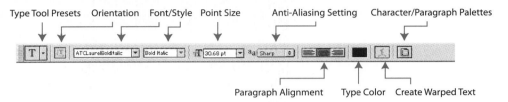

As you select the Type tool, you need to choose an orientation for the text. To do so, select either the Horizontal Type tool or the Vertical Type tool from the Toolbar pop-up menu. You can also select the font, weight, size, anti-aliasing options, alignment, color, and warped text options from the Options toolbar. The final button on the bar enables you to access the Character and Paragraph palettes, which we'll discuss shortly. Any favorite type set-up options may be saved as tool presets and accessed from the pop-up menu at the top left of the Options toolbar.

Type created using the Type tool can be converted to a vector-based shape by applying the Layer>Type>Convert to Shape command. Type layers can be used to create a work path by applying the Layer>Type>Create Work Path command (more about work paths in a later chapter), or they can be rasterized directly to allow for the application of special effects (such as filters) that are not available for type layers.

Point Text

Photoshop allows two methods of setting text. Simply clicking anywhere in the image and typing creates what is known as *point text* as show in this example.

Point text works fine for headlines or titles; but as line breaks must be added manually, it becomes cumbersome when more than a few words are placed.

Text Boxes

A *text box* is created by clicking the Type tool on the page and dragging to create a box. You can then place the cursor inside the text box and begin entering text. In the following example, you can see the handles that allow the text box to be resized as necessary.

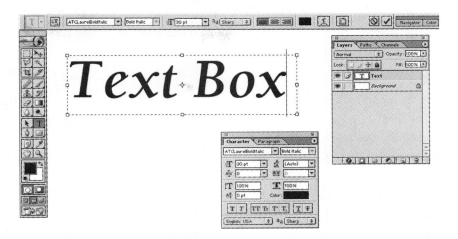

Hold the cursor over the handle of a text box. Wait a moment for the cursor to change to a little arrow; then you can resize the box. If the box is too small to hold all of your text, a small plus sign (+) appears in the lower-right handle.

Depending on what you intend to do with the type, text boxes can be more flexible than point text. Once you've created the box, it can be resized, rotated, and repositioned anywhere on the image.

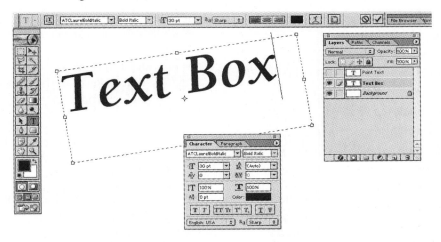

Here the Point Text layer has been turned off to show the text box. Text boxes may be rotated or resized at any time.

Layers are not available in Bitmap, Indexed Color, or Multichannel modes. If you are working in one of these modes, the Type tool only creates Type masks or selections.

Since the release of version 6 of the program, all the typographic controls that are necessary to create beautiful type have been included in Photoshop. Control of leading, kerning, tracking, point size, and much more is possible using Photoshop. In addition, layer styles such as drop shadows, and bevel and emboss allow users to create effects that are difficult or impossible to achieve using other software. All of these effects and the type remain editable as long as they are on a type layer in the native Photoshop (.psd) format.

Type Palettes

There are two palettes used for detailed text formatting — the Character palette and the Paragraph palette.

Character Palette

The Character palette provides controls that affect individual characters or selected ranges of text.

For a detailed study of typography, we suggest you read "The Type Companion for the Digital Artist", available from Against The Clock (http://www.againsttheclock.com).

In this illustration, the first line was set with no tracking or kerning. The second line applies specific kerning values to letter pairs. In the third line, a tracking value of +100 was applied to the entire kerned line.

Typography
Typography
Typography

Note the difference in these three lines of type; pay particular attention to the distance between the upper case "T" and the lower case "y".

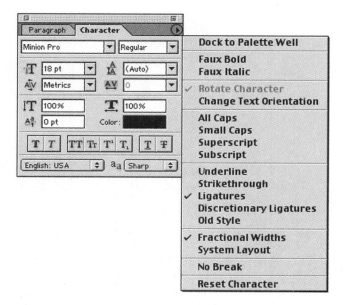

In this example, Minion Pro was selected as the font because it is an Open Type font. Ligatures are only available in certain typefaces, such as Open Type and Expert families.

The Character palette provides additional control over the attributes of individual text characters: the leading (line space), kerning (tightness or looseness between two characters) in .001 of an em, and tracking (tightness or looseness over a range of characters) in .001 of an em.

The Character palette also allows you to control the horizontal and vertical scale of letters, shift the baseline of individual letters up or down (baseline shift), and specify the color of the characters.

Other characteristics may be applied from the Options pop-up menu. Faux (imitation) bold or italic (oblique) may be applied to characters that do not have bold or italic included in their type family. When type is being set with a vertical orientation, the type may be rotated (more information about this later).

Type may be changed to all caps, small caps, superscript, or subscript. If the font does not have true small caps, superscript, or subscript, Photoshop generates faux versions.

Underline and strike-through may be applied to any type, but you may not identify a specific drop for the underline. When Ligatures and Old Style numbers are selected, Photoshop substitutes the ligature or the old style. Under normal circumstances, ligatures and Old Style numbers are only found in specialized, Expert typefaces as well as within Open Type font families.

On the left are character sets that do not use Ligatures or Old Style; on the right, these attributes have been turned on.

Fractional widths are turned on by default. When producing a document for Web use, the feature should be turned off when characters are smaller than 20 pt. to aid legibility at these small (for the Web) sizes. When No Break is selected, a word will not hyphenate, even if hyphenation is enabled. Reset Character resets the Character palette to its default settings.

The Paragraph Palette

While the Character palette provides enhanced control over individual characters within the document, the Paragraph palette provides control over entire blocks of text. The palette itself allows control over justification: left, center, right, and justified with the last line left, centered, right, or justified. Left, first line, and right indents can be defined, as can space before and space after a paragraph. Hyphenation for the paragraph is turned on and off via the Hyphenate check box at the bottom left of the palette. There is also a pop-up Options menu for both the Character and Paragraph palettes.

From the Options pop-up menu, Roman Hanging Punctuation places a number of punctuation marks outside of the right or left margin, depending upon how the paragraph is justified. This results in a smoother looking margin, especially with point sizes of 14 and below.

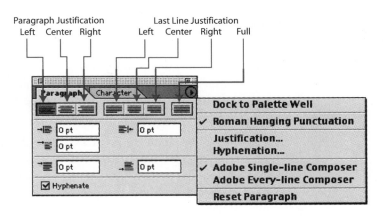

The Justification option allows you to define letter space and word space parameters, and has its own menu.

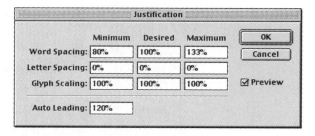

Photoshop applies the desired Word Spacing, Letter Spacing, and Glyph (character) Scaling options to non-justified text. When text is justified, it applies (in order) a variety of Word Spacing options, followed by Letter Spacing options. As a last resort, it applies Glyph Scaling. The Auto Leading amount, defined as a percentage of the type size, is also specified in this dialog box.

Hyphenation has its own secondary Options palette. Here, the size of letters and the specifications that allow hyphenation are controlled.

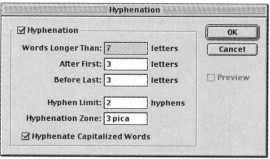

If bold or italic fonts are available, always use them in preference to using Faux Bold or Faux Italic. Faux fonts do not reproduce nearly as well as the actual bold or italic styles of a font.

In the first section of the menu, you define details about words to be hyphenated: the minimum length of the word, and how many characters must appear before or after the hyphenation point. You may also specify how many hyphens are allowed to appear in succeeding lines.

The Hyphenation Zone is defined as the distance — measured from the end of the line — in which a hyphenation point must fall without an intervening word space before hyphenation occurs in unjustified type, when using the Adobe Single-Line Composer option.

The Adobe Single-Line Composer uses the rules in both the Justification and Hyphenation dialog boxes to arrive at appropriate break points for a line of type. The line-breaking decisions using Single-Line Composer are made as follows: word spacing, hyphenation, compressed letter spacing, expanded letter spacing, and glyph scaling.

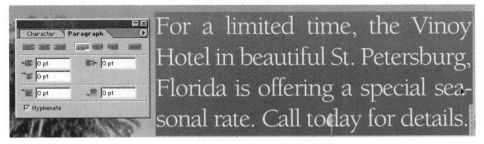

Hyphenation is sometimes necessary to avoid unsightly spacing in blocks of text. Adobe Composer options are available from the Paragraph palette's pop-up menu.

If you must have precise control over the line breaks in the document, you should use the Single-Line Composer option. Adobe Every-Line Composer looks at several lines of type, applies the rules to all of them, and arrives at an overall hyphenation and justification decision that provides evenness of type and the fewest hyphens. This almost always creates a tighter, better-looking paragraph. It can take longer to reflow text when you use the Single-Line Composer option, but since we you're not setting multiple pages of type in Photoshop, it is an excellent option.

There is a check box to allow or disallow hyphenation of capitalized words.

Positioning and Modifying Text

Text may be horizontally or vertically oriented. Most of the time, you'll work with horizontally oriented text, since vertically oriented text can be difficult to read. When horizontal text orientation is selected, there are no other options available.

When vertical orientation is selected, the Rotate Character option becomes available from the Character palette. The Rotate Character option rotates each character 90° counter-clockwise.

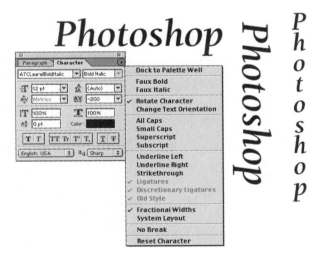

This example shows type set normally at the top, vertically in the center, and with character rotation (applied via the pop-up menu) at the right. The example that shows character rotation is set in a smaller point size and is tracked in so it would fit in the space provided.

Creating a Type Mask or Selection

When you create a Type mask or selection, a new layer is not automatically created. By default, the selection outline of the type is placed on the active layer. As a selection is active on the active layer, it is easy to activate the layer of interest. Type created in this way is not editable after the type has been committed.

The text remains editable as long as the Type tool is active. You can fill a Type mask or selection with an image, or apply gradient or filter effects. These effects cannot be applied to type in vector format.

It is a good idea to create a separate layer for text using the Create a Type Mask or Selection option, and to retain that layer as a separate entity for as long as possible; otherwise, you may find it necessary to completely redo a portion of the image.

Many experienced Photoshop users have settled on a workflow that always sets type as vectors on a type layer. Command/Control-clicking on the type layer creates an instant selection that may be used on any active layer. The advantage of this process is that the vector layer is available for edits, spell checking, or use in another document.

Use Type in a Document

1. Open the file **bike.psd** from the **RF_Intro_Photoshop** folder. This image from Chuck Ealovega, a world-class motor vehicle photographer, was originally a studio shot. The background was added later. Save the file into your **Work_In_Progress** folder using the same name. This ensures the original remains intact in case you want to repeat the exercise at a later time.

2. Use the Eyedropper tool to select the red color from the stripe on the bike to make it the foreground color. Select the Type tool, click the Center Alignment icon, and click in the upper middle of the image. Type "Not for the Weak of Heart", using the ATC Oak Bold Italic font. It probably isn't exactly the right size, but you'll fix that in a minute.

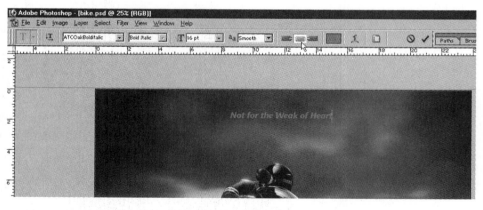

The point size shown in the Character palette reflects a slight resizing of the line using Free Transform. The exact size is less important than getting a feel for transforming type. Play with the line until you are satisfied with how it looks.

3. With the text cursor still in the line of type, press Command/Control-A to select all. Now press Shift-Command/Control, and then press the Greater-Than symbol (>) to increase the point size of the headline; 50 pt. worked well for us.

Once you make a selection, don't forget that you may add to the selection by Shift-Command/Control-clicking on any type layer in the document. Alternately, Command/Control-Option/Alt-clicking subtracts from the selection.

4. Add a layer style of Bevel and Emboss. For this example, we used an Inner Bevel with a Smooth Technique and a Size of 6 pixels. The Shading Angle was set to 48 degrees with an Altitude of 30 degrees. Click OK to close the dialog box.

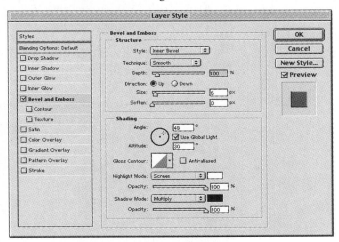

5. Command/Control-click on the type layer to turn the text into a selection. Add a new layer (above the type layer), by clicking on the New Layer icon. Press Option/Alt-Backspace to fill the selected area with the same red you used for the original text.

6. Deselect the headline (Command/Control-D). From the Filter menu, select Stylize>Wind, click the button for Blast, and set the Direction to be From the Left.

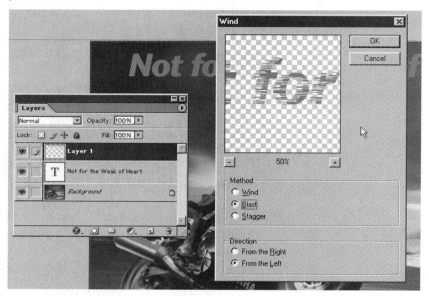

7. From the Filter menu, select Blur>Motion Blur. Set the Angle to 13 degrees and the Distance to 12 pixels. Click OK, and then reduce the Opacity of the layer to 70%.

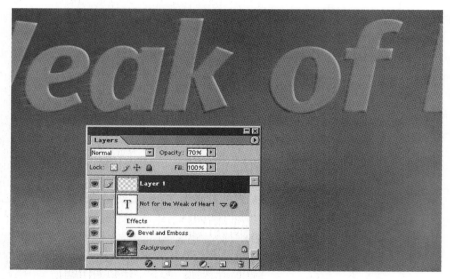

8. The result should be the interesting type effect shown below.

9. Save and close the file.

Warping Text

In addition to modifying type layers using the Layer>Layer Style menu, you can actually modify the appearance of the text itself while the text remains completely editable. You can do this by selecting the Create Warped Text button from the Text Options toolbar.

The Warp Text dialog box appears. It features a pop-up menu containing 15 Warp options.

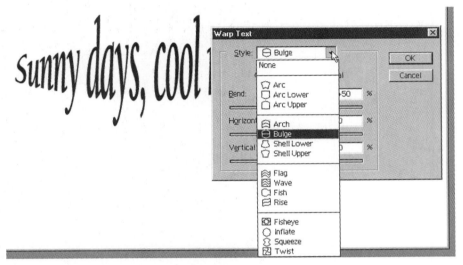

In addition to using the standard warps, you can further alter them to achieve a variety of effects. Even after text has been warped, it can be edited and layer styles can still be applied.

Each of the 15 Warp effects can be modified through the use of the sliders that appear in the dialog box. There are so many available variations that it would be impossible to show them all — you'll have to spend some time experimenting on your own. The following exercise introduces you to the basic concept of warping text.

Warp Text

1. Create a new RGB document, 8 in. x 8 in., with a White background and a Resolution of 150 pixels/inch. Name the file "warp_text.psd".

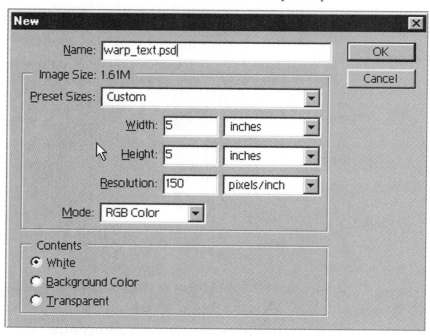

2. Select the Type tool, and choose the Horizontally Orient Text option from the dialog box that appears.

3. At about the middle of the page, type the words "Warp Text" in 72-pt. ATC Oak Bold with a Smooth Anti-alias setting. Using the Character palette, apply appropriate kerning values. (We kerned the "WA" character pair —50, and the TE pair -100.)

4. From the Type Options toolbar, select the Warp Text button. Select the Flag style and apply the settings shown. Click OK.

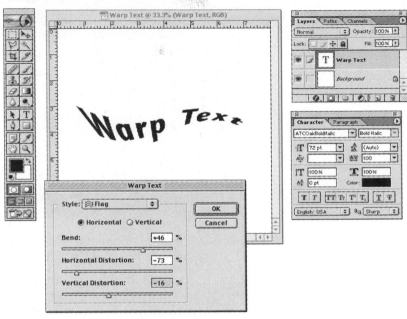

You may need to reposition your text after you have typed it. To do so, move the Type tool out of the active text area; it will function the same as the Move tool.

5. Experiment with the other Warp options and observe the control you can exercise over each distortion. When you've settled on one you prefer, click OK, then click the check box in the Options toolbar to commit the warp.

6. Save the file to your **Work_In_Progress** folder as "warped_text.psd".

Vector Output

Type layers can be converted to shapes that maintain their vector attributes (Layer>Type> Convert to Shape).

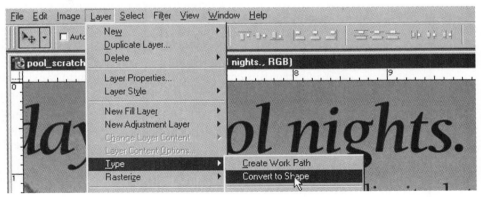

Files containing type that was converted to paths and then saved as an EPS file prints the vector objects at the highest available resolution of the output device. Once you convert a type element to a shape, you're presented with the option of saving the vector data along with the EPS file.

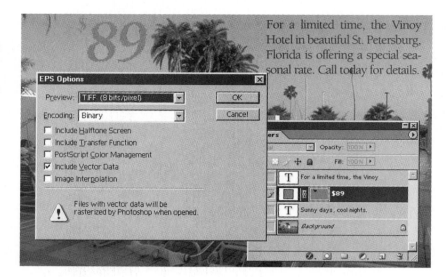

Type elements can also be converted to paths — the same vector format used by Adobe Illustrator or Macromedia FreeHand. You'll get a chance to work with paths a little later in the book.

These files can also be placed into page-layout programs in the same way as Illustrator EPS files, and can be processed through a PostScript Raster Image Processor (usually called a "RIP"). EPS or native Photoshop files containing normal type layers (those not converted to shapes) require the font information to accurately reproduce text elements; be sure to include any fonts used in your documents when you send them to an output service.

Chapter Summary

You began this chapter with an introduction to the difference between raster (bitmap) graphics and vector graphics — the format that Photoshop uses for text elements. You learned that using the Type tool automatically creates a layer containing the type elements, and that type layers behave the same as normal layers. You learned the difference between point and paragraph text, and how to use the Character and Paragraph palettes. You learned to create Type masks and apply layer styles to type layers. Finally, you saw how Photoshop can convert type into vector shapes, and export those shapes as part of an EPS file.

Complete Project B: Fallsbridge Menu Cover

Blending Modes

Chapter Objectives:

Blending modes and layers are very similar in nature; they both add depth and complexity to images. Using layers alone can create exceptional artwork; but using layers in combination with Blending modes results in even more compelling images. In Chapter 8, you will:

- Learn how to activate the Blending modes from the Layers palette.

- Learn how Blending modes control how pixel colors and tones interact between layers.

- Practice using different Blending modes including Darken, Lighten, Dissolve, Luminosity, Color, and Multiply.

- Discover how to combine Blending modes and Paint tools.

Projects to be Completed:

- Gulls Poster (A)
- Fallsbridge Menu Cover (B)
- Jazz Postcard (C)
- USA Poster (D)

Blending Modes

Blending modes specify how Photoshop combines image information from two different sources. Most of these modes are available when using painting tools and the Edit>Fill command, and when compositing layers. You don't have to worry about the actual mathematical calculations that go on behind the scenes; but it is important to understand how Blending modes affect your image.

Blending Modes and Layers

Blending modes can be found in several places. First, you can access them from a pop-up menu on the Layers palette — as long as you're not working on the Background layer (you can't apply Blending modes to the default Background layer; it has to be converted to regular layer before they'll work).

Next, you can see them in the Options bar whenever you're using a painting tool, a shape tool, or the Path tool.

Blending modes are separated into six groups, based on the type of operation they perform.

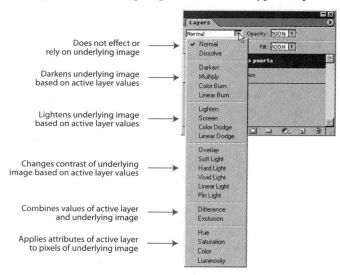

As you know from previous chapters, layers work as though photographs are stacked on top of each other; anything on the upper layer obscures what is on the layer below it. Each Blending mode, however, affects the way a layer interacts with the layer beneath it.

Mode Effects

To access Blending modes, you can either use the pop-up menu on the Layers palette, or, if you're using a painting tool and need to apply a mode, you can use the menu on the Options bar.

Most modes are available on both the Options and Layers palettes; the exception is the Behind mode, which is available only when using the painting tools. This mode allows you to paint only the transparent areas of an image — similar to painting on the back of a piece of acetate. Clear mode is also only used with the painting tools and removes a portion of the blend layer, much the same as the Eraser tool.

For most of this chapter, we'll discuss the use of Blending modes in the Layers palette. The concepts are the same, however, whether using a painting tool, or a Fill command.

The Behind and Clear modes only work with painting tools. Behind mode paints only on transparent areas, and the Clear mode tool erases pixels to a transparent state (as opposed to the current background color).

The following list contains all the modes that are available from the Layers palette:

- **Normal**. A layer set to Normal at 100% opacity obscures the layer below it, except where the upper layer is transparent. If the layer opacity is reduced, the upper layer fades into the lower layer.

- **Dissolve**. This mode behaves identically to Normal at 100% opacity. If the blend layer is partially transparent, Dissolve mode randomly makes the layer pixels either 100% opaque or 100% transparent. The ratio of pixels that become 100% transparent is determined by the pixel opacity. A layer with 30% opacity set to Dissolve mode turns about 30% of the pixels opaque and leaves the remaining pixels transparent.

- **Darken**. This mode displays the pixels of the upper layer only when they are darker than the pixels on the underlying layer; otherwise, the base layer pixels are displayed.

- **Multiply**. This mode literally multiplies the values of the pixels on the upper layer and the underlying layer to produce a new color. The color produced is always darker than the original color. White pixels, which have a value of 0, are transparent. Multiplying any color by black produces black. Adjusting the opacity softens the effect.

- **Color Burn**. This mode darkens the base color based on the blend color; 100% white is transparent.

- **Lighten**. This mode displays the blend layer pixels if they are lighter than the pixels on the underlying layer; if they're not, the base layer image is displayed.

- **Screen**. This mode is the opposite of the Multiply mode; it always creates a color lighter than the original color. Screening with black leaves the underlying pixels unchanged; screening with white produces pure white.

- **Color Dodge**. This mode brightens the base color based on the blend color; 100% black is transparent.

- **Linear Dodge**. Much like Color Burn, this mode has a tendency to make areas of the underlying image go all the way to white, producing a higher contrast result.

- **Overlay**. This mode multiplies or screens the blended layer with the underlying layer, depending upon the color of the base layer. The upper color is blended with the lower color, not replaced, which preserves the highlights and shadows of the image.

- **Soft Light**. In this mode, the closer the blend layer pixel is to white, the more the underlying image is lightened; the nearer to black, the more the base layer is darkened. Using black and white on the blended layer creates a color much lighter or darker than the original, but never changes to pure black or pure white.

- **Hard Light**. This mode behaves almost the same as Soft Light, except that instead of simply lightening or darkening, the mode adds black or white to the image. If pixels in the blend layer are 100% black or 100% white, the resulting color is totally obscured by black or white. In both Hard Light and Soft Light modes, 50% gray is transparent.

- **Vivid Light**. This mode combines Color Dodge and Color Burn modes.

- **Linear Light**. This mode combines Linear Dodge and Linear Burn modes.

- **Pin Light**. This mode combines Darken and Lighten modes.

- **Difference**. This mode compares the pixels on the upper layer to the pixels on the lower layer. It subtracts the value of whichever is the darker from the brighter. Since black has a brightness value of 0, it does not affect the underlying image. White inverts the colors in the underlying image.

- **Exclusion**. This mode behaves in much the same way as the Difference mode — but produces a softer effect.

When creating a new layer with a special Blending mode, you can ask Photoshop to automatically fill the layer with a neutral color — one that is transparent in that mode. For example, if you create a layer in Hard Light mode, you can ask Photoshop to fill it with 50% gray. The layer appears transparent, but filters such as the Noise filter can be run on it without filling it first.

- **Hue**. This mode uses the hue (the named color) of the blend layer, but preserves the luminance and saturation of the original image. It allows you to preserve the highlights and shadows in the image while changing the color.

- **Saturation**. This mode uses the saturation of the blend color and the hue and luminance of the base image. It is the intensity of the color that changes, not the color itself. Grays have 0% saturation, and, therefore, they are transparent. Very bright colors, such as pure reds and greens, over saturate areas of the image.

- **Color**. This mode blends the hue and saturation of the image. It's extremely useful for tinting or colorizing images since it maintains the grays, and therefore, much of the detail of the base image.

- **Luminosity.** This mode is the opposite of Color mode. The grays, or luminance, of the blend layer are used with the hue and saturation of the base image.

Blending is more easily understood when it is seen, so let's try some blending. These effects are best seen in color, so only a limited number of examples are shown.

Use Normal and Dissolve Modes

1. Open the file called **blends.psd** from the **RF_Intro_Photoshop** folder. The file contains four layers: Clouds, Gray Gradient, Layer 1, and Layer 2. Only Layers 1 and 2 are currently visible. The Blending mode for Layer 1 and Layer 2 is set to Normal.

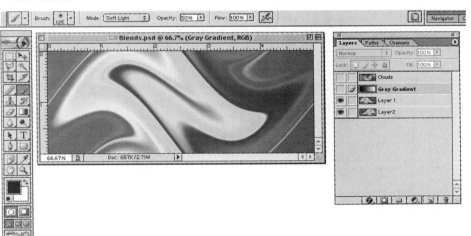

2. Select Layer 1. Move the Opacity slider to 60%, or enter the value directly on the palette. Layer 1 is now 40% transparent — 60% of the image data on the layer is visible, blended with 40% of the layer underneath.

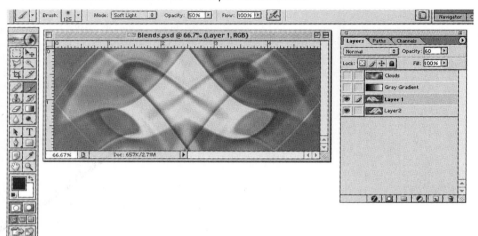

3. Return the Opacity of Layer 1 to 100%. Activate the visibility icon for the Gray Gradient layer and select that layer. The layer hides the underlying color layer. Click the word Normal to bring up the Blending mode drop-down list. Select Dissolve. The image stays the same; when a layer is set to 100% Opacity and there are no partially transparent pixels, Dissolve mode behaves identically to Normal mode.

4. Move the Opacity slider down to 50%. Half of the pixels display the image on the lower layers; the other half display portions of the black-and-white blending layer. Spend a minute adjusting the slider back and forth to get a feel for how Dissolve mode affects your image.

5. Move the layer's Opacity slider back to 100% and change the Blending mode back to Normal.

6. Leave the file open for the next exercise.

Use Modes that Work with Highlight and Shadow

1. In the open file, hide the Gray Gradient layer by clicking its visibility icon. Select the Clouds layer, and change the Blending mode to Screen. Reduce the Opacity of the layer to about 50%; the underlying image looks as though it is being viewed through fog.

2. Change the Blending mode to Multiply and leave the Opacity value at 50%. The black portion of the blend layer darkens the image, as if that portion of the picture were in deep shadow. The white portions of the blend layer allow the brighter underlying base layer to show through.

3. Turn off the visibility icon for the Clouds layer and select the Gray Gradient layer. Set the Blending mode to Overlay. The image is darkened or lightened (multiplied or screened) according to the information in the Gray Gradient layer (the blend layer).

4. Soft Light and Hard Light modes behave in a similar manner, but with markedly different results. Change the Blending mode to Soft Light, and set the Opacity at 100%. The image is lightened or darkened according to the blend layer, but never changes to pure black or pure white.

5. Change to Hard Light mode. Note the difference. Spend some time experimenting with both the Gray Gradient and the Clouds layer as blend layers. Turn them on and off, and change the Blend modes and Opacities to get a feel for what is happening.

6. Wherever Layer 1 is 100% white, the image is obscured with white; black in the blend layer turns the image black. Hard Light and Soft Light modes are especially useful for adjusting the highlights and shadows in an image. In addition, Hard Light mode can be used for special effects such as compositing a texture onto a grayscale image, and creating buttons used in multimedia and Internet graphics. Reduce the Opacity to about 20%; notice that the effect now resembles Soft Light mode.

7. Turn off the visibility eyeballs for the 2 top layers. Select Layer 1 and return it to 100% Opacity. Layer 2 is a copy of Layer 1 that has been flipped horizontally. Turn the visibility icon off and on to see the effect.

8. Keep the file open for the next exercise.

Use Darken, Lighten, Difference, and Exclusion

1. In the open file, change the mode to Darken for the Clouds layer. The layer is pure black and pure white, so Darken mode shows only the areas that are painted with white.

2. Now change the mode to Lighten. Lighten allows everything but the dark areas to show through.

3. Change the Blending mode to Difference. This mode is used primarily for special effects. Since black has no brightness, it does not affect the underlying image. White pixels invert the pixels underneath.

4. If Layer 1 contains colored pixels, Difference mode subtracts the mathematical value of one color from the other. Click on Layer 1 to activate it, and select the Paintbrush tool. Choose a bright foreground color such as red. Paint a bit on Layer 1 to see the effect.

5. Change the Blending mode to Exclusion. Notice that it is very similar to the Difference mode, only not as harsh.

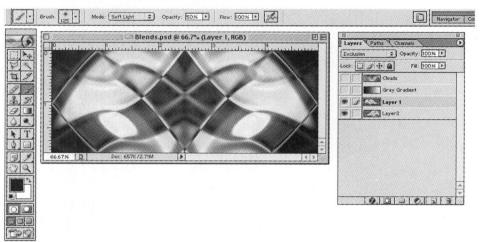

Combining the two-twisted gradient layers using the Exclusion mode creates this intricate pattern.

6. Included in your **RF_Intro_Photoshop** folder is a file called **blends2.psd.** This file has a blend layer made up of both a gradient and some clouds. Open the file and experiment viewing each of the Blending modes and trying to see the relationship between the tone of the blend layer and what happens to the underlying layer. Close both files when you are done experimenting.

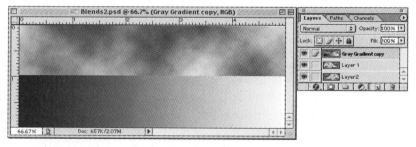

Practical Usage

At first glance, it may seem that the Blending modes are useful only for surrealistic special effects. There are many real-world Photoshop problems, however, that can't be easily handled in any other way.

For example, colorizing grayscale images is easy when using painting tools and the Color mode. Hard Light mode may be used to intensify highlight and shadow areas of low-contrast images. Darken mode makes it simple to superimpose black line art onto an image. Hue mode allows you to recolor items in an image without changing the saturation or brightness of the pixels in the image.

Chapter Summary

In this chapter, you had the opportunity to experiment with the Blending modes and observe how they affect an underlying image. You also had the chance to note the difference between modes that affect the color of an image and those that manipulate other facets of the image, such as its light, luminance, saturation, and hue.

9 Creating and Managing Paths

Chapter Objectives:

For those familiar with vector drawing applications — such as Adobe Illustrator or Macromedia FreeHand — the pen tools and the concept of vector paths will be second nature. For those new to creating vector paths using anchor points, segments, and curves, this chapter will provide insight into the importance and effectiveness of vector paths. In Chapter 9, you will:

- Understand that the pen tools are shape tools, and are controlled from the shape tools Options bar.

- Learn that paths are vector objects, similar to type and vector shapes.

- Learn how to create paths with the pen tools, how to create a path on its own (new) layer, or as an object on the currently active layer.

- Explore the use of the Pen tool and its variants, including the Freeform Pen, Add Anchor Point, Delete Anchor Point, and Convert Point tools.

- Find out how to turn a path into a selection.

- Discover the use of Clipping masks.

- Learn that you can export paths as vector objects to Illustrator and to other programs using EPS formats to retain their vector attributes.

Projects to be Completed:

- Gulls Poster (A)

- Fallsbridge Menu Cover (B)

- Jazz Postcard (C)

- USA Poster (D)

Creating and Managing Paths

Paths are customized vector shapes that you can create with the Pen tool. The tool is used to create line segments that are connected and defined by points. Paths are not bitmapped lines or painted strokes; they are objects that can be saved, edited, converted to selections, and used for other special purposes.

When you select the Pen tool, the Shape tools Options bar becomes active. You're familiar with the shape options from the chapter on layers, where we introduced shape layers.

Profile Mismatch Errors: When you're opening an image, you may get an error message that says that the embedded color profile contained in the image doesn't match the one you're currently using. If this happens, refer back to the Getting Started section to learn how to disable the warning. Color profiles will be discussed in Chapter 10.

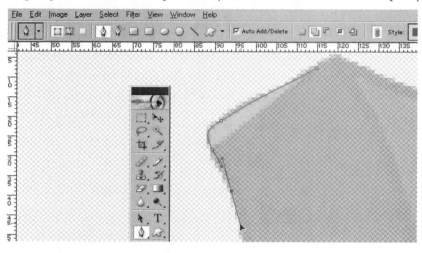

Paths are not part of the image itself. They are available to the Photoshop file for other functions: they can serve as stencils, borders, or routes that the other Photoshop commands and tools can follow. Unlike the other shape tools, objects created with the pen tools can only exist as shape layers or as paths — the Fill Pixels option available for other shape tools is disabled when you're using a pen tool.

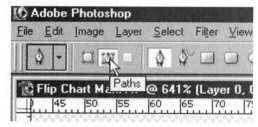

The two most often used path functions are:

- **Selections**. A path can be converted to a selection. At times, the Pen tool is the best bet for tracing an object. Even after you learn sophisticated channel-based masking techniques, there will be times when the Pen tool is the best choice. When all else fails, the Pen tool always works; it may be a tedious process, but you can select anything with the Pen tool.
- **Clipping Paths**. A clipping path strips out (does not allow to print) the area that falls outside of the path. They can be saved in most Photoshop formats, but are most often seen in EPS files.

There are five pen tools:

- **Pen Tool.** This is the basic tool. It draws paths by placing corner or curve points.
- **Freeform Pen Tool.** This tool works similar to the Lasso tool — by clicking and dragging. It sets anchor points and direction lines according to the shape that is drawn.
- **Add Anchor Point Tool.** This tool allows the addition of a point to a path already drawn.
- **Delete Anchor Point Tool.** This tool permits removal of an existing point.
- **Convert Point Tool.** This tool changes a curve point to a corner point and vice versa. Line segments between corner points are straight; between curve points, line segments are usually curved.

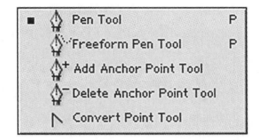

Used in conjunction with the pen tools are the path selection tools:

- **Path Selection Tool.** This tool is used to select an entire path, which may then be moved or acted upon with the pen tools or the Direct Selection tool.
- **Direct Selection Tool.** This tool is used to move path points and reshape curves after a path has been drawn.

The Paths Palette

The pop-up menu in the upper right of the Paths palette holds most of the commands available for creating and applying paths.

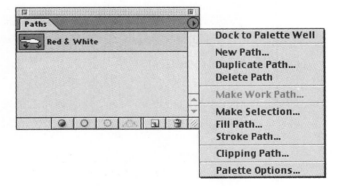

The palette also has icons along the bottom that serve as shortcuts to the most commonly used commands. The icons (left to right) are shortcuts for the following:

Holding the Shift key and pressing the "P" key cycles through each of the pen tools.

• The first icon fills an active path with the foreground color by default, or with the last used settings from the pop-up menu command.

• The second icon strokes (traces) the path with the active painting tool (or the last painting tool used to stroke a path if a painting tool is not currently selected) using the foreground color.

• The third icon turns an active path into a selection (marching ants).

• The fourth icon turns an active selection into a path.

• The fifth icon creates a new empty path.

• The sixth icon deletes the targeted path.

Basic Tool Techniques

The Pen tool in Photoshop is quite similar to its counterpart in Adobe Illustrator. Drawing with this type of vector curve tool can at first seem counter-intuitive; but stick with it — the skill is very valuable. Since the Pen tool in Photoshop is most often used to trace pixel-based images, either to select them or to create a clipping path to silhouette them in a page-layout program, we will concentrate on a drawing method that addresses this task. Option/Alt-clicking on each point before adding the next line segment allows each curve to be drawn without consideration of the one before. This can be a little slower than more conventional methods; but overall, it is far easier for those who are new to the tool to grasp this method, and it has the added advantage that the first paths you create should be quite usable. Advanced drawing methods are discussed in the Adobe Illustrator book, published by Against The Clock.

Draw Simple Paths

1. Open the **lure3.tif** file in the **RF_Intro_Photoshop** folder. If the Paths palette isn't visible, go to the Window menu and select Paths. Select the Pen tool from the Toolbox. On the Options bar, make sure the Paths option is selected on the left. This ensures that the path you create doesn't automatically generate a new shape layer.

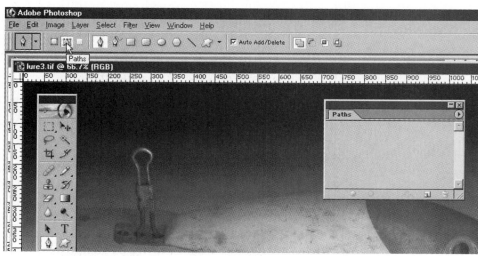

2. Click the Pen tool at the top of the lure — right where the white and red sections meet. Drag the tool to the right about half way to the eye. A line and two control handles appear.

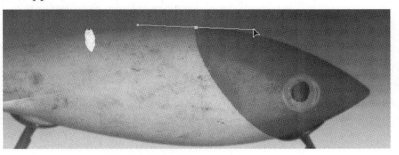

3. As you drag, notice that the line segment curves. Move the handle until the curve matches the curve of the lure. You may want to zoom in to make it easier to follow the edge of the lure.

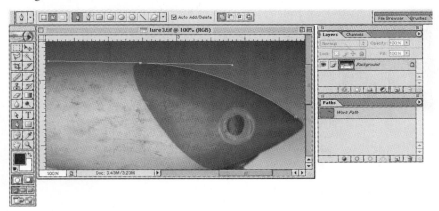

When the Pen tool hits the edge of the window, it causes the image to scroll; it often scrolls so quickly that control of the tool is difficult. Working in full-screen mode (press the "F" key on your keyboard) is more Pen-friendly.

4. Now click the tool again at a spot just before the nose begins to curve around to the bottom of the lure. When you click, drag the mouse to the right and down, and notice how the curve can be made to fit the object. It takes some practice to become adept at placing anchor points and fitting curves, but it's well worth the effort.

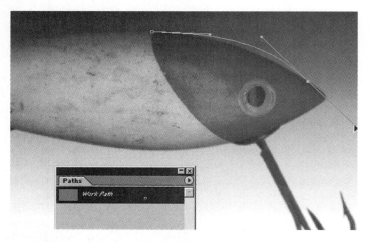

5. Hold down the Option/Alt key. The cursor changes to a hollow pointer. You can use it to adjust only one side of the curve. Try it. Adjust the curve until it perfectly fits the shape.

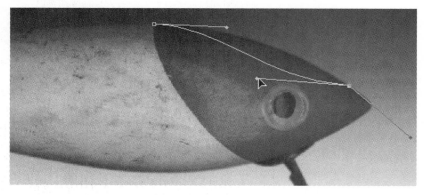

6. Click the tool to place another anchor point underneath the curve of the nose. You'll probably have to use Option/Alt-drag to adjust the curves until they properly fit the shape.

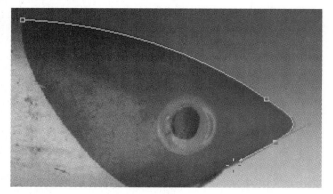

7. The trick to creating efficient paths is to create as few anchor points as possible. This is particularly true when you're working on big curves. Click the tool on the lower curve of the lure. If necessary, adjust the handle to the right so the path fits the shape.

8. The last anchor point on the stomach of the lure is just above the rear hook. Place the point and adjust the curves as necessary. You'll have to make the next point go in a different direction.

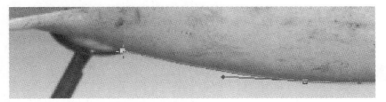

9. Zoom into the detail of the image. Before you do anything, hold down the Option/Alt key. Now click on the last point you created, and pull a handle off to the lower left.

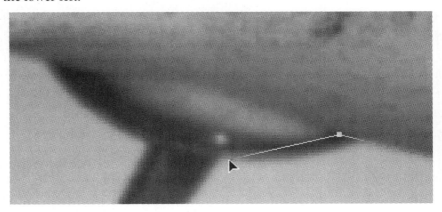

10. Place another anchor on the other (rear) side of the curve. Adjust the handles as necessary.

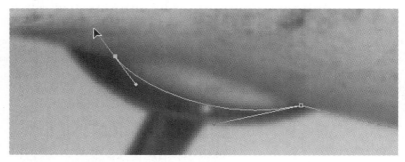

11. Option/Alt-click this new anchor point, and pull a handle toward the back of the lure. Continue adding and adjusting points as you work around the shape.

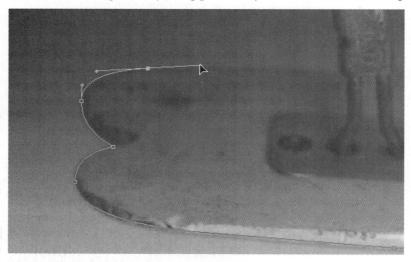

The Direct Selection and Path Selection tools (accessed by pressing the "A" key) can also help to create the perfect path; but in most cases, doing it correctly, one segment at a time, takes less time overall. This is especially true for those who are new to the Pen tool.

12. Complete the path for the entire lure. When you are ready to close the path, notice the icon for the Pen tool changes slightly. This Closing Path icon automatically appears as you end the path by placing the cursor over the first anchor point.

13. After you have closed the path, edit it with the Direct Selection tool to improve its shape (if you need to). Now is a good time to practice with this tool even if you have created an accurate path. Save your file before editing if you are satisfied with your path. The Direct Selection tool is in the Toolbox along with the Path tool, and is accessed by pressing the "A" key. You can:

   • Click on an anchor point to activate its direction lines. You can then adjust the lines' lengths and directions by dragging the direction handles.

   • Drag an anchor point to edit the path shape.

   • Drag the line segment to improve your path.

14. You may also need to add and/or delete points before the path is complete. Delete extraneous anchor points by clicking them with the Delete Anchor Point tool. Add needed anchor points by clicking on the path at the point where you would like to add an anchor point.

15. When you're done, double-click the name Work Path in the Paths palette, and name the path "Red & White". Click OK.

16. Click and hold on the Paths palette pop-up menu in the upper-right corner of the palette, and select Clipping Path. Change the name of Path to "Red & White".

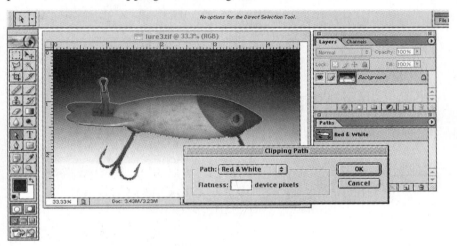

17. Save the file as a Photoshop file, and call it "lure3.psd".

18. Leave the file open for the next exercise.

Some Tips for Using the Pen Tool

If you find it difficult to work with the Pen tool, don't worry. This tool requires quite a bit of practice before it feels natural when you use it. Every expert user of the Pen tool struggled in the same way you may be struggling. Here are some tips for successfully using the Pen tool:

- The direction handles indicate where the line segment is coming from and where it is headed. The best way to know in which direction to drag the handles is to simply drag along the edge of the object you are trying to trace.

- The length of the direction handles control the *torque* (bend strength) applied to the line segment by the handle. The shorter the handle, the closer to the handle end of the segment the curve will be; conversely, a long handle makes the bend more acute near the previous anchor point.

- Simplify your paths. The fewer points the better. You could use 20 points to draw a circle, or 2. Always try to figure out the most economical way to develop a shape.

- Don't scrimp on your points. When you're making a tight, round corner, use a point going in and another going out.

- Pull, look, and pull some more. Get in the habit of pulling your curves around once you've placed the anchor points.

- When you are working around the points on the hooks, try placing a point on either side of the point and bending the path around the point.

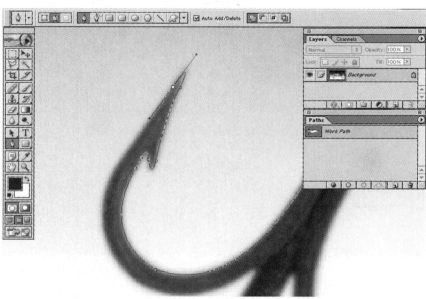

Work with Paths

1. The Red & White path should be active (highlighted in the Paths palette). Click the pop-up menu in the upper-right corner of the Paths palette, and examine the options. Most of them are self-explanatory. For example, Turn Off Path deactivates the path so it's out of the way (clicking on it reactivates the path). For now, choose Make Selection. You can accomplish the same thing by clicking the third icon in the bottom row of icons (the one with the dotted circle). Do not change any settings. Click OK. The program creates a selection region that matches the path's shape. You can also stroke a path with any of Photoshop's many brushes. Try this next experiment.

2. Copy the selection to the clipboard (press Command/Control-C). Press Command/Control-D to deselect the selection.

3. Select a bright yellow as the foreground color, and then choose the Paintbrush tool. Pick a large soft brush (the illustration below shows a 45-pixel-diameter brush). Select the Red & White path again, and click the icon with the dark black ring around a white circle; it is the second icon. This is the Stroke Path icon. Watch what happens.

4. Click the Load Paths as a Selection icon, and press Command/Control-V. The inside image is restored, leaving the neon glow around the outside edges. This is a particularly useful technique when you want to create neon type, glowing lines or shapes, or when you want to otherwise paint paths.

5. Turn off the path and look at your work.

A completed path is included in the file for your reference. Click on Reference Path in the Paths palette to see an efficient path shape. Select the Direct Selection tool from the Pen tool cluster, and click on the path itself — the anchor points appear. Click on an anchor point, and its direction lines become visible.

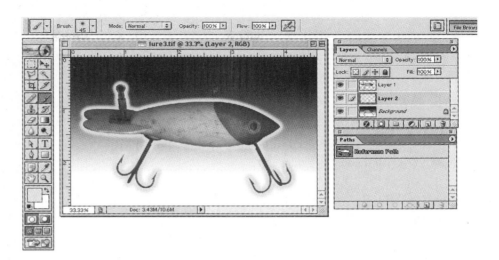

6. Close the file without saving.

Now that you are beginning to understand the workings of the path tools, its time to practice. Located in a folder called **lures** in the **RF_Intro_Photoshop** folder are all the components needed to complete the image below. Draw your paths carefully and examine the reference image (also included) as a guide to shadow placement. Experimenting on your own without relying on step-by-step instructions is the best way to get a firm grasp of the concepts you have been learning. The only photograph in this image is the water; all the other elements were scanned on a flatbed scanner using a piece of white paper as a background (items were placed on the scanner glass with white paper laid over them). Each was outlined with the Pen tool and pasted onto a gradient background.

Write with Neon

1. Create a new RGB document, 5 in. wide by 1.5 in. high at 200-ppi Resolution. Fill the background with Black. Name it "sale.psd".

2. Set the word, SALE!, in 72-point ATC Pine Heavy Italic using all caps. Any color is acceptable, as we are only using the type to create a new path.

3. From the Layer menu, select Type>Create Work Path.

4. Select the pop-up menu from the Paths palette again, and choose Save Path. Name the path "neon". Turn off the visibility eyeball for the type layer. Make a paint layer for your neon light. Name it "Sign".

5. Create a new RGB document, 200 pixels wide by 50 pixels high at 200-ppi Resolution with a White background. Name the document "blue_gradient.psd". Click on the Swatches palette, and Option/Alt-click to select a very dark blue for your background color. Click to select a very light blue for the foreground color.

6. Select the Linear Gradient Fill tool. Set the gradient options to 100% Opacity, and choose the Foreground to Background gradient. Draw a gradient in the new document from left to right. This provides a complete range of blues from which to select your colors.

7. Make certain that both documents are visible on your screen. Select the Paintbrush tool, and click the Airbrush option from the Options toolbar. Set the Flow Rate to 15%, and select a 100-pixel soft brush. Option/Alt-click in the lightest blue area of the Blue Gradient image. Change to the SALE! image, and stroke the path by clicking on the circle with the solid outline at the bottom of the Paths palette.

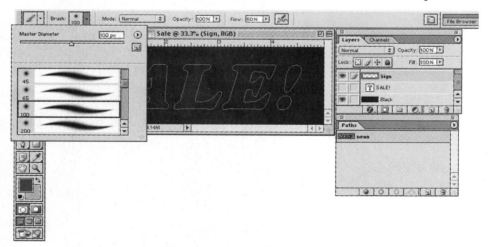

8. Change the Flow Rate to 50%. You have to reselect the Airbrush option each time you change brush sizes. Select the 45-pixel soft-edge brush, and Option/Alt-click to select a dark blue from the far right of the Blue Gradient image. Click the outlined circle again to stroke the path.

With a path active, you can select any painting tool and press Enter on the number pad (not Return/Enter on the keyboard) to stroke the path with that tool at its last used settings.

If you have a selection tool selected with an active path, pressing the Enter key changes the path into a selection.

9. Change to the next smallest brush (35 pixel), and select a little lighter blue, about 3/4 of the way across the Blue Gradient image. Stroke the path again. Continue working this way with smaller brushes and lighter colors until you've reached the lightest area in the Blue Gradient image.

10. Select the smallest soft brush (5 pixel), and change the foreground color to White. Stroke the path once more. Activate the Paths palette pop-up menu by clicking on the black triangle, and select Delete Path.

11. Now you can put your sale up in lights. Save both files to your **Work_In_Progress** folder, and close them.

Chapter Summary

In this chapter, you learned to add vector paths to images and used them to create special effects. You created clipping paths and converted paths to selections. In the process, you developed some expertise using the Pen tool. In addition, you used other tools in conjunction with the paths you created to achieve special effects, such as a neon sign.

10 Filters

Chapter Objectives:

Filters are add-on components in Photoshop (as well as several other graphic programs, including Adobe Illustrator) that can be used to apply a wide variety of different effects and techniques — including the ability to turn photographs into watercolors, frescoes, glass images, and much more. In Chapter 10, you will:

- Learn how filters are organized in the Filters menu, and how to reapply the last filter you used for a cumulative effect.

- Find out why the Extract, Liquify, and Pattern Maker filters are different from all the other Photoshop filters.

- Explore the primary categories of filters, including Artistic, Blur, Sharpen, Render, and Distort.

- Learn the difference between filters that enhance the appearance of an image, and the filters that are utilitarian in nature — such as sharpening and blurring filters.

- Learn to use the Noise, Blur, and Distort filters to create realistic textures, materials, and surfaces from scratch.

Projects to be Completed:

- Gulls Poster (A)

- Fallsbridge Menu Cover (B)

- **Jazz Postcard (C)**

- USA Poster (D)

While filters are critically important tools that can help you achieve effects that would either be extremely time consuming or (in some cases) impossible to create without them, they can definitely be over-used. Simply applying an artistic or style filter to an image doesn't make it a work of art. Make sure you apply filters judiciously; and that the resulting image suits the purpose for which it's intended.

Filters

Filters are specialized tools that allow you to apply a seemingly endless number of special effects to your images — whether they're photographs, line art, or paintings. A large number of filters are already built into Photoshop, and an array of additional filters are available from a variety of third-party developers.

Filters fall into several specific categories that we'll explore in more detail as we move forward. Filters can be applied to entire images or to portions of an image (by using them in conjunction with selections, channels, or masks).

In this example, the image on the left is the original, the second (middle) picture had a Dry Brush filter applied to it, and the one on the right shows the effect of a filter called Ink Outlines.

In this chapter, we're going to spend time learning about filters and the Filter menu, find out how filters affect your artwork, and how filters are organized and managed. There isn't enough time to cover every single filter, because, as we said, the possibilities are virtually endless. You will enough to get you started on the path to successfully using filters.

The Filter Menu

All filters are accessible from a single source: the Filter menu. You might find — as we do — that many projects don't require the use of filters. On the other hand, some projects can't be completed without them. What's important is that you know when to use filters and when to rely on other techniques, such as Layer effects or Blending modes.

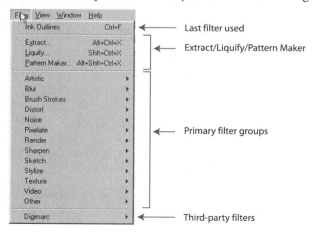

You have the option of re-applying the last filter you used by pressing the keyboard command Command/Control-F. Whatever settings you used for the filter will automatically be applied. If you want to apply the last filter again, but with different settings, add the Option/Alt key to the Command/Control-F combination. The dialog box for the filter will appear, and you can adjust the appropriate values.

Other programs can often make use of Photoshop-compliant filters; these include other Adobe programs (Illustrator and Premiere) as well as third-party applications such as procreate Painter.

Menu Organization

At the top of the Filter menu, you'll see the last filter that you used, and to the right, its keyboard equivalent — Command/Control-F. Please note that this keyboard command isn't specific to a particular filter; the space is reserved for whatever filter you used last, and is the one that will be reapplied if you press Command/Control-F.

If you use the Command/Control-F command, whatever filter you just used is applied without displaying the filter's dialog box. If you want to re-apply the last filter you used, but also want to access its dialog box, add the Option/Alt key to the combination (Command/Control-Option/Alt-F).

The first group on the Filter menu contains three filters: Extract, Liquify, and Pattern Maker. They're actually mini-programs. Most filters display a dialog box where you can edit settings that control the effect they have on your images. These three filters provide independent workspaces, where you can edit and tweak them in ways not possible from a dialog box.

Next is the primary filter groups. In this section of the menu, you'll find the most commonly used filters. Some of them are incredibly complex, such as the Lighting Effects found under the Render submenu; others are fairly simple.

The last group, which by default contains the Digimarc watermarking filter, contains third-party filters. There are dozens of commercial filters available for Photoshop (and any other program that can use the Adobe Plug-in specifications). You buy them, install them, and they are stored in this group.

Types of Filters

There are different types of filters, and they're organized according to the type of effect they have on your images. First, let's explore the use of the stand-alone filters, and then we'll look at the various categories of regular filters.

Stand-Alone Filters

As we mentioned earlier, the three stand-alone filters — Extract, Liquify, and Pattern Maker — are essentially mini-programs dressed up to look like filters. In some ways, they're similar to the ImageReady companion application, but not as powerful or complex.

Extract Filter

The first of the three, the Extract filter, is basically a selection method that makes it far easier to extract a portion of an image, and then use pens, brushes, and other painting tools. It does not, however, create masks.

Use the Extract Filter

1. Start Photoshop. From the File menu, select Open to navigate to the **RF_Intro_Photoshop** folder, and open the file named **desert_rose.psd**. Save it into your **Work_In_Progress** folder. You'll see that it's a picture of a desert rose in bloom. Our task is to separate the plant from the cluttered background.

2. From the Filter menu, choose Extract. The Extract dialog box appears. Dominating the view is a preview of the image. In the upper-left corner is the Edge Highlighter tool. It's the heart of the filter. It allows you to draw a rough outline around even the most complex images. Select the Edge Highlighter tool. You can see the tool in the upper-left corner of the following image.

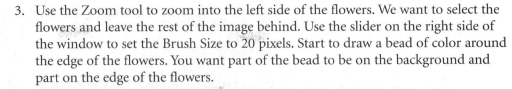

The default highlight color for the Edge Highlighter tool is Green — but you can change it to any color you want by choosing it from the Highlight pop-up menu in the Tool Options section of the dialog box (on the upper-right side).

3. Use the Zoom tool to zoom into the left side of the flowers. We want to select the flowers and leave the rest of the image behind. Use the slider on the right side of the window to set the Brush Size to 20 pixels. Start to draw a bead of color around the edge of the flowers. You want part of the bead to be on the background and part on the edge of the flowers.

4. You can make the painting process even easier; turn on Smart Highlighting by clicking the check box on the right of the dialog box. Now, as you paint the edge, the cursor actually snaps to the edge and perfectly positions the bead of color. Notice that when you use Smart Highlighting, the size of the brush remains the same, but the bead itself becomes just wide enough to straddle the edge of the flowers and the background.

5. With Smart Highlighting turned on, continue to develop the edge bead.

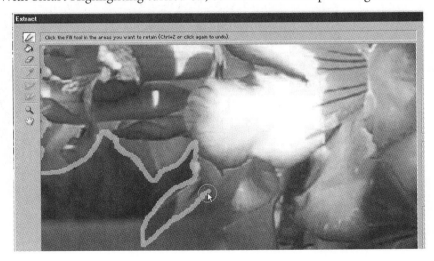

Smart Highlighting works best where you have a well-defined but very complex edge — as is the case in this example. If you're trying to extract something like hair or bubbles, turn off the option, use a bigger brush, and cover the whole area.

6. If you accidentally highlight an area that you don't really want to keep, you can select the Eraser tool, which removes sections of the bead.

7. If you look carefully, you'll notice that there are areas within the flowers where background material needs to be removed from the image to achieve a natural result. Use the Highlight Edges tool to enclose these areas so they won't appear when we perform the extraction.

8. Keep working to refine the edge highlighting. Don't forget to find and highlight all the holes.

This is a complex image and requires a good deal of patience to properly extract. If you try filling the protected area with the Paint Bucket tool and the entire image turns blue, use Command/Control-Z to undo the Fill command, and check the edge bead. It's likely there is a hole in it somewhere, allowing the paint to spill out.

The Matte option allows you to blend a silhouette into a colored background. It changes the color of the edge pixels; instead of fading into white, they fade into the selected color.

9. When you think you've selected it all, zoom out (or use Command/Control-0 (zero) to fit in the window) and check the results of your work.

10. Select the Fill tool — the one that looks like a paint bucket. Click it inside the edge highlight you just drew. The flowers should be filled with a blue tint (or whatever color you've set in the Fill Color pop-up field).

11. It's time to see the filter at work. Click the Preview button on the upper-right corner of the dialog box.

If you hold down the Option/Alt key, the Cancel button turns into the Reset button, which restores the preview image to the state it was in when you first chose the filter. This also works for the Liquify filter, which you'll work with later in the chapter. In fact, it works in many of Photoshop's dialog boxes, such as Levels, Curves, Brightness and Contrast, and others.

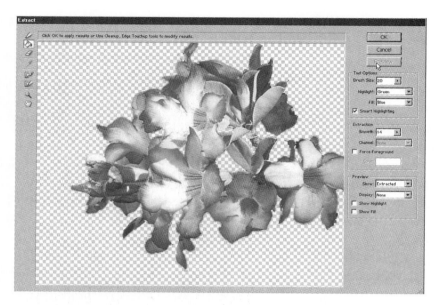

12. Once you're in Preview mode, you gain access to two additional tools — the Cleanup tool (which reduces the opacity of any unwanted background elements) and the Edge Touchup tool, which smooths and refines the edges of the silhouette.

13. Select the Edge Touchup tool (or press the "T" key) and zoom into the image so you can see the edges clearly. Run the tool along the edge. It will smooth out as you apply the tool.

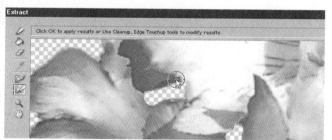

14. You can change the Smooth setting as well. It changes the edge clarity. In some cases it can blur details too much, so you should normally start out with a setting of 0 or 1, and take a look at the results before you set it higher.

15. Look around the image to make sure there aren't any unwanted background areas showing. If there are, use the Cleanup tool to reduce their opacity. It's a cumulative tool; each time you pass over an area, it disappears a little bit more until it's completely gone.

16. Continue working on the edges, smoothing and cleaning, until you're satisfied with the results. This filter works much faster than older silhouetting tools; very detailed work requires much less time to complete than before.

17. Click OK to perform the extraction. You'll have an opportunity to keep or discard any cleanups you made. Back in the Photoshop application, use the Layers palette to flatten the image.

18. Save and close the file when you're done. If you want, you can always go back to the original image and try the exercise again. The more you practice using the Extract filter, the more comfortable you'll become with its functions — and the cleaner your silhouettes will be.

Extracting a single element from a background — as you did in the previous exercise — has many implications. You are able to blur a background to simulate depth of field — or create the blurriness that occurs when you take photographs with wide apertures and high shutter speeds.

Using the Extract filter only creates the silhouette; in many cases, you may want to use the Magic Wand tool to select the transparent background and use the selection to create a mask.

Simulate Depth of Field

1. Open the file named **amsterdam_biker.psd** from the **RF_Intro_Photoshop** folder. Activate the Layers palette.

2. Drag the Background layer onto the New Layer icon. We want to keep the original image intact and perform the extraction on a copy.

3. From the Filter menu, choose Extract. Zoom into the bottom of the picture. Use the same techniques you used in the previous exercise to highlight the edges of the biker. Fill him with the Paint Bucket tool once you've defined the edges of the extraction. Click the Preview button, and check the extraction. Click OK when you're satisfied with the results. This closes the filter dialog box.

4. Double-click the Background layer to turn it into a regular layer (it is named Layer 0 by default). Lock the Background Copy layer and select Layer 0.

5. Let's apply the Gaussian Blur filter. This filter is the most sophisticated of the blur filters, and has a lot of uses when creating textures — or in this case, changing the apparent focus of a camera shot. From the Filter menu, select Blur>Gaussian Blur, and set the Radius value to 6.5 pixels. Click the Preview box to view the results.

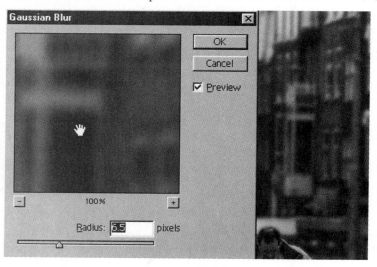

You might try using Edit>Transform>Scale to slightly enlarge the image of the rider on the extracted layer. Making him 2% or 3% larger will help hide the slight halo that might have resulted from the extraction.

6. Click OK to apply the filter to the image. Since the layer containing the extracted biker is locked, only the copied image — which is on the currently selected layer — is affected by the blurring. The result is a change in the focus of the background — something that didn't exist in the original photograph.

7. Save and close the file when you're done.

This technique is critically important when you're doing photo compositing. In many cases, when you drop an object (or person) onto a background, they're both in total focus — something that doesn't often happen in the real world.

Now that you've had a chance to see how the Extract filter works, we can move on to the Liquify filter — the second stand-alone filter.

Liquify Filter

The second stand-alone filter is the Liquify filter. This powerful distortion tool allows you to push pixels around as if they were wet paint. There are eight different Liquify tools; they all work on the concept of a *mesh* — an underlying geometric grid that is distorted by the tools — and in turn, distorts your artwork.

Apply the Liquify Tools

Remember, you can use the Left and Right Bracket keys to interactively reduce ([) or enlarge (]) the size of the current brush.

1. Create a new RGB document, 600 pixels high by 600 pixels wide. Set the Resolution of the document to 150 ppi.

2. From the File menu, select Place and navigate to the **RF_Intro_Photoshop** folder. Double-click the **checkerboard.eps** file. It appears in the center of the document. Press Return/Enter to complete the process and place the graphic on the page. Save the file in the **Work_In_Progress** folder under the name "liquify_practice.psd".

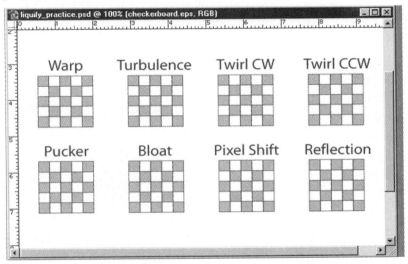

3. Activate the Layers palette (if it's not already visible) and choose the Flatten Image command from the pop-up Options menu.

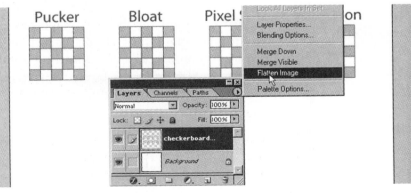

4. Choose the Liquify filter from the Filter menu. The Liquify dialog box appears. On the left side of the window, there are a number of different tool icons. The first one — at the top of the stack — is the Warp tool. Select it.

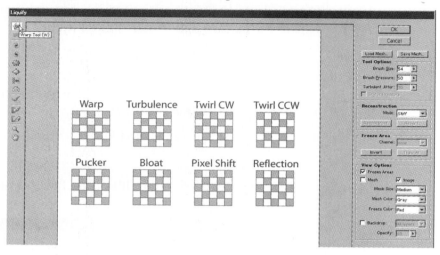

5. On the upper-right side of the window there's a field (and slider control) that determines the size of the brush. Change the Brush Size to 60 pixels, which is about the size of the individual checkerboard graphics.

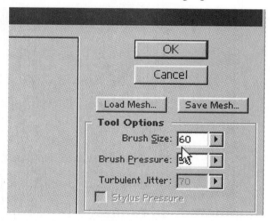

6. Click in the center of the Warp graphic and push up and to the right. The pixels move and you see the effect on the pattern. The more you push, the greater the effect. Try pushing all four corners out from the center.

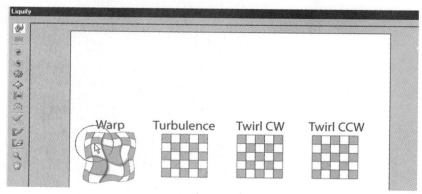

7. Select the tool directly below the Warp tool — it's called the Turbulence tool. Click it in the center of the Turbulence graphic and hold down the mouse button — there's no movement required. The longer you hold the mouse button, the greater the effect of the tool. The Jitter setting (underneath the Brush Size field) controls the intensity of the tool.

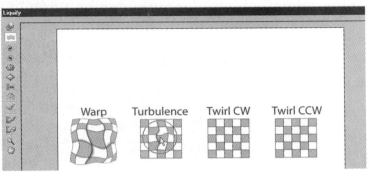

8. Continue on to the two Twirl tools. The first one twirls pixels in a clockwise direction, and the second twirls them counterclockwise. Again, you don't have to do anything but click the tool on the graphic and hold down the mouse button.

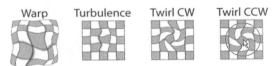

9. Apply the other four tools to the appropriate graphics. The Pucker tool sucks the pixels into the center of the brush; the Bloat tool does the opposite — pushing pixels out from the center of the brush. The Pixel Shift tool is similar to the Warp tool, but it's more intense. The Reflection tool creates the illusion of an object being reflected on a curved surface.

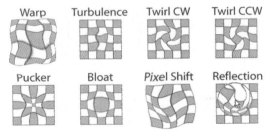

10. The next tool — the one that resembles a paintbrush — is the Reconstruct tool. Select it and drag it across one of the graphics. It restores and repairs the grid to its original appearance.

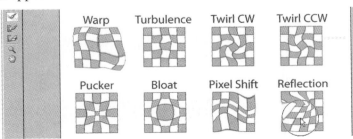

11. The next brush is the Freeze tool. It can be used to protect portions of an image from the effects of the tools. Try painting a border around one of the graphics.

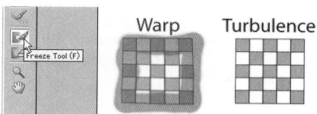

12. Frozen areas are protected from the Liquify tools. You can erase frozen areas using the Thaw tool; it's the one directly below the Freeze tool.

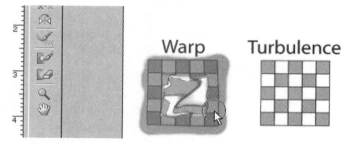

13. Turn on the Mesh (in the View Options area). You'll see the virtual grid on which the tools work. It's the Mesh that affects the image. You can save the Mesh and apply it to other images — a useful method when designing cloth, reflections, and other repetitive techniques.

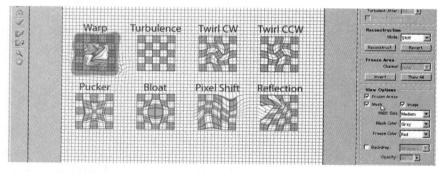

14. Continue working with the tools and trying different options. When you're done, save and close the file.

The Liquify tools are very interesting — but they should be applied with some care. On the other hand, there are some cases where these filters can lend themselves to the creation of some very engaging artwork.

Build an Entrance to Another Dimension

1. Open the file named **pergola.psd** from the **RF_Intro_Photoshop** folder. It's an old path situated at the Vinoy Hotel in St. Petersburg, Florida. You're going to use the Liquify tools to turn it into something out of a science fiction movie. Save the file in your **Work_In_Progress** folder using the same file name.

2. Select the Liquify filter and when the image appears, select the Freeze tool. Hold down the Left Bracket key and watch the Brush Size field — the number begins to decrease. When it reaches 5, release the key.

3. Zoom in to the bottom of the first two columns. Use the Freeze tool to freeze the edges of the white tiles. You're going to warp the bases of the columns, but the effect will be more realistic if the outer tiles remain intact.

4. Change the Brush Size to 2 and with the Warp tool, pull out the lower corners of the columns. This makes them look a little more "organic."

5. Select the Thaw tool and increase the Brush Size to around 40 or 50. Remove the frozen areas.

6. Select the Pucker tool and position the brush over the opening at the end of the path. Use the Bracket keys ([or]) to resize the brush so it fits directly over the space. Apply the Pucker tool to pinch the opening.

When we talk about the "door," we're referring to the opening at the end of the path.

7. Freeze the door with the Freeze tool.

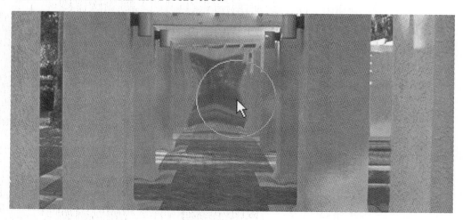

8. Make the brush big enough to cover about a third of the image. Select the Twist Clockwise tool. Click it on the door and hold the mouse down for a moment.

9. Use your imagination as you continue to work on the graphic. Use large Warp tools, Bloats, or whatever you choose. When you're done, close the file without saving it.

The Pattern Maker dialog box is similar to the Extract and Liquify dialogs in the sense that it allows you to edit the filter effects until you're happy with the results. Most filters work as soon as you click OK.

Pattern Maker

The Pattern Maker filter offers an alternative method of creating patterns (compared to the Edit>Define Pattern technique). It's particularly effective if you want to create a number of different patterns from the same image. It also does a better job when you're creating seamless and random patterns.

To access the filter, you would select Pattern Maker from the Filter menu. The image, layer, or selection would appear in the Preview window. Using the Rectangular Marquee tool, you would select the portion of the image you want to use for the pattern.

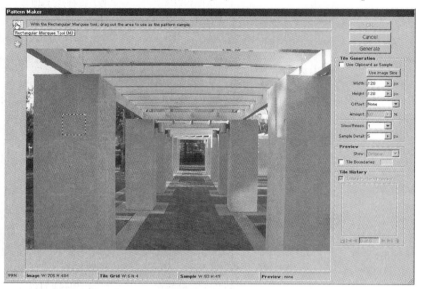

Clicking the Generate button would create a pattern from the selection area. When you generate a new pattern, it fills the entire Preview window. This would allow you to see how the pattern looks over a large surface.

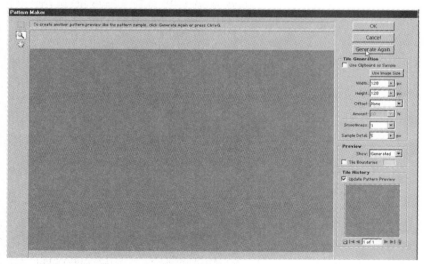

Once you've generated a pattern, you can change back to the original preview by using the Show pop-up menu (found under the Preview section on the lower right of the window). You can then repeat the process to generate other patterns from the image. Here, we selected a portion of the brick pavement and generated a second pattern.

Tile History commands — found on the lower right of the window — display a preview of the patterns you've generated. These commands also allow you to move forward, backward, or to the start or end of the list using the VCR-like controls. You can delete patterns with the trash can icon or save them for use in other documents by clicking the floppy disk icon.

When you generate a pattern, you have the choice of creating numerous small tiles or one large tile based on the size of the image. If you choose to use smaller tiles, you can use the Tile Boundaries check box (in the Preview section) to display the seams.

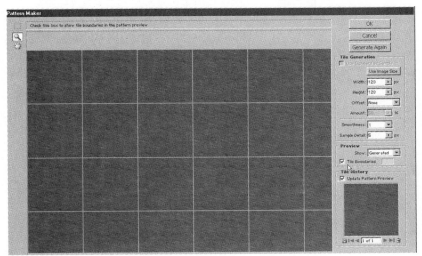

You should experiment and compare the differences between small tiles and document-sized patterns. The latter sometimes produces a more seamless effect.

Once you've generated and saved your patterns, you can use them as you would any other custom pattern — select an area, and use the Edit>Fill command. When you select Pattern from the Use pop-up menu, you'll see your new patterns. You can select the pattern you want to use, set the opacity level, and fill the selection.

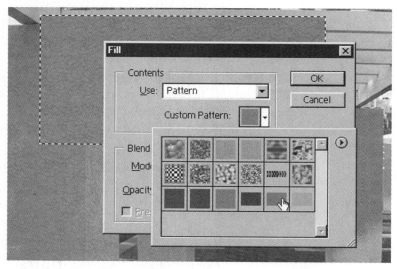

Standard Filters

The next grouping of filters contains nearly 100 filters that are organized into 14 submenus. In reality, the 14 submenus more accurately represent 3 categories:

- **Artsy and Painterly Filters**. These filters include the Artistic, Brush Strokes, Pixelate, Render, Sketch, and Stylize filters. They can also be used to create new artwork from scratch.

- **Retouching Filters**. These include the Sharpen and Blur filters, as well as the Noise filters. They're used to fix problems in scanned images, and can also be used to create new artwork.

- **Distortion Filters**. Distortion filters reside in a single menu — but also include the Liquify filter you worked with earlier in the chapter.

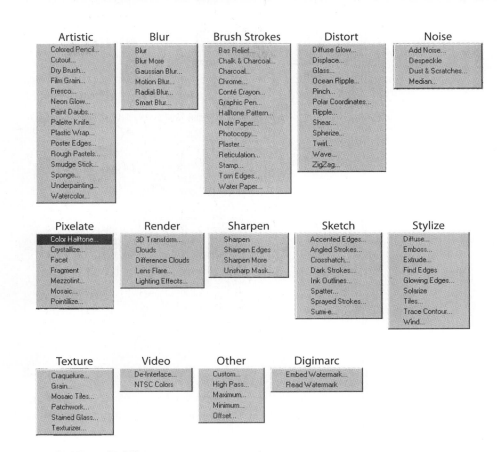

Artistic
Colored Pencil...
Cutout...
Dry Brush...
Film Grain...
Fresco...
Neon Glow...
Paint Daubs...
Palette Knife...
Plastic Wrap...
Poster Edges...
Rough Pastels...
Smudge Stick...
Sponge...
Underpainting...
Watercolor...

Blur
Blur
Blur More
Gaussian Blur...
Motion Blur...
Radial Blur...
Smart Blur...

Brush Strokes
Bas Relief...
Chalk & Charcoal...
Charcoal...
Chrome...
Conté Crayon...
Graphic Pen...
Halftone Pattern...
Note Paper...
Photocopy...
Plaster...
Reticulation...
Stamp...
Torn Edges...
Water Paper...

Distort
Diffuse Glow...
Displace...
Glass...
Ocean Ripple...
Pinch...
Polar Coordinates...
Ripple...
Shear...
Spherize...
Twirl...
Wave...
ZigZag...

Noise
Add Noise...
Despeckle
Dust & Scratches...
Median...

Pixelate
Color Halftone...
Crystallize...
Facet
Fragment
Mezzotint...
Mosaic...
Pointillize...

Render
3D Transform...
Clouds
Difference Clouds
Lens Flare...
Lighting Effects...

Sharpen
Sharpen
Sharpen Edges
Sharpen More
Unsharp Mask...

Sketch
Accented Edges...
Angled Strokes...
Crosshatch...
Dark Strokes...
Ink Outlines...
Spatter...
Sprayed Strokes...
Sumi-e...

Stylize
Diffuse...
Emboss...
Extrude...
Find Edges
Glowing Edges...
Solarize
Tiles...
Trace Contour...
Wind...

Texture
Craquelure...
Grain...
Mosaic Tiles...
Patchwork...
Stained Glass...
Texturizer...

Video
De-Interlace...
NTSC Colors

Other
Custom...
High Pass...
Maximum...
Minimum...
Offset...

Digimarc
Embed Watermark...
Read Watermark

Artsy and Painterly Filters

Each of the filters works in a similar manner — through filter-specific dialog boxes. This applies to all of the Artistic filters. They're used to change scanned images or illustrations into artistic renderings, pencil sketches, charcoal drawings, stained glass windows, and other traditional "natural" media. These filters can be combined, and the intensity with which they affect the original image can be modified through the use of dialog boxes. Each filter has its own dialog box, with the exception of a few that simply perform their task with no input on your part.

Work with Artsy Filters

1. Open the file named **amsterdam_train.psd** from your **RF_Intro_Photoshop** folder. Save it into your **Work_In_Progress** folder.

2. From the Filter menu, select Artistic>Watercolor. The filter's dialog box appears. You'll see a Preview window containing a portion of the image. Take a moment to study the controls for the filter.

3. Try enlarging and reducing the preview pane using the (-) and (+) icons. Adjust the Brush Detail, Shadow Intensity, and Texture settings. The preview provides instant feedback. Click OK to apply the filter to the entire image; it might take a second or two for the program to calculate the changes to the pixels in the original image.

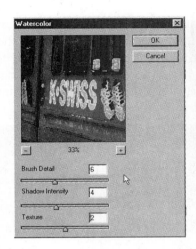

4. Undo the filter (Command/Control-Z). If you would like to see how the train would look if it were painted on a piece of canvas, select Filter>Texture>Texturizer, and select Canvas from the pop-up menu. There are several different textures you can try. Make sure you undo them as you go along.

5. Select the Polygonal Lasso tool, and draw a selection area around the train.

6. From the Filter menu, select Blur>Motion Blur. Change the Angle of the blur effect so it more naturally parallels the position of the train in the image. Set the Distance of the blur to 99. The filter's effect was limited to the selection area. Click OK to apply the blur to the image, and press Command/Control-H to hide the selection area. The effect is quite realistic — a speeding trolley moving through the camera field set to a slow shutter speed.

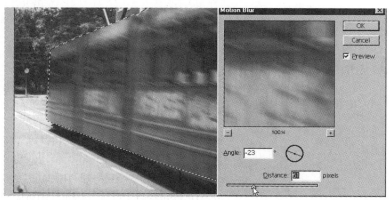

7. Undo the Blur. Use the Oval Selection Marquee tool to draw a fairly large circle over the surface of the image. Use the Select>Feather option with the Feather Radius set to 100 pixels to soften the edge of the circle.

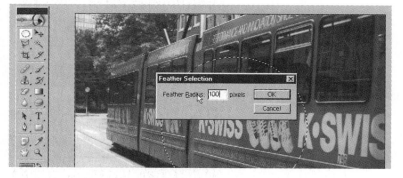

8. Apply a filter to the selection. Here, we used Sketch>Chalk & Charcoal. If you look closely, you can see how the feathering effect causes the filter to blend smoothly into the unaffected area.

9. In your free time, continue to experiment with this image and various filters. You'll soon understand why it is not possible to introduce and work with every filter in the confines of this book. When you're done experimenting, close the file without saving it.

You might try taking a placed image, duplicating it, and creating grids that display all of the filters available in the different categories. When you're a more experienced user, and you are capable of performing file repair and image retouching tasks, you can use those grids as references. We include a grid in your **RF_Intro_Photoshop** folder. It's an Illustrator EPS file named **artistic_grid.eps**, which you can open directly in Photoshop.

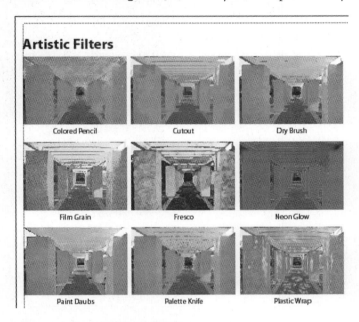

Artistic Filters

Colored Pencil	Cutout	Dry Brush
Film Grain	Fresco	Neon Glow
Paint Daubs	Palette Knife	Plastic Wrap

Using Filters to Create Textures and Drawings

Using various combinations of Noise, Blur, and Distortion filters, you can achieve some dramatic and realistic effects. In this last section of the chapter, you'll have a chance to learn about some of the common textures and painting effects, including the use of displacement maps — a relatively advanced but extremely effective way to simulate cloth and other random appearances.

Create Custom Textures

1. Create a new document, 600 pixels high by 600 pixels wide. Set the Resolution to 300 ppi. This resolution is suitable for textures destined for printed materials, such as brochures or print ads.

If you're creating textures or effects for print, use 300 ppi resolution; for the Web, use 72 ppi resolution.

2. Set the Fill to White and the Stroke to Black (if they are not already at these default settings). From the Filter menu, select Render>Clouds, and then Render>Difference Clouds. The canvas fills with a mottled black, white, and gray pattern.

3. Use the Stylize>Emboss filter, and set the Angle to 135, the Height to 4, and the Amount to 250%. The clouds turn to what appears to be stone.

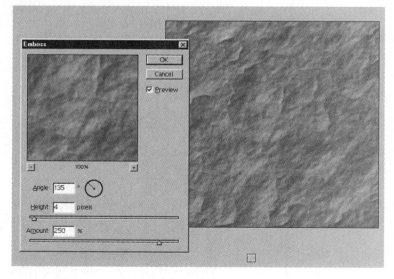

4. Try colorizing the stone texture. From the Image menu, select Adjustments>Hue/Saturation. Check the Colorize box, and then set the Hue to 40, the Saturation to 15, and the Lightness to +10. The stone assumes the color of light brown slate.

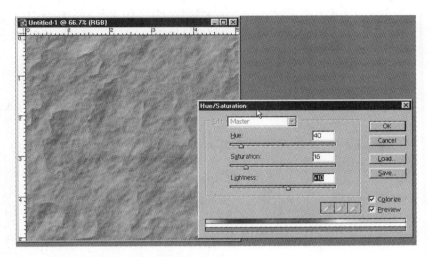

5. Save the file into your **Work_In_Progress** folder as "slate.psd". Select all, delete the contents of the page, and save the file into your **Work_In_Progress** folder as "cloth.psd". Next, we're going to create some cloth.

6. Flatten the document from the Layers palette Options menu. From the Image menu, select Mode>Grayscale to discard the color information. Click OK in the dialog box. Select Filter>Render>Difference Clouds. Click the Save button, and check Save as Copy. Save the file as "cloth_map.psd". This texture is going to be used as a *displacement map*. The Displace filter will use this texture to add depth and shading to the cloth we're going to create.

7. From the Image menu, select Mode>RGB to change the document back to color.

8. Delete the contents of the image again (select all, and then press Command/Control-Delete), and then fill it with White. From the Filter menu, select Noise>Add Noise. Set the Amount to 300, Distribution to Gaussian, and check the Monochromatic option. Click OK.

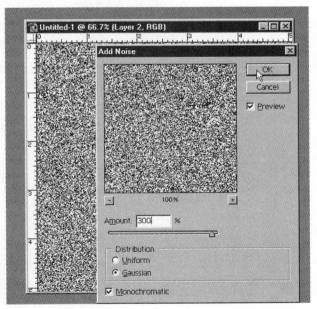

9. In the Layers palette, drag the layer onto the New Layer icon to create a copy of the layer.

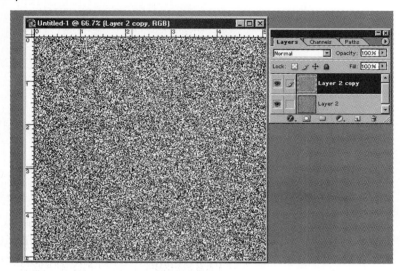

10. On the top layer, from the Filter menu, select Blur>Motion Blur. Set the Angle to 0 degrees and the Distance to 50 pixels.

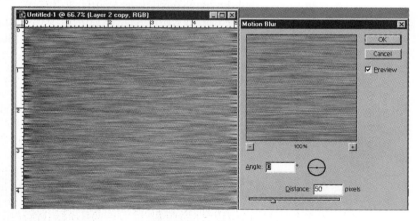

11. Now, hide the top layer and select the bottom layer. Once again, choose the Motion Blur filter, but this time set the Angle to 90 degrees. The blur runs vertically, compared to the horizontal blur on the top layer.

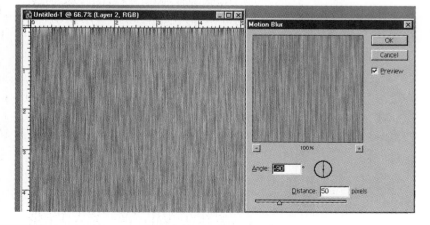

12. Select the top layer — it becomes visible when you select it. Use the pop-up Blend Mode menu to select Multiply. What appears to be linen cloth appears.

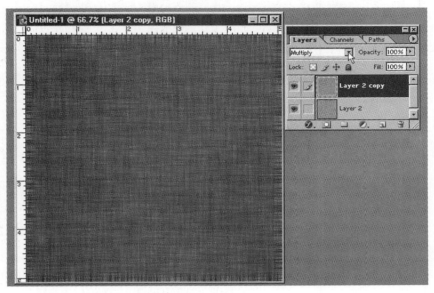

13. Flatten the layers. Save the file as "linen.psd" in your **Work_In_Progress** folder.

14. Use the Image>Adjustments>Hue/Saturation to colorize the cloth. Here, we made the linen a light greenish-yellow.

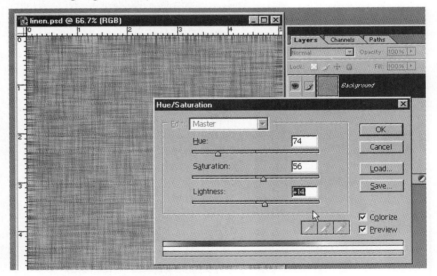

15. Real cloth is rarely flat. We're going to use the map file we created earlier to add depth to the linen through the use of the Distort>Displace filter. Choose this filter and set the Horizontal and Vertical Scale values to 20%. Click the Stretch To Fit and the Repeat Edge Pixels radio buttons.

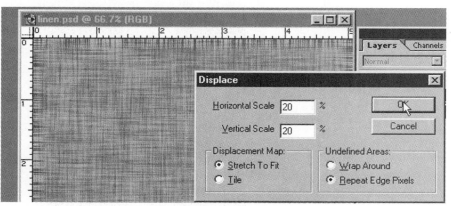

16. As soon as you click OK, the open dialog box appears. The program is looking for a displacement map on which to base the filter. In the map file you created earlier, the darker gray areas push pixels up and to the right by 20%. The lighter areas result in pixels being pushed down and to the left by 20%. Navigate to the **Work_In_Progress** folder and select the **cloth_map.psd** file.

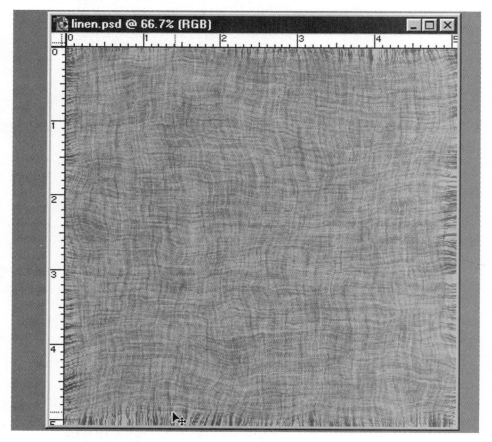

17. Save and close the file.

Chapter Summary

In this chapter, you learned about filters — how they're organized, how they're applied, and how to use them to create original artwork and textures. First, you learned about the stand-alone filters, including the Extract filter, used to isolate complex objects from their backgrounds; the Liquify filter, an interactive distortion filter offering eight different tools; and the Pattern Maker, which can generate any number of patterns from a single document and save them for later use. Lastly, you learned how to apply artistic and painterly filters to your images, and how to use filters to create realistic and useful textures and objects.

Complete Project C: Jazz Postcard

NOTES

11 Printing and Publishing

Chapter Objectives:

Unless we are capable of correctly preparing our images for output services and commercial printers, or ensure their compatibility with established Web performance standards, our work will go unseen and unappreciated; we also stand the chance of slowing down workflows and incurring unforeseen costs. Artists must be knowledgeable about correct file output, which file formats best suit specific requirements, and how to ensure the highest possible quality from finished projects. In Chapter 11, you will:

- Learn how to print your work directly from within the Photoshop environment, and how to use the Print with Preview dialog to control a variety of output-related options.

- Review the relationship between pixels per inch (ppi), dots per inch (dpi), and lines per inch (lpi).

- Become familiar with the concept of effective image resolution, and why it's important to scan and capture images at the correct size and resolution for their intended use.

- Learn how to resize and resample images, and the potential pitfalls involved with the process.

- Work with process color separations, and learn how to manipulate and print individual color channels.

- Learn about spot colors and the use of custom inks, and how to accommodate for their application using channel techniques and the proper file formats.

- Become comfortable with using file formats that are compatible with external applications, such as page-layout and illustration programs.

Projects to be Completed:

- Gulls Poster (A)
- Fallsbridge Menu Cover (B)
- Jazz Postcard (C)
- USA Poster (D)

This chapter is somewhat different from the others in this book because it is not possible for us to anticipate exactly what type of printer you're using in your current environment. This somewhat limits our ability to provide the same kind of hands-on activities you've had in previous chapters.

There are physical limitations relative to film, plates, paper, and printing presses that have historically stood in the way of printing extremely high-resolution color (higher than 200 lpi). The advent of a process known as "waterless" printing — combined with devices that can image a file directly to a printing plate without the interim film stage — allows printers to achieve lines screens as high as 400 lpi.

Printing and Publishing

In this chapter, we explore ways to use your Photoshop images after they're finished. Completing your images is only half of the publishing equation; the other is presenting the work to your audience. There are only a few options:

- You can print the image directly from Photoshop, producing what is commonly called "hard copy."

- You can export the file to an appropriate format, import it into another application, and then print the file from the application. This is a very common workflow used for magazines, newspapers, advertisements, packaging, and other print applications. In this scenario, the images are created in drawing programs, Photoshop, or a combination of the two, and then exported for use in a page-layout program (such as QuarkXPress, InDesign, or Framemaker, to name a few). Once the image is placed onto a page, the layout application is used to output hard copy.

- You can export the file in a Web-compatible format. This is accomplished through the use of ImageReady — a companion application that's included with Photoshop. ImageReady is engineered to optimize and generate Web-compliant graphics. We discuss ImageReady in the last chapter of this book.

In this chapter, we focus on printing from within Photoshop and preparing files for use in other applications. In the next chapter, we cover the issues relative to generating images for use on the Web.

Resolution

When you're preparing your image for print, it is important to remember that no matter what kind of printer you're using, it reproduces your images by converting the square pixels you see on the screen to dots of ink on paper.

 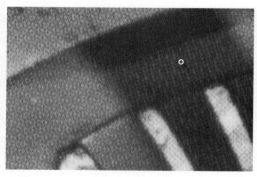

When you print a Photoshop document (or a document from another application containing a Photoshop image), screen pixels are converted into the dot patterns required for hard copy output. This process is called *screening*.

The dots that result from the screening process are arranged in lines. The number of *lines per inch (lpi)* determines the quality of the hard copy. Applications such as newsprint and other relatively low-cost, high-volume publications like flyers, racing programs, and instructions supplied with appliances typically use between 85 and 120 lines per inch; higher-cost publications such as magazines or art posters are often produced using line screens as high as 300 lpi — although 150 lpi and 175 lpi are more common.

Quality Factor

Whenever you're preparing an image for printing, you first must determine the line screen value that's going to be used for the reproduction process. Once you know that value, you must adjust the resolution of your images so you have the precise amount of data for the screening process. If there's too little data (a low-resolution image), the results are not crisp and clear; if there's too much data, the image can take a long time to output, and shadow areas in many types of common images can become muddy and dark. Although this naturally depends on the exact image in question, quality often suffers if the resolution of your image is too high for the application.

The general rule is to multiply the intended line screen times a factor of 1.5 or 2; if your image is going to be output using a line screen value of 150, you should provide an image that's between 225 and 300 pixels per inch on your system. This factor — which we've already talked about earlier in the book — is called the *quality factor*, or *QF*.

You should never provide an image whose effective resolution is higher than 2 times the line screen at which the document is being printed; exceeding a QF of 2 times results in slower print times and a loss of detail — especially in darker (shadow) areas.

Resizing Images

Making an image larger or smaller is quite simple. In Photoshop, you use the Image>Image Size command and enter new values for width, height, or resolution. In a page-layout program, it's even easier; all you have to do is select the image and adjust the control handles until it's as large (or small) as it needs to be to fit the layout.

Unfortunately, as easy as it is to resize an image, it's hardly ever a good idea to do so. Granted, you can make an image 10% or 15% larger or smaller without any significant adverse effects; but beyond that, the quality of the image begins to degrade. The more you reduce or enlarge an image, the worse the results. Even Photoshop, which offers very sophisticated formulas (called *algorithms*) for sizing an image, cannot generate perfect results.

If you have to resize an image beyond these narrow limits, you should either re-scan the original, or, if you're using a digital camera, re-shoot the image with a bigger lens or stand closer to the subject (if it's possible to do so). These alternatives might sound drastic, but the science of image resolution makes it necessary to do so.

Let's say you're preparing a school newsletter that's to be sent to a commercial printer for reproduction at a line screen value of 150. The quality formula dictates that we scan the image at 300 ppi — at the exact size of the final image. We talk to the designer, and find that the image will be placed in the article at 2.5 in. wide by 4 in. high. You start the scanner, place the photograph on the glass, and set the scanning resolution to 300 ppi.

You click the button, and the image is captured. You save the image and hand it off to the layout artist.

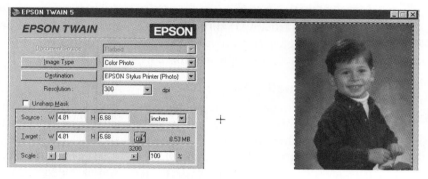

In a perfect world, the size and resolution specifications provided during the early stages of the design process would never change; everything would go exactly as the designer planned, and the image would work perfectly. The image would be dropped on the page, it would fit perfectly into the article layout, and everyone would be satisfied with the results.

In the real world of graphic design, however, things seldom go exactly as planned. Soon after you scan the image, the editor may announce that a late-breaking news story must be included in the newsletter. After considering the impact of the insertion on the layout, the designer decides to reduce the size of several images to provide some additional space. Your scan is one of the pictures that must be resized.

A designer can easily change the size of an existing scan, so this is usually the resizing method that's used; simply grab the handles of the (already placed) image, and make it smaller.

The problem with resizing a scan in a page-layout program is that it changes the *effective resolution* of the image. If the image is reduced by 50%, the effective resolution is doubled; if the image is scaled up to twice its original size, the effective resolution is cut in half. What was a 300-ppi image ends up at 600 ppi if it's scaled to 50%, or 150 ppi if it's enlarged to 200%.

Original Scan
Resolution x 1
300 ppi

Reduced 50%
Resolution x 2
600 ppi

Enlarged 200%
Resolution x .5
150 ppi

For a print job using a line screen value of 150, the second image contains twice as much data as necessary, and the third image provides only half the required resolution.

Effective resolution isn't the only problem that comes into play when you need to resize an image; image details are also affected.

Change Resolution

1. Inside the **RF_Intro_Photoshop** folder are 2 scans of the same original photograph. One is named **mikey150ppi.psd** and the other is named **mikey300ppi.psd**. Open them both, and position them so they're side-by-side with the 150-ppi scan on the left and the 300-ppi scan on the right. Click the Title bar of the 150-ppi image, and then select Image Size from the Image menu.

2. There are 2 things to note: the Pixel Dimensions of the image show a Width of 719 pixels and a Height of 1033 pixels. The Document Size shows a Width of about 5 in. and Height of about 7 in. This is the size at which the image will appear if placed into a page-layout program at 100%. The resolution of the image is 150 ppi. The file weight is slightly larger than 2 megabytes.

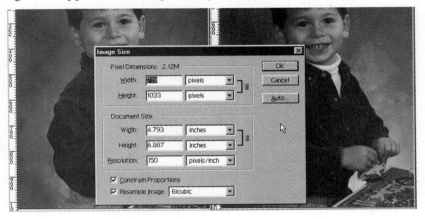

3. Click OK, and then select the 300-ppi image. Select Image>Image Size again. Look at the values. The Resolution is 300 ppi and the file size (Pixel Dimensions) is almost 9 megabytes. It's 1445 pixels in Width and more than 2,000 pixels in Height. The Document Size, however, hasn't changed at all — it's still about 5 in. wide. If placed side-by-side in a layout program, they would appear to be the same.

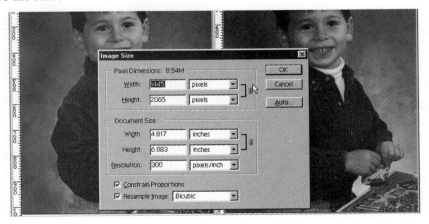

4. If you look closely, the child featured in the images is seated in front of a board game. Select the 150-ppi image. Select the magnifying glass (Zoom tool) and zoom

into the board. You'll see the word "WILD". Now select the 300-ppi image and zoom into the same detail. Look at the difference between the images.

5. Select the images one at a time, and press Command/Control-0 (zero) to fit them back into their windows. Now zoom into the child's right eye. Notice the substantial difference in the number of pixels used to render the details.

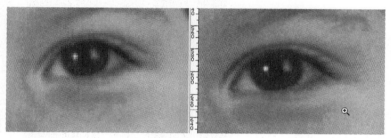

6. Select the 150-ppi image, and then select Image Size from the Image menu. Change the Resolution of the image to 300 ppi. Don't change any other values. Click OK to apply the change.

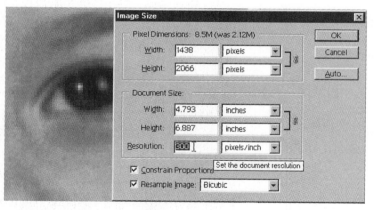

7. Now that the images are the same resolution, zoom back into the eye detail. You can see that simply changing the resolution of the 150-ppi image doesn't create detail that wasn't there before. Even though the images are both 300 ppi, the image that was scanned at that resolution is clearly superior in quality.

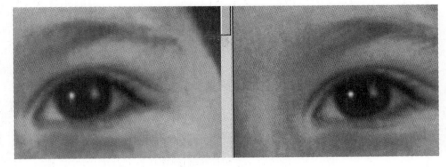

8. You can somewhat improve the appearance of the resized image by using a sharpening filter. First, make sure the **mikey150ppi.psd** image is still selected, and choose Sharpen>Unsharp Mask from the Filter menu. This specialized filter is used to subtly sharpen an image based on the values of adjacent pixels. Enter 40 for the Amount, 3.0 for the Radius value, and keep the Threshold setting at 0 (zero). Click OK to apply the filter.

When applying an Unsharp mask, make sure the Preview check box is checked so you can see the results before you apply the filter. You can also use the + (plus) and - (minus) buttons below the Preview window to zoom in and out of the image. This helps you carefully inspect the effects of different settings. If you set the values too high, the image begins to degrade; if you don't sharpen it enough, you won't pull out any details.

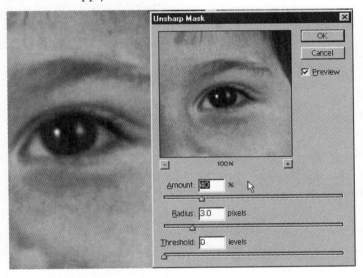

9. The sharpening process definitely improves the resized image — but still fails to achieve the quality and detail of the original. Zoom into different areas of the images and you'll quickly see what we mean. Individual hairs, small wrinkles, and details in shadow areas just aren't the same. Another negative effect can be seen in the skin tones. What were smooth blends between subtle colors (called *gradations*) begin to appear blotchy and uneven.

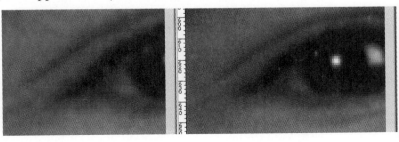

10. When you're done inspecting the images and comparing the details between the original and the resized image, close them both without saving the changes you've made.

When you absolutely must resize an image, it is important to consider how Photoshop will approach the change. In most cases, you'll want the program to perform a process known as *resampling*. Resampling uses a mathematical formula called *interpolation* to determine how to add pixels (when you're increasing the size), or which pixels it needs to discard (when you reduce the size).

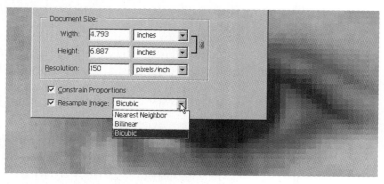

There are three different interpolation methods available. Each offers a tradeoff between quality and speed:

- Nearest Neighbor is the fastest method, but produces the poorest quality results.
- Bilinear is slightly slower than Nearest Neighbor, and offers mid-range quality.
- Bicubic — the slowest of the three — produces the highest quality results. In the past, this was important information to know; but most new computers are so fast, it isn't worth using anything but the Bicubic option.

Printing from Photoshop

While most of the images you generate in Photoshop will be imported into other applications for final output, many projects are suited for output directly from Photoshop. Examples might include posters, photographs for an album or portfolio, greeting cards, package designs, and silkscreen graphics. This is what we explore in the next section of the chapter — printing directly from Photoshop.

Page Geometry

Some printers are limited to using regular letter-size paper. Others can print on larger stock, such as tabloid size (11 in. × 17 in.). Devices found at commercial service bureaus and graphic arts service providers can place your files onto film. Each device offers different resolutions; a typical laser printer can output at 600 or 1200 dots per inch (dpi). The more specialized equipment can image pages at 2,000 dpi and higher. The higher the resolution of the output device, the finer a line screen it's capable of rendering. Today, even some laser printers can achieve a line screen value of 140.

Page geometry is defined as the size and shape of your document. Generally speaking, documents are either taller than they are wide, or wider than they are tall. You may find yourself working on perfectly square documents, but in general, your images will fall into one of these two categories: a tall document is called a *portrait*; a wide document is called a *landscape*. The term for this positioning is the *orientation* of the page.

To complete the following exercises, you need access to a printer. It can be directly connected to your computer (called a *local printer*), or available over a network (a *network printer*). As every printer is a little different, your dialog boxes might not look exactly the same as ours — but this shouldn't affect your ability to follow the steps of the exercises.

Work with Page Setup

1. Open the file named **revolucion.psd** from the **RF_Intro_Photoshop** folder. It's an image taken by Tampa photographer Chris Dunn in Havana, Cuba. Save it into your **Work_In_Progress** folder.

2. Examine the size of the image. Select Image Size from the Image menu, and take a look at the values. You'll see the Width of the document is a little less than 8.5 in.

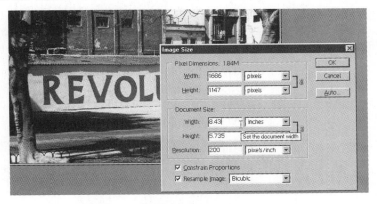

We don't have the time or space to discuss every possible printing device; there are so many available that it would take volumes to cover every possible combination — not to mention that by the time we finished the book, we would have to start over because all the printers we described would have been upgraded or replaced by something newer and faster.

3. Click OK to close the dialog box. Now select Page Setup from the File menu. Below the generic preview image at the top of the dialog box, you'll see a section for Paper settings. The Size is likely to be set for Letter (8.5 × 11 in.). If not, use the pop-up menu to select that size from the list. This is the default paper size that's going to be used to output your file. In the Orientation section, if Portrait isn't selected, click it now.

A local printer is one that's connected directly to your computer. A network printer is available to any workstation that is connected to that particular network.

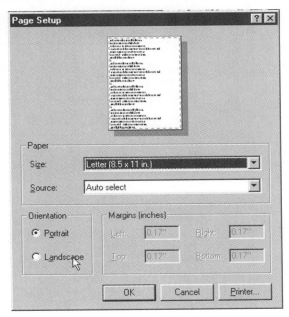

4. Select Print from the File menu. The image is too large for a letter-size page set to Portrait orientation, so you'll receive a warning message.

5. Click Cancel. Return to Page Setup (File>Page Setup) and change the Orientation of the page to Landscape. This causes the document to print across the wide access of the page, which offers plenty of room to print the image.

6. This time, instead of selecting Print from the File menu, select Print with Preview. Instead of sending the document directly to the printer, Photoshop presents the Print with Preview dialog box. If the Show More Options box is checked, uncheck it. We'll explore those options shortly.

From the Print with Preview dialog box, you can reposition an image on the paper and change the scale at which it prints. Remember — this changes the effective resolution of the image; in this case, it's very useful if you need to print a large image on a small piece of paper; it allows you to check a hard copy version of the image without actually changing its resolution or size.

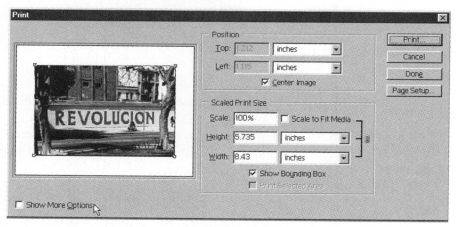

7. Click the Print button. The regular Print dialog box appears. The pop-up menu in the Printer section shows all the printers connected to your machine or your network. Pick the one you use the most, and then click OK.

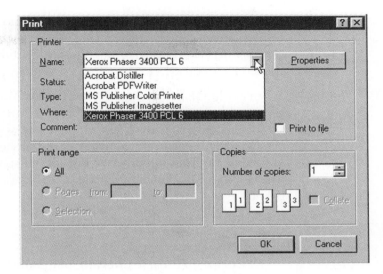

8. If everything went well, you should have a hard copy of the image. Save and close the file when you're done.

Composite Images and Separations

When you're printing from Photoshop, you have one of two options: you can print what's called a *composite* image (all colors in one file), or you can print each color on its own piece of paper. This process, called *color separation*, is normally performed by professional graphic arts service providers (service bureaus and print shops).

A composite image prints all of the channels contained in the image in one piece. When you're working with a grayscale document such as the one you used in the previous exercise, there's only one color, and, therefore, only one channel.

Color images contain multiple channels. An RGB document contains three channels: one for red, one for green, and one for blue. A CMYK image contains four channels: one each for cyan, magenta, yellow, and black. When the tonal values from each of the channels are combined, the result is displayed in a *composite* channel.

CMYK is the standard screening method used in commercial printing. Although a color image in a magazine or newspaper looks as though it contains thousands of colors, a closer inspection reveals that there are actually only four ink colors being used. The screening process generates four different films containing four sets of dots; one each for cyan, magenta, yellow, and black. These screens are positioned on top of each other in

All non-digital printing presses (and some digital printing presses as well) use a "plate" to place ink onto the paper. The ink is first transferred to a roller, and then from the roller onto the plate. The plate is pressed (or rolled) over the paper, transferring the ink onto the paper.

If you have a color printer, the composite channel is output in full color. If your printer can only print black and white, then the composite image is printed in shades of gray corresponding to the color areas of the image.

such a way that your eye is fooled into seeing more color than is actually there. Look through a high-powered magnifying glass at an image in a magazine and you'll see exactly what we mean. Color images must be converted to CMYK before they can be properly reproduced.

When a color image is being prepared for the commercial printing process, each channel is printed on a separate piece of film (or plate material). This process requires very expensive equipment that is normally found in professional environments. Many of the fine details relative to generating quality separations are very technical and outside the scope of this book. What's important to understand about color separation is what's happening when an image is split into four colors. This next exercise should help you visualize the process.

View Separations

1. Open the file named **florida_pompano.psd** from the **RF_Intro_Photoshop** folder. It's a CMYK file. If it's not already showing, activate the Channels palette by selecting Window>Channels.

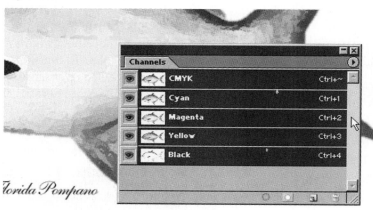

2. Select Preferences>Display & Cursors from the Edit menu. Make sure Color Channels in Color is turned off (not checked).

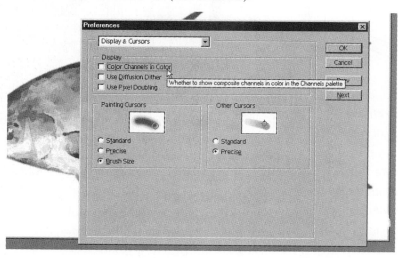

To view the composite channel, use Command/Control-~ (tilde). Use Command/Control-1, Command/Control-2, and Command/Control-3 for viewing the red, green, and blue channels (respectively) in an RGB document, or Command/Control-1 through Command/Control-4 for viewing the channels in a CMYK document. If you have additional channels in a document, use Command/Control and the number of the channel to isolate its view.

3. Click the visibility icons (eyeballs) to hide the Black, Yellow, and Magenta channels. When you hide them, the CMYK composite channel is also hidden.

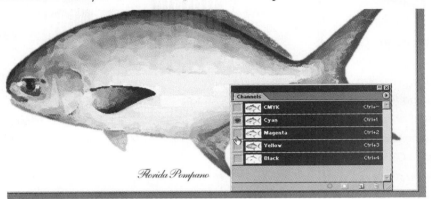

4. The channel is displayed in grayscale. When film is output for this image, this plate will carry only the cyan ink. It's the ink that colors the image — not the film. The cyan film will be imaged with the tonal values you see on this channel. In particular, look at the fish's stomach. In the composite image, you may have noticed that the fish has a distinctive yellow coloring on its stomach. Since there isn't going to be much cyan ink in this area of the image, there isn't much tonal value on the Cyan plate; in fact, there's almost none.

5. Click the visibility icon for the CMYK channel and examine the stomach to see what we mean. Now click the visibility icon again, and drag down to the Yellow channel. All the other channels are hidden, and only the Yellow channel is visible. Not surprisingly, the tonal values in the stomach area are much higher on this channel. The darker the area, the more yellow ink ends up on the page.

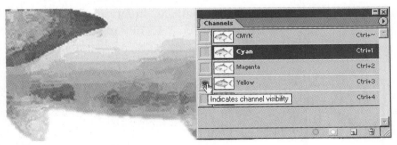

Not everyone agrees with our statement that you should always work in RGB color mode — even if your images are ultimately going to be converted to CMYK or Grayscale for printing purposes. Many traditionalists believe that you shouldn't use anything but CMYK color mode because that's the way the image is going to be reproduced. Another consideration is that in today's environment, the "highest and best use" of your images isn't necessarily a traditional ink-on-paper printing press; many advanced color reproduction technologies (not to mention the Web) rely on RGB or L*a*B formats to achieve maximum-quality output.

6. Turn on the composite image again by clicking the CMYK visibility icon. Look closely at the image. There's not a great deal of black. Click the CMYK channel, and slide down to the Black channel.

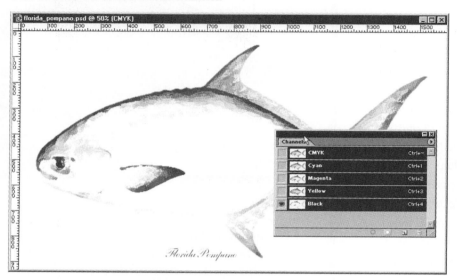

7. Hide all the channels except the Cyan channel by clicking their visibility icons. Look at the image, and then turn on the Magenta channel so both channels are visible at the same time. You can now see the interaction between the cyan and magenta inks. This is exactly what's going to happen on press. Although the inks aren't transparent, the arrangement of the line screens (each color is run at a slightly different angle) ensures a very similar result to what you're seeing on your monitor.

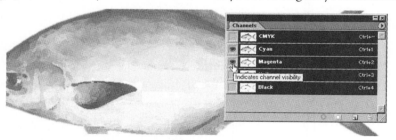

8. Add the yellow ink by turning on the Yellow channel's visibility icon. The image is almost complete. In fact, the only things missing are the fine, dark details. Turn on the Black channel now, or simply press Command/Control-~ (Tilde) to re-access the composite (CMYK) channel.

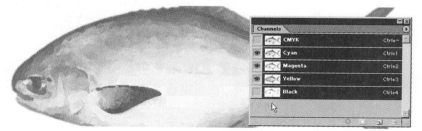

9. When you're done, close the file without saving the changes.

Theoretically, you can create black simply by printing 100% Cyan, Magenta, and Yellow in the same spot on the page. In practice, though, this produces only a dark brown/grey. Black ink is added to the image to bring out details, reproduce type and line elements, and to reduce total ink coverage.

You can access the Levels palette by pressing Command/Control-L.

This exercise demonstrates how inks interact on press during the production of a four-color print job. The films only carry tonal values — they only contain grayscales. When an individual film is used, dark areas result in more ink being used. The yellow plate is dark in the fish's stomach region because that's where the yellow ink is going to be when the job is printed. Mixing yellows and cyans produce the green shades; adding magenta brings out reds, pinks, and browns; the black plate provides details and reduces ink coverage.

Interestingly enough, you can modify the intensity of an individual channel in a four-color print job and affect the color produced on press. In fact, many experienced pressmen reduce or increase a specific ink during press runs in order to adjust the intensity of the colors within certain ranges.

You can experiment with this concept quite easily on your own. In this example, we selected Image>Adjustments>Levels, and then picked the Yellow channel from the pop-up menu on the Levels palette.

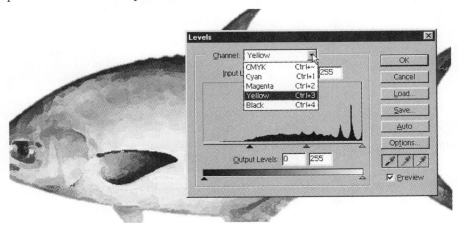

If you move the sliders for the shadows, midtones, and highlights, the color of the image changes accordingly. This is an excellent technique for adjusting specific colors before final output.

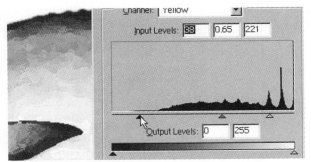

Spot Colors

Some colors can't be perfectly reproduced using four-color process printing. There are many examples of this, but the one that most readily comes to mind concerns the colors of a corporate logo. Many companies — especially large, household-name companies — are fanatical about the colors of their logos. It is often true that the exact colors they require can't be reproduced using CMYK inks — they require ink that is specifically mixed for that particular graphic.

The printing process isn't limited to ink-on-paper. You can see dozens of examples of alternative printing methods: images appear on plastic, soda cans, t-shirts, golf balls, cups, pens, and many other objects. The actual material on which an image is printed is called the "substrate." Different substrates often require different physical processes — but image preparation is largely the same with only subtle differences.

By mixing solid ink colors, a printer can match (or *hit*) almost any color — including metallic, pastel, and fluorescent colors. In a four-color print job, however, this requires adding a fifth ink to the press run. A solid color ink used in the printing process is called a *spot color*. Spot colors aren't only used in four-color printing; a simple two-color poster might use black as one color and a solid ink (spot color) for a second color.

Another use for spot color channels is for applying varnish to a project — a technique that's often used to add gloss (or a matte finish) to specific areas of the page. Many designers varnish photographs in order to make them stand out from the rest of the image.

There are two ways to add a spot channel to an image:

- The first method is to Command/Control-click the New Spot Channel icon at the bottom of the Channels palette. From there, you can name the color and determine how solid the ink appears on your monitor. This setting has no impact on actual ink coverage when the project is printed on a printing press or digital imaging device.

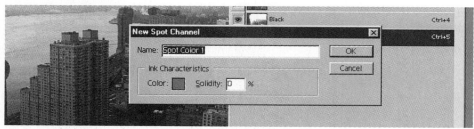

Before you decide to add a spot (or custom) color to your image, make sure you talk to your printer about color values and other technical requirements they may have.

- The second way to incorporate a spot color into one of your documents is to first add a new alpha channel. From the Channel Options dialog box, you can define it as a Spot Color channel.

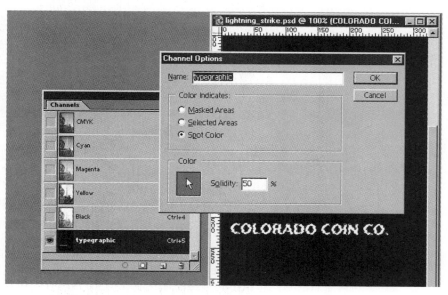

Using duotones, tritones, and quadtones are other ways to add custom colors to your print projects; simply select the mode and pick a custom color for the second, third, or fourth color. This is a particularly good way to add tone to black-and-white images.

There's a useful tool on the Color Picker called the Gamut Checker. If you pick a color and you see an exclamation point, you know that the color will not reproduce properly on a printing press. Click the exclamation point icon and the color shifts to the nearest press-compliant color. Click the cube icon and the color shifts to the nearest Web-safe color.

Whichever method you use to create the spot channel, you'll have to click the color chip, and from the Color Picker dialog box, click the Custom button. This provides you with access to a number of different spot color definition "books," including several from the popular Pantone Color Matching System. You can type in a number, or pick a color from the scrolling list.

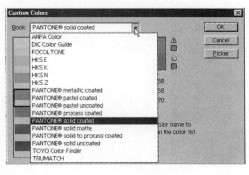
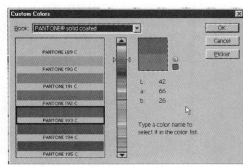

Remember that when you're specifying a spot color, be sure to pick it from a physical swatch book; don't trust your monitor display when selecting custom colors. Even if your system is calibrated, spot colors are tricky to reproduce on screen since they're comprised of custom pigments.

Printing Options

The Print with Preview dialog box offers a number of additional options. To access them, click the Show More Options check box on the bottom left of the dialog box.

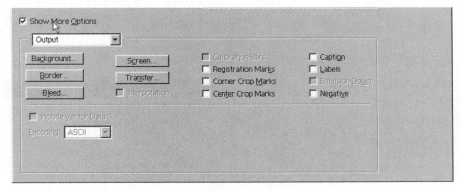

There are two sets of additional options. The first group controls the output function, and the second controls color management and separation settings.

Output options include:

- **Background.** Clicking this button accesses the Color Picker. It can be used to place a colored background behind your image.

- **Border**. You can use this button to place a black border around your image. A dialog box provides a field where you can enter a pixel value for the width of the border.

- **Bleed**. If you want ink coverage to extend all the way to the edge of the paper, you have to print the image slightly larger than the size of the finished piece and then cut off the excess (all output devices require some amount of margin for holding — or gripping — the substrate). This option allows you to determine how much of the image needs to be cut off by placing cut marks inside the image area.

Captions are part of the information maintained for each image. Select File>File Info to access the File Info dialog box.

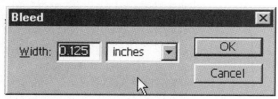

- **Screen**. This option controls the angle and shape of the screen dots. It's best to allow your service provider to determine the values for these options. Changing them can — and will — produce unexpected results on press.

- **Transfer**. Transfer functions affect the intensity of the dots in specific areas of an image — such as shadow areas or areas containing highlights. Until you're fully familiar with press conditions and screening algorithms, avoid making changes to these options.

- **Printer's Marks**. Printer's marks include gradient bars, calibration strips, registration targets (which allow the printer to align film separations), captions, and labels. The rest of these options are best handled by your service provider.

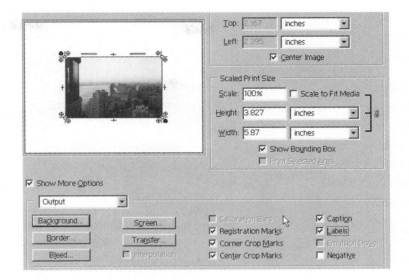

You can resize an image within the Print with Preview dialog box by simply grabbing the corners of the image and dragging in or out. Remember, resizing the image changes its effective resolution.

Besides the output options available in the Print with Preview dialog box, there's also a set of controls relative to color management.

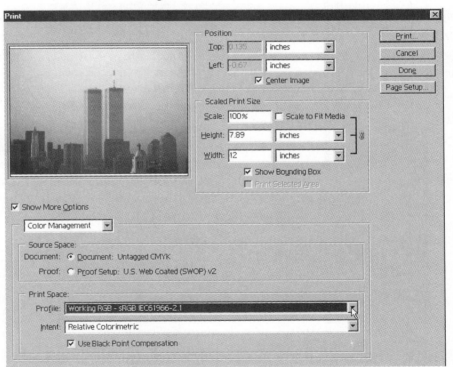

If you hold down the Option/Alt key while you're looking at the Print with Preview dialog box, the Print button changes to Print One (which, when pressed, immediately sends one copy of the document to the selected printer with no further input on your part); the Cancel button changes to Reset; and the Done button changes to Remember. This third option provides the only way to save your print settings.

If you want to print separations from your own machine, this is the place to do it. If you have a CMYK document open, you can pick Separations from the Print Space Profile pop-up menu. The Document>Source Space radio button must be checked in order to activate the Separations selection in the pop-up menu; if it's not, the option will be grayed out and unavailable.

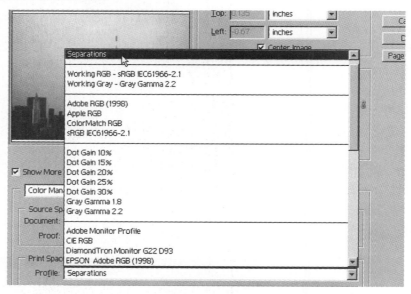

Once you select Separations from the Print Space pop-up menu, clicking the Print button outputs each channel separately. This is usually done by service bureaus or printers who output the channels onto film or plates.

Profiles

Color calibration is the process whereby you match the colors you see on your monitor to the colors you can expect from whatever printing process you're going to utilize to reproduce the project in quantity (even if the quantity is 1 and it's being printed on your personal color printer). Calibration also takes into consideration the source from which you're getting your images, be it a digital camera, a scanner, or a digital stock service.

Learning how to calibrate your entire system is a fairly broad subject, and one that's best delayed until you are completely comfortable using the Photoshop program. There are, however, several things you should understand about how profiles work.

Profiles are small pieces of software that contain information about how specific printing processes and devices reproduce color. There are profiles for monitors, printing processes, specific printers, and specific scanners.

When you load these profiles, Photoshop adjusts the view on your monitor to match — as closely as possible — what an image is going to look like when it's run through a specific printing process.

To load profiles, simply use the View>Proof Setup>Custom command. A dialog box will appear that provides access to the profiles that are already available — ones that were placed on your hard drive when you first installed Photoshop.

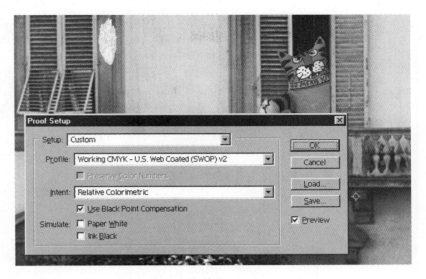

We encourage you to load an image and go through several different profiles and watch what happens to the monitor display. Different profiles can have a dramatic affect on the image. Just be careful — sometimes the monitor display looks a little flatter than the actual results. This is better than having the monitor show you something that looks brighter than it will actually appear when printed.

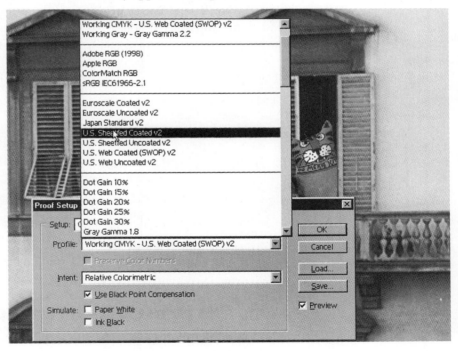

The second profile collection to which you have access is found in the Print with Preview dialog box. From the pop-up menu at the bottom of the dialog, simply select Color Management.

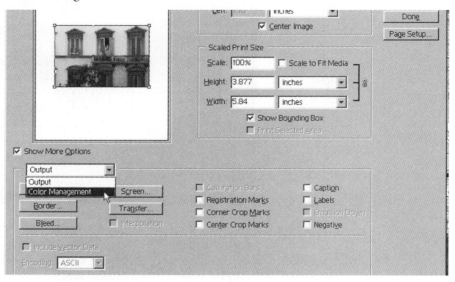

Many devices such as printers and monitors are supplied with their own custom profiles, and you can actually purchase third-party color profiling systems that range from a few dollars to many thousands of dollars. As is often the case, the more expensive the solution, the more complex — and arguably — the better it is.

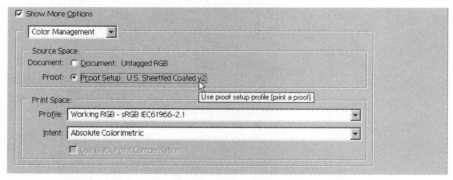

Until you've reached the point where the color you see on your monitor absolutely must match the finished results you expect to get from the printing process, using the supplied profiles will provide you with satisfactory results.

Preparing Files for Use in Third-Party Applications

As you learned earlier in this book, you can save Photoshop images in a wide variety of file formats, but only a few of them are commonly used. All of the other formats are either old, out-of-vogue formats used by a dwindling number of applications, or are necessary to move files back and forth between specialized software tools (such as engineering and computer assisted drawing programs — commonly called *CAD* programs).

The process of preparing files for use in other applications isn't very difficult to learn; it's simply a matter of understanding which file formats work best with which applications.

File Formats

There are four file formats most often used for printing. Let's take a moment to review each of them.

TIFF Files

Tagged Image File Format, better known as TIFF, is the standard bitmapped format and can be used by any program that processes bitmapped images. In the past, TIFF images were quite simple, containing only the pixel information that comprised the image. Today, the format can also contain layer information, masks, and other components that may or may not be compatible or compliant with page-layout programs.

When generating a TIFF image for use in another application, save the file as a copy without layers, masks, or any other enhancements. Saving the original image as a native Photoshop file retains layers, color channels, and alpha channels. Using the industry-standard TIFF format ensures that you won't run into problems when/if you repurpose the image.

Photoshop EPS

EPS (Encapsulated PostScript) files allow a combination of bitmap information and vector image data to be present in the same file. For files containing fonts and paths, using the EPS format ensures those vector objects are rendered at the highest resolution available from the output device.

As you've already learned, Photoshop supports the inclusion of vector objects. These objects include type elements, paths, and shapes.

This image contains three shapes and a "live" text object.

Photoshop documents are comprised of pixels and are, therefore, bitmap documents. This is the reason for the quality breakdown that occurs when you resize an image — especially scaling up an image by more than 20%. Vector objects, however, aren't subject to this quality degradation; they can be scaled up or down by any amount. Since they're described as mathematical formula, they maintain the quality of their edges, color blends, and shapes.

In order to achieve this constant level of quality, you must make sure that when you save the EPS file, you select the Include Vector Data option by clicking the appropriate check box in the EPS Options dialog box.

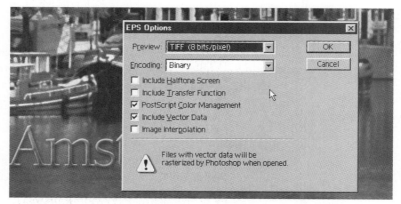

EPS/DCS

Several layout programs require that you "pre-separate" your CMYK images before they can be used in a four-color document. To accomplish this, you must first convert your image to CMYK, and then use the EPS/DCS option to save the file. The option allows you to save a preview image (which is used in the layout process) along with the four files (four films) required for the printing process. DCS files are also used in the event that you've added a spot color to your image.

There are two types of DCS files, both based on evolving standards. The type that is appropriate for your artwork can only be determined by reviewing the manual that came with your layout software.

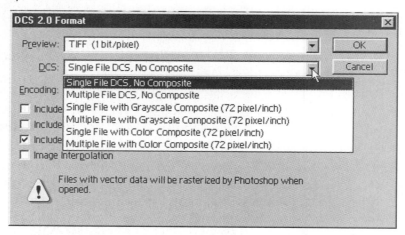

This is the DCS 2.0 Format dialog box. DCS 2.0 is one of two DCS options available from the Save dialog.

There are a number of different options for creating DCS files; the exact combination is determined by your layout application and the workflow in place between you and your service provider. You can save a single file containing a composite preview and all the color components, or you can choose to generate separate files for the composite (preview) image and each color channel contained in the image.

JPEG

JPEG (Joint Photographic Experts Group) files are not often viewed as suitable for print applications because of the "lossy" compression scheme the format relies upon; however, JPEG files can be used successfully in print projects under certain conditions. When transmitting RGB files electronically to your service provider, for example, JPEG can significantly reduce the upload and download times. Negative effects on print quality are often unnoticeable, even to trained eyes (this depends on the quality level you choose when generating the file; if you compress the image too much, the degradation becomes apparent). All current versions of popular page-layout packages support the use of JPEG formats.

Photoshop opens and prints JPEG files to any desktop printer; the problem reveals itself when a file is opened, modified, and resaved as a JPEG; compression is applied each time the file is saved, and eventually degrades the image quality until it's no longer useable.

PDF

As Adobe Acrobat becomes ever more sophisticated and capable, more and more files are finding their way into this useful format. Photoshop allows you to save directly to PDF (Portable Document Format) from the Save As dialog box. There are options for Save, Layered Data, Vector Data, and Embedded Fonts.

PDF is a very useful format for sending proofs or samples to clients, as the files can be viewed in Acrobat Reader —the clients are not forced to install Photoshop on their systems. Since many people don't own Photoshop, PDF offers a viable alternative to physically distributing hard copy of your images.

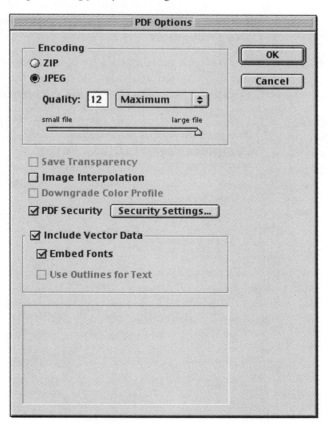

The PDF Options dialog box provides a variety of save and security options. This provides a way for clients to view files, while at the same time restrict them from printing and changing the file. This helps the artist to stay in control of the artwork.

Below is the PDF Security dialog box that shows some of the built-in security features of this file format.

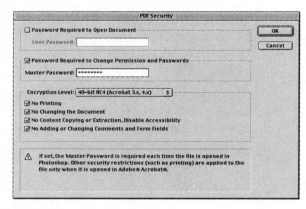

PDF files generated from within Photoshop can be opened in Adobe Acrobat and made interactive through the use of the program's buttons, navigation tools, annotation, and text objects. For more information about Acrobat, visit Adobe at http://www.adobe.com.

Chapter Summary

In this chapter, you learned how to print from within Photoshop. You saw how the resolution of an image affects the final print quality, and that resizing images can result in poor print quality.

You saw how color images are broken into four separate films used on printing presses, and how colored inks interact to create the illusion of thousands of colors where only four exist. Lastly, you learned how to prepare Photoshop images for use in other applications.

Complete Project D: USA Poster

12 Web Design with Photoshop

Chapter Objectives:

It is true that Photoshop is not a fully-functional Web site authoring tool. It is also true that Photoship is an excellent vehicle to design, plan, and produce mock-ups of Web sites that can then be exported to a Web-authoring product for final production and publication. Photoshop provides all the tools and features necessary to create powerful Web objects. In Chapter 12, you will:

- Learn the basics of HTML, and how it is used in Photoshop.

- Learn HTML limitations with regard to text element creation and placement, and table usage.

- Discover the differences between print file formats and those used for Web distribution.

- Find out why it is necessary to keep the size of your Web images and files to a minimum.

- Discover the differences between global, parallel, and local navigational structures.

- Find out the importance of using Web-safe colors for images destined for the Internet.

- Learn to use the Save for Web command to optimize files for output to the Web.

- Discover the benefits of creating slices of your images, how they can reduce download time, and how they can be used to add interactivity to your projects.

Projects to be Completed:

- Gulls Poster (A)

- Fallsbridge Menu Cover (B)

- Jazz Postcard (C)

- USA Poster (D)

HTML isn't actually a language in the pure sense of the term; it doesn't offer logical branching or the definition and use of variables. Strictly speaking, HTML is a markup system – it makes use of "tags" that are interpreted by a Web browser.

Web Design with Photoshop

Designers use Photoshop to create the initial mock-up and the final design of their Web sites before they export the images and recreate the design in an HTML authoring tool. In this chapter, we explore ways to take advantage of Photoshop's powerful imaging and formatting tools for the creation of designs and actual Web objects.

Understanding the Limitations of HTML

While many Web site designs don't require you to be a Photoshop wizard, they all necessitate a solid understanding of the design limitations of HTML (Hypertext Markup Language). HTML is the "structural language" that is used on the Web. Let's examine some of the limitations you must take into consideration when using HTML.

Absolute Positioning

HTML offers very little in the way of absolute positioning. Designers have worked around this deficiency by placing text and images in invisible tables (that is, tables with the Border attribute set to 0). HTML also offers layers that were supposed to be the solution for the lack of absolute positioning. At first glance, having the ability to stack elements on top of one another, as well as having complete control over the placement of elements, seemed to work well; but it was soon found that using layers is not the best solution for Web layout. Text can flow differently on various computers, and the length of a text layer can't be predicted; this makes it difficult to place items in proper relation to one another.

Earlier versions of Netscape Navigator have an additional quirk: if the browser window is resized after the page has been loaded, the layers get mixed up. Layers can be used safely only for animation (with DHTML) where one layer with some text or an image moves across the screen.

For this reason, Web designers still generally use tables to position elements. This solution works quite well, as long as the tables only contain elements with clear and fixed measurements (such as images). As soon as text enters the equation, the matter becomes more complicated. Due to the differences in browsers and computer platforms, there is no certainty about the text flow. When designing in Photoshop, you must be aware of table cells that contain text, and understand the relationship of one cell to its neighboring cells.

Limited Text Formatting

Arguably the worst limitation – from a design standpoint – is that HTML doesn't handle text very well. Formatting is limited to basic attributes such as style (bold, italic) or color. Text size is measured not in points or pixels, but in relation to other text characters, and the browser determines the actual appearance of the text on screen. The use of Cascading Style Sheets (CSS) is an extension to HTML that was supposed to solve most of these issues; but CSS is not implemented consistently across browser platforms. This inconsistency means that some of the features are missing in some browsers, or they don't produce the same results; however, the most basic CSS features are reliable and allow the user to perform certain operations, including precisely setting the font size.

HTML is not capable of embedding fonts, a feature that Adobe Acrobat possesses; to display correctly, all fonts that you use in your design must be installed on the users computer. This is a drawback that limits you to using Arial/Helvetica and Times/Palatino — cross-platform fonts that are present on both Windows and Macintosh systems. If

The browser being used to view your designs establishes the default font size (called the "basefont"). Any settings you establish for text elements on your page (with the exception of graphic objects that look like text) are determined relative to this basefont attribute.

It's a good idea to test your designs not only in the current versions of Internet Explorer and Netscape Navigator, but in older versions as well. Also be sure to check your pages on several different platforms — at the very least on both Windows and Macintosh systems.

your design requires a headline to appear in a special font, you must rasterize the type, and turn it into an image to ensure that it will be viewed correctly.

Limited Table Formatting

Since tables are so essential when designing Web pages, there are some important factors you should keep in mind when using them in your site designs:

- The main limitation of HTML tables is that you can only set the cell pad (the distance of the cell content from the cell border) and the cell space (the space between the cell borders of two neighboring cells) for an entire table, as opposed to individual cells. If you need to individually set any of these attributes, you must nest tables inside each other. This is done quite extensively by HTML authors; they nest as many as three tables when working on complex designs. Nesting too many tables can cause problems in some browsers, however, so simplicity is often the key to good (consistently viewable) Web design. It is also important to know that table cells can be merged.

- The dimensions of a table can be set to a fixed value in pixels, to a percentage (of the browser window), or even a relational value (all the available space). This allows for some design concepts and techniques that are not available in the world of desktop publishing.

- Table cells can have a background, either a color or an image. This adds a layer in the code, and increases the complexity of the image.

- Netscape Navigator and Internet Explorer handle image backgrounds differently; if your design incorporates this technique, be sure to test it in both browsers before distributing to the Web.

Images

If you're making a career move to Web site design from a background in print design, you're probably accustomed to using graphic formats such as TIFF and EPS, which offer the best possible image quality. On the Web, these formats are largely irrelevant, while JPEG, GIF, and PNG formats prevail. As you probably already know, bandwidth is a big concern on the Web, and large data transmissions are considered unacceptable. Images commonly make up 60 to 80 percent of the data on a Web page; consequently, image file compression is a significant concern. JPEG and GIF are popular formats on the Web because they employ effective compression algorithms that can compress graphics into relatively small files. This efficiency, however, comes at the expense of image quality.

JPEG, GIF, and PNG formats all have their advantages and drawbacks, which pertain mainly to their various compression algorithms. Generally speaking, JPEG is used for photographs, GIF is used for graphics with solid-colored areas, and PNG can straddle both types of images.

Bandwidth

One of the restrictions of the Web medium is connection speed. Many people still access the Internet with 56 Kbps modems. For designers, the bandwidth problem means that 40 to 60 Kb should be the maximum amount of new transferred data per Web page. Browsers store downloaded text and images in a local cache on the user's hard drive; stored data can be recalled from this cache much faster than new content (new

The size of an image — in Kbytes — is referred to as the "weight" of the file. Files that weigh too much take too long to download, and visitors using modems often lose patience and leave the site before they've had a chance to view the content.

Print design requires high-resolution images — often in excess of 300 dpi (dots per inch). On the Web, images require only 72 dpi. A 4-inch photograph in a magazine can be as large as 15 megabytes, while the same size image on the Web requires only about 15k due to the differences in resolution/quality.

transferred data) can be downloaded from the Web. If the browser detects that an image on a page has been previously downloaded, it will load that image from the user's cache.

When you develop the design concept for your Web site, it's a good idea to use the same image elements as often as possible across your pages. For example, a company logo placed on multiple pages is downloaded and stored in a visitor's cache after he or she visits the first page; this speeds up your viewer's browsing of other pages on the site. Reusing graphics in this manner allows you to add new graphics to other pages on the site while still minimizing user download time.

Web-Savvy File Formats

Let's spend a minute discussing the primary file formats in use today for Web graphics.

JPEG

The JPEG (Joint Photographic Experts Group) file format can store up to 16 million colors, making it an excellent choice for photographs. It is not well suited for text or graphics, since its block-by-block compression algorithm introduces a blurring effect to the images. Within each block, differences in brightness are retained, but subtle color changes are lost. Despite this loss of color information, the image quality is acceptable, even at maximum compression.

Compression factors range from 10:1 to 100:1; this means that at the highest compression rate (100:1), a 1 MB image can be compressed into a 10 Kbyte JPEG file. This makes it ideal for use on the Web. Since JPEG compression is not lossless (you lose quality), always keep the original file intact so you can refer back to it at any time. JPEG files also lack transparency — a feature offered by both GIF and PNG formats.

GIF

GIF (Graphical Interchange Format) files use a compression algorithm based on pattern recognition: if several adjacent pixels have the same color, GIF can compress them better. This explains why GIF is used for images that are graphical in nature (rather than photographic). GIF is not as successful as JPEG at compressing photographs, but it compresses large areas of flat color extremely well.

GIF's compression factor with photographs is only 4:1; but it has the advantage of compressing losslessly. *Lossless* means that after decompression, the picture looks exactly the same as it did before compression, and that repeated saves (compressions) don't degrade the image as they do with the JPEG format. GIF images are limited in the number of colors they can incorporate; the maximum is 256 colors.

GIF has two more useful features: the format supports both transparency and animation. In order to produce transparency, one color is defined as the chroma key color during storage. The browser then disables this color and replaces it with the background image. With GIF animation, you can set the duration of each image and define whether the animation should run once or in a continual loop. GIF's transparency and animation features have greatly contributed to its popularity.

PNG

PNG (Portable Network Graphic format), developed in response to the restrictions of JPEG and GIF formats, was supposed to be the next step in image formatting for the Web. PNG combines the best of both worlds: lossless compression with up to 16 million colors, and 256 levels of transparency that allow for semi-transparent color areas. Semitransparency is particularly important when you want the edges of an image to blend smoothly with the browser background.

PNG also includes an excellent gamma correction function that guarantees images will be equally bright on all platforms. Since Windows monitors are inherently darker than Macintosh monitors, Web pages created on a Macintosh system look too dark when viewed on a Windows browser; conversely, pages designed on a Windows-based system look too pale on a Macintosh. PNG's gamma correction feature resolves this discrepancy, so PNG images display with the correct brightness on both platforms.

The PNG format is actually two formats in one. PNG-8 supports 8-bit color with lossless compression, much the same as the GIF format does. PNG-24 also uses lossless compression while supporting 24-bit color. The compression is lossless, so the files are larger than corresponding JPEG files.

Unfortunately, PNG is not supported by all browsers; older versions still require a plug-in to view PNG images, and might not take advantage of the 256 levels of transparency. Other limitations include the fact that PNG does not support animation, and some of the formats – particularly the higher-resolution versions – can be much larger than GIF or JPEG formats. Eight-bit PNG files are exactly the same size as an 8-bit GIF files.

Navigation

Some Web designers create fancy interfaces and expect visitors will be able to navigate them. Very often this is not the case, and visitors may have serious difficulties finding desired information. You can avoid this pitfall by using clear and consistent *global*, *parallel*, and *local navigation*:

- Global navigation allows the visitor to move between the main sections of the site. It should be present on every page.

- Parallel navigation applies to subcategories or subsections within each section that require a consistent navigational structure. It should be present on every page within a section.

- Local navigation works much the same as a table of contents. You use it to find information within a page. It may resemble a table of contents at the beginning of the page, or it might be a list of links in a sidebar.

With this basic information in mind, you can create a design in Photoshop that can later be recreated in an HTML authoring program.

Web Techniques

Over the years, Web designers have devised standard techniques to develop sites. One of these techniques is to dim an image and blend it with the background color. Combined with smaller images in the foreground, this creates an interesting dynamic and lends depth to the page.

In the following exercise, you're going to define colors using the Color Picker and a naming system called Hexadecimal notation. Hexadecimal notation is a series of 6 characters, ranging from AA to FF, and from 00 to 99. As an example, a yellow color might be named FFCC66. This notation is necessary for proper color interpretation by modern browsers. You can directly enter "hex" codes in a field on the Color Picker dialog box.

Photoshop can generate entire Web pages, but shouldn't be viewed as an Web-authoring package. Dedicated applications such as Adobe's GoLive or Macromedia's Dreamweaver offer critically important site management, form, table, and other tools that aren't contained in Photoshop. Nonetheless, using Photoshop is still one of the best ways to design your pages.

Simply double-click the foreground or background color swatch on the Toolbox (or create a new color swatch in the Swatches panel), and enter the appropriate code.

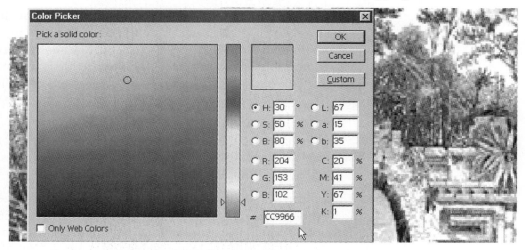

Create a Dimmed Image Background

1. Create a new (File>New) 72-ppi RGB document measuring 640 pixels high by 600 pixels wide. Fill it with a yellow foreground color (FFCC66) using the Paint Bucket tool.

2. Open the document **1082.jpg** from the **RF_Intro_Photoshop** folder, and use the Move tool to drag it into the new document.

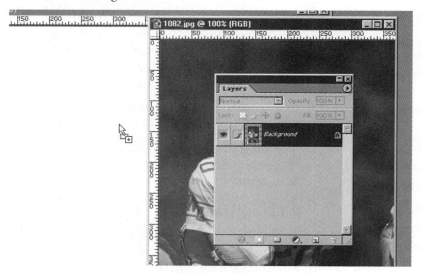

3. Use the Opacity slider in the Layers palette to dim your image to 30%.

4. Apply a Layer mask to the layer (Layer>Add Layer Mask>Reveal All). Use the Airbrush tool with a Black foreground color to paint on the Layer mask. All the dark areas of the Layer mask turn transparent: use a large brush size with soft edges from the Options palette. Make sure the Layer mask is activated when you paint into the image, otherwise you will paint over the image.

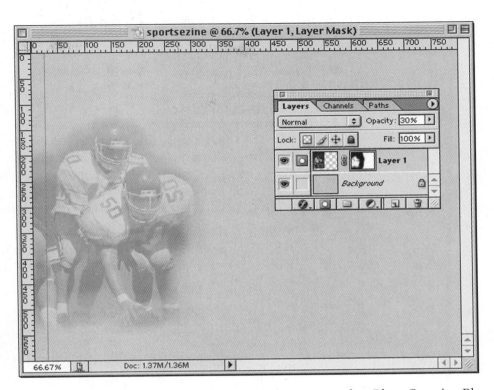

5. Add a blur effect to the image. From the Filter menu, select Blur>Gaussian Blur, which creates an interesting background texture. A small amount of blurring helps to improve the readability of any applied text elements. Experiment with different settings. Keep the Preview option checked to see the results before you apply the filter.

6. If you want to change the color of your image, select Adjustment>Hue/Saturation from the Image menu, and check the Colorize option in the dialog box. Once activated, you can use the sliders to change the hue, saturation, and lightness of the color.

To apply a Blending mode to a layer, double-click its name in the Layers palette and select the mode from the pop-up menu.

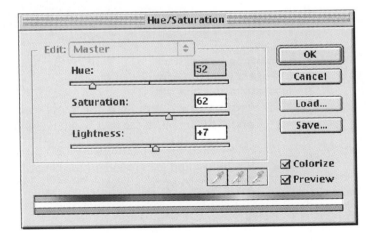

7. If you want to experiment with different effects, try applying a layer Blending mode — Multiply, Soft Light, Hard Light, and Luminosity work very well.

8. Keep the file open for the next exercise.

Create Solid-Colored Areas

1. With the **1082.jpg** document still open, draw a horizontal rectangle across the top of the document and fill it with a brown color (996633). Below this rectangle, draw a smaller rectangle and fill it with grey (666666). If you want to change the color of the shape layer, either double-click on the shape layer icon to access the Color Picker, or click on the color field in the Options palette.

2. To adjust the size of a rectangle, select Free Transform from the Edit menu (or press Command/Control-T). Use the control handles to resize the rectangle, and double-click (or press Return/Enter) when you're done.

3. Leave the file open for the next exercise.

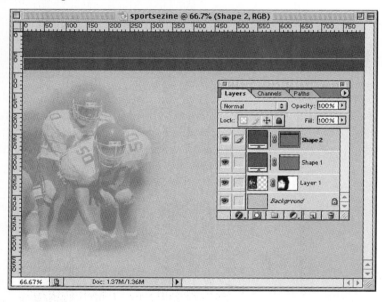

Create a Fill Pattern

1. Create a new 72-ppi RGB document with a Width of 1 pixel and a Height of 3 pixels. Enlarge it to the maximum possible size using the Zoom tool.

2. Select the Pencil tool and paint the 3 pixels in the image brown (996633), yellow (CC9933), and grey (666666) as shown. Save the file as "pattern.psd" into your **Work_In_Progress** folder

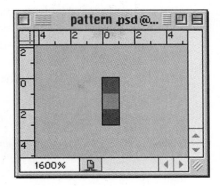

3. Define this document as a pattern by selecting Define Pattern from the Edit menu.

4. Return to the open document from the previous exercise (the Web design document). Create a new layer. Draw a rectangle in the upper-left corner and fill it with the new pattern you created in Steps 1 and 2.

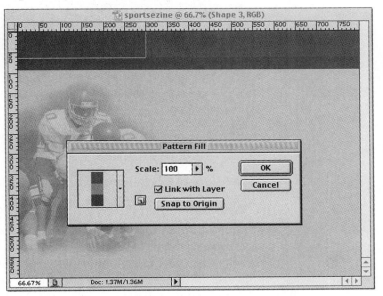

5. Save the file into your **Work_In_Progress** folder as "web page.psd".

6. You can modify this design as much as you want – add text, logos, and other elements as you prefer. We've provided a slightly more developed version of the document. You can see it by opening the **sportsezine.psd** file from your **RF_Intro_Photoshop** folder. To see the type, use the visibility icon to turn on the Contents folder on the Layers palette.

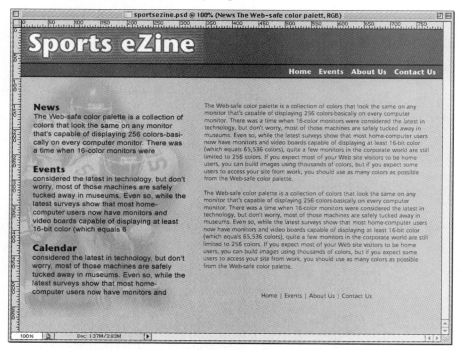

7. When you're done, save and close both files.

The Web-Safe Color Palette

The Web-safe color palette is a collection of colors that look the same on any monitor that's capable of displaying 256 colors - which is basically every computer monitor. There was a time when 16-color monitors were considered the latest in technology, but this is not the case any longer. While the latest surveys show that most home computer users now have monitors and video boards capable of displaying at least 16-bit color (which equals 65,536 different colors), quite a few monitors in the corporate world are still limited to displaying 256 colors. If you expect most of your Web site visitors to be home users, you can build images using thousands of colors; but if you expect some users to access your site from their offices, you should restrict your use of color to the Web-safe color palette whenever possible.

The Web-safe color palette actually consists of only 216 colors; the remaining 40 are reserved for the operating system (Windows). Those 216 colors are evenly divided and assigned to different shades and intensities of red, green, and blue (for the RGB color mode used for computer graphics). In addition, the palette uses a linear system in which every color value is increased or decreased by 20%; this was done largely for convenience, since the resulting hexadecimal values (00, 33, 66, 99, CC, and FF) are easy for programmers to remember. If you want to create an element in GoLive using a Web-safe color, use these hexadecimal values (in any combination) to ensure you get a Web-safe color that won't dither on 256-color monitors (you'll learn more about dithering later in the chapter).

The linear division of the color space means that the Web-safe color palette doesn't provide you with many choices if you want to create, for example, shades of brown or skin tones. The palette would have been much more useful if it had been modeled after the color perception of the human eye, but unfortunately that wasn't considered a top priority at the time the palette was devised.

Working with Web Colors

When designing a Web site, it's important to restrict your color choices to Web-safe colors whenever possible; this helps you avoid many color display problems. This is very easy to do when you're designing and colorizing elements — all you need to do is use the Only Web Colors option in Photoshop's Color Picker. If you happen to forget to turn this option on, you can always convert to Web-safe colors when you optimize and export GIF images in the Save for Web dialog box.

Let's explore one method to use non-Web-safe color and ensure that its appearance is acceptable on 256-color monitors.

Change to a Web-Safe Color Before Exporting

1. Open **solidcolor.psd** from the **RF_Intro_Photoshop** folder. Set the foreground color swatch on the Toolbar to CC6666. Make sure that the Only Web Colors option is checked in the Color Picker.

2. Select the Background layer. Choose the Paint Bucket tool from the Toolbox. On the Options toolbar, check Anti-aliased, Contiguous, and All Layers.

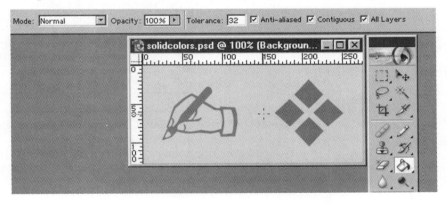

3. The hand fills as expected. Undo this operation by pressing Command/Control-Z.

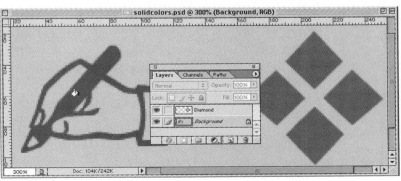

4. Now select the second layer with the diamond-shaped object, and then select Contiguous from the Options toolbar. Click with the Paint Bucket tool on one of the diamond squares. As you see, only this portion of the element fills. You also notice that the anti-aliased edges vanish, even though the Anti-aliased option is selected.

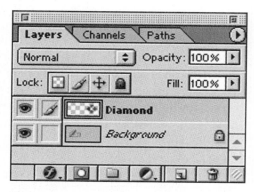

5. Go back through these steps by repeatedly pressing Shift-Command/Control-Z. Click on the Lock Transparent Pixels button in the Layers palette to preserve the anti-aliasing. Deselect Contiguous on the Options toolbar. Now when you click the diamond shape with the Paint Bucket tool, it will fill correctly.

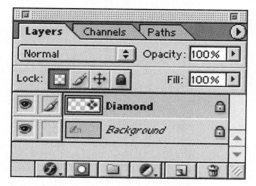

6. Undo the previous step (Command/Control-Z) and select the All Layers option. Deactivate the Lock Transparent Pixels button in the Layers palette. Now when you

click with the Paint Bucket tool on the diamond shape, the hand shape also fills (on the same layer as the diamond shape).

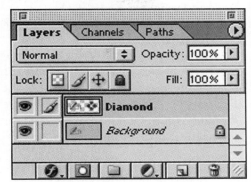

7. Save and close the file when you're done.

It's not always necessary to make a color Web-safe before you optimize it as a GIF in the Save for Web dialog box. Since GIFs work with a Color Table, all the colors in the image are listed and you can easily convert them to Web-safe colors. (You'll learn more about Color Tables later in this chapter.)

Optimization

After creating a design in Photoshop, it is necessary to export the images in order to use them in the HTML-authoring tool. It is possible to save a JPEG, GIF, or PNG using the Save or Save As command, but it is not recommended to do so. When you use these commands, there are fewer options for optimizing a file. Using the Save for Web command is a better choice.

The Save for Web Command

This command is found in the File menu. It offers many tools to optimize your image, all of which are located in one dialog box. At the upper-left corner are tabs that allow you to switch between the original view of the file and an optimized view. The 2-Up view provides you with the original and optimized view at the same time; the 4-Up view allows you to compare 3 different optimized versions at one time.

The Image Size tab on the right side of the dialog box enables you to downsize the image without having to alter the original file. A click on the Image Size tab reveals the same commands that are in the Image>Image Size dialog box.

The tools in the upper-left corner are:

- The Hand tool to move the views in case they are not fully displayed.
- The Slice Select tool to activate any slices that were created before.
- The Zoom tool to zoom in and out of the image.
- The Eyedropper tool to select a color in the image, which is then automatically used in the eyedropper color field. This field can also be set manually be clicking on it.
- The last element in this list of tools is the View Slices selection, which alternatively hides or displays the slices.

In the Optimized File Format pop-up menu, you can select between GIF, JPEG, PNG-8, PNG-24, and WBMP. *WBMP* is an image format used for wireless devices, such as hand-helds and cell phones.

Optimizing GIFs

The basis of GIF optimization is the Color Table. This table includes up to 256 colors of the image, and each color in the table contains 24-bit color information. The pixels in the image store a reference to the color in the table, which only requires 8-bit information. This already saves up to two-thirds of the image; but in order to decide which colors should be included in the table, you have to select one color reduction algorithm. The color reduction algorithms include:

- **Perceptual and Selective.** Adobe suggests Selective as the best choice for Web design and uses it as the default setting. The Selective Color Table is similar to the Perceptual Color Table, but it favors broad areas of color and the preservation of Web colors. Perceptual gives priority to colors to which the human eye has greater sensitivity. You can clearly see the effect if you set the Web Snap slider to 25% and then switch between the Selective, Perceptual, and Adaptive palettes. The Selective reduction algorithm usually generates more Web-safe colors than Adaptive or Perceptual.

- **Adaptive.** This palette adapts to the colors in the image, meaning that it picks the most frequently occurring colors for the Color Table.

- **Web.** The advantage of the Web palette is that all 216 colors display almost identically on all platforms. This Color Table is not used very often because you must save your image in the worst possible color mode to be sure the results will be acceptable on 256-color displays.

Pick a Color Reduction Algorithm

1. Open the file **colorspectrum.psd** from the **RF_Intro_Photoshop** folder. From the File menu, select Save for Web.

2. From the ensuing dialog box, choose the 4-Up view. Select Perceptual as the Color Reduction Algorithm in the second view, and reduce the Colors to 16. Set Dithering to None, 0% Lossy, and 0% Web Snap.

3. Choose Selective as the Color Reduction Algorithm in the third view, and reduce the Colors to 16. Set Dithering to None, 0% Lossy, and 0% Web Snap.

4. Select Adaptive as the Color Reduction Algorithm in the fourth view, and reduce the Colors to 16. Set Dithering to None, 0% Lossy, and 0% Web Snap.

5. When you compare the three views, you can see how the different color reduction algorithms produce different results, with all other variables remaining the same. Keep the file open for the next exercise.

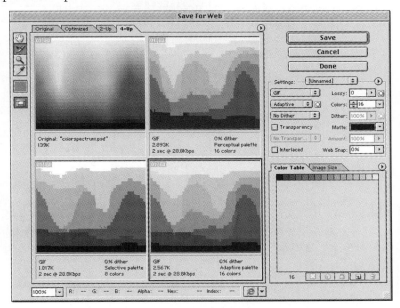

At the bottom of the Color Table are buttons that allow you to make changes to colors in the table. The first button (Transparency) makes any selected color transparent. The second button (Web Palette) shifts any color to the closest Web-safe color. The third button (Locking) locks a color and prevents any changes. The fourth and fifth buttons are there to add and delete colors, respectively.

The Color palette menu in the upper-right corner of the Color Table is useful for sorting the colors according to different criterion, such as hues or popularity.

The Web Snap slider is helpful if you're using a non-Web-safe color reduction algorithm and you have too many color shifts in your image when viewed in a browser. Use the Web Snap option to increase the number of Web-safe colors in your image, making the colors more predictable when viewed on various monitors.

Use the Web Snap Slider

1. With the 4-Up view still open from the previous exercise, click in the second view (with the Perceptual algorithm) and set the Web Snap slider to 50%.

2. Click in the third view (Selective algorithm) and set the Web Snap slider to 50%. Do the same for the fourth view (Adaptive algorithm).

3. Compare the three views and note the colors that shifted. They are marked with a little diamond in the color fields. Keep the file open for the next exercise.

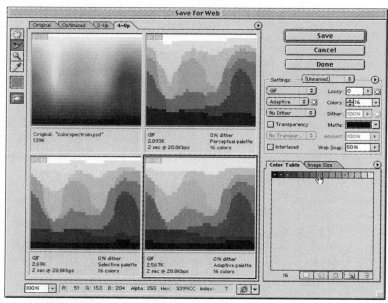

Lossy

The Lossy option works miracles with many GIF files. It uses the patterns identified by the LZW algorithm and stores them in a compression table. You can then use the Lossy slider to specify how much you want to reuse those patterns in the image, further improving compression.

Dithering

Dithering improves the visual quality of an image by simulating a color by using two colors from the Color Table. In general, dithering makes GIF files compress less efficiently, resulting in larger files. At the same time, it allows you to reduce the number of colors used in the image, which usually saves more space than is gained through the dithering process.

Photoshop and ImageReady allow you to choose from three dithering options: Diffusion, Pattern, and Noise. Pattern dithering mixes the two colors in a regular pattern that is easy for the eye to detect; because of this, Pattern dithering is not recommended. Diffusion and Noise dithering, which use similar algorithms, achieve much better visual results. Noise dithering does a better job, but Diffusion dithering has the advantage of allowing you to set the amount of dithering via a slider.

Set the Dithering

1. With the Save for Web dialog box still open from the previous exercise, go to the second view and set the Dithering to Pattern

2. In the third view, set the Dithering to Noise; and in the fourth view, set the Dithering to Diffusion. Compare the file sizes. As you can see, the Noise dithering produces the largest file; the best result comes from the Diffusion dithering. Keep the file open for the next exercise.

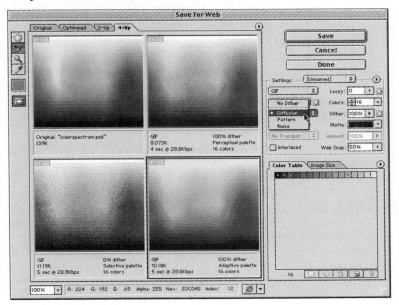

Transparency and Matte

Photoshop's Save for Web dialog box and ImageReady's Optimize palette both offer a Transparency option. This option allows you to make parts of your image transparent; the background color of your Web page shows through and allows the GIF image to blend with the browser background. There is only one problem with this option: if the edges of your object are anti-aliased (and they are in most cases), you might end up with a "halo" effect. This is where the *Matte option* comes into play. The Matte option allows you to select a color - usually the background color of your Web page - and Photoshop uses this color to blend the anti-aliased pixels in your image, creating a much more acceptable appearance for your edges.

Use Transparency with Single-Color Backgrounds

1. Create a new RGB document, 90 pixels wide by 30 pixels high at 72ppi. Choose White for the background color. Select the Type tool and enter the word "Headline" in 12-pt. ATCPineHeavy. Center the text object on the page. Hide the Background layer by toggling off the visibility in the Layers palette by clicking the eyeball icon.

2. From the File menu, choose Save for Web. Check the Transparency box, and select a Matte color that matches the color of your HTML page background. Even though you see a halo in the Optimized preview, it blends seamlessly with the background in a browser window with no halo effect.

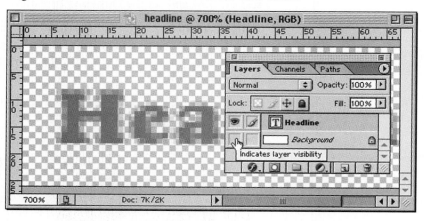

When images are put on white backgrounds, they often look fine — but when they're floated on top of colored backgrounds, an unsightly "halo" can appear around the edges. Make sure your images blend seamlessly into the page background.

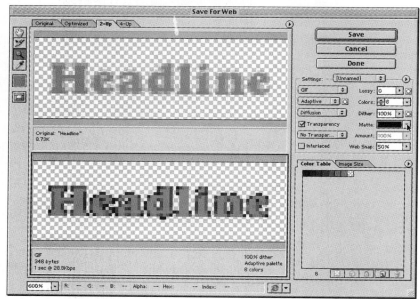

3. Close the file when you're done.

Use Transparency with Multi-Color Backgrounds

1. Open the file **headline.psd** from the **RF_Intro_Photoshop** folder. This file is similar to the one you created in the previous exercise. Make sure all the layers are visible, and then select Save for Web from the File menu. You may receive a message indicating that Photoshop needs to update the text layer. Click OK to proceed.

2. Choose GIF as Image Format, set the number of Colors to 16, and check the Transparency option. Then use the Eyedropper tool to select a color from the background of the image. Click the Transparency button at the lower left of the Color Table. This setting maps selected colors to transparent.

3. If you need to select several colors, press and hold the Shift key while using the Eyedropper tool before selecting the Transparency button.

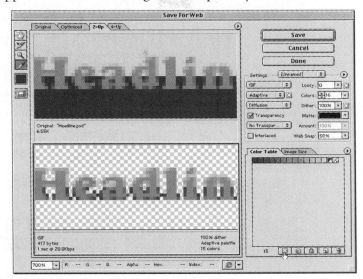

4. Close the file without saving your changes.

Interlaced

The Interlaced option is important when you have many images on your Web site. Browsers can display a low-resolution "preview" of the image while downloading the remaining data. (Some browsers, such as Internet Explorer, actually display interlaced GIFs line by line.) Gradually, the resolution gets sharper and clearer until the image is completely downloaded.

Using Alpha Channels to Optimize Files

With Photoshop, you can control the application of the color reduction algorithm, Diffusion dithering, and the Lossy option by making selections that are saved as alpha channels. It is important to understand how you should create your selections in order to generate the best results.

If you want to create an alpha channel for the color reduction algorithm, use the Lasso tool to select areas in the image that are most significant in terms of color, but might not necessarily be the dominant colors in the picture. Take, for example, the red lips of a face. While they're only a small part of a photo, they might be crucial to a natural-looking face. While pressing the Shift key, you would select all of these areas with the Lasso tool, and then save them as a channel (Select>Save Selection).

To control the dithering in your image, you would select all the areas that should get the maximum amount of dithering. Later, when using a channel to modify the dithering, the selected pixels would represent the areas for the Maximum slider, while the unselected pixels would represent the areas for the Minimum slider.

The exact opposite is true for the Lossy command. The selected pixels would represent the part of the image that gets the least amount of lossy compression, while the unselected pixels would represent the part of the image that gets the most. When creating a selection for the Lossy command, you would select the most important parts of the image, and then save the selection (or select the areas where you want to apply Lossy, and then inverse the selection before saving).

Optimize a GIF

1. Open **bannerad.psd** from the **RF_Intro_Photoshop** folder, and then select the Save for Web command from the File menu. Choose 4-Up. Use the second view to select the number of colors you think your image requires (a GIF should use 32 colors or less). For this example, start with 16 colors.

2. Pick one of the color reduction algorithms for each of the three Optimization views (Perceptive, Selective, and Adaptive).

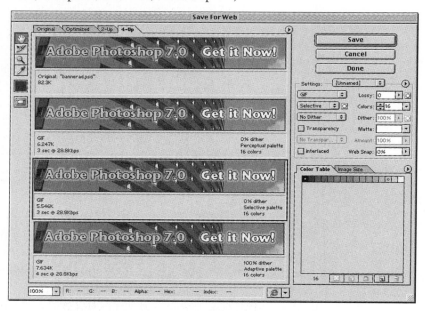

3. Gradually reduce the number of colors for each view, using the arrows in the Colors box. At some point, you will notice a sudden drop in quality. For the first view (Perceptual), this happens when the colors drop below 8; for the second view (Selective) the quality degrades below 9 colors; and for the third view (Adaptive), the quality limit is 10 colors.

4. Now select a dithering method. Take note of the file size before switching to Diffusion dithering so you can compare the results after you switch. Increase the amount of dithering until you arrive at the best result; then start reducing the number of colors. If the quality of the image is not better (and the file size at least the same as before) then undo everything (Command/Control-Z). In this example, only the last view (Adaptive) benefits from dithering (50% Diffusion dither and 8 colors produce the best image quality and file size).

5. Use the Lossy option if the current quality of the image is still acceptable and you need to reduce the file size. Note that the Lossy option is only accessible if Interlaced is deactivated. All the views improve in file size with a value of 30% Lossy while still retaining good visual quality.

6. Every image is different, but in this particular case, the best result is with the second view: Perceptual algorithm, 8 Colors, 30% Lossy, and 0% Dithering.

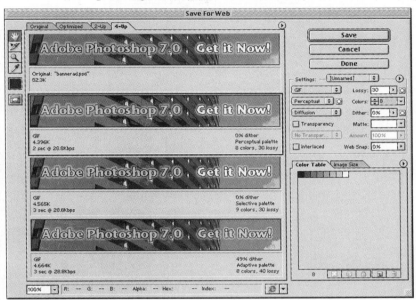

7. Close the file without saving.

Optimizing JPEGs

If the image is a photograph, you should choose JPEG from the Image Format pop-up menu in the Save for Web dialog box. There are considerably fewer settings for JPEGs — the Quality slider is virtually the only setting to make. Usually, the best results are achieved with quality settings between 20-30. Values below 20 cause the image to deteriorate dramatically, and there are other (better) ways to improve the file size.

One of the best-known tricks for reducing the file size of a compressed JPEG image is to apply a Gaussian blur before saving it. There is also a blurring value in the Save for Web dialog box that applies a Gaussian blur to the image. There are alternatives to applying a Gaussian blur to maximize JPEG compression: you can use a Smart blur filter, or a Despeckle noise filter as well (filters must be applied before using the Save for Web command).

Save for Web also allows you to optimize the Quality slider through an alpha channel. Unfortunately, this procedure never produces smaller file sizes. In most cases you gain almost as much as you save, so this is not a highly-recommended feature.

Optimize with an Alpha Channel

1. Open the file **theteam.psd** from the **RF_Intro_Photoshop** folder. Use the Lasso tool to create a selection around the players. JPEG uses 8 × 8-pixel blocks in its compression algorithm, which means that you should not make a tight selection; otherwise, the edges of the two different quality settings will appear more obvious.

2. Save the selection using the Select>Save Selection command, and name the new alpha channel "players".

3. Open the Save for Web dialog box and select the 4-Up view. In the second view, set the Quality slider to 0. In the third view, set the Quality slider to 30. For the fourth view, click the Channel button next to the Quality text field.

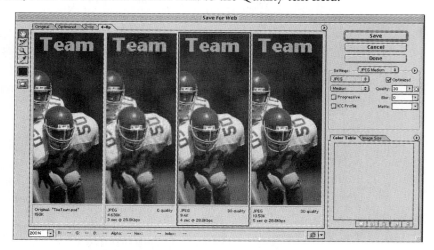

4. In the Modify Quality Setting dialog box, choose the players alpha channel that you saved in Step 2, and select the Use All Text Layers option. The white areas in the thumbnail represent the Maximum slider (marked in white) and the black areas represent the Minimum slider. Set the Maximum value to 30 and the Minimum to 0.

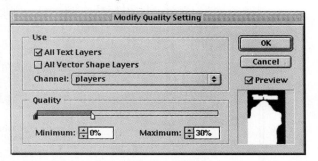

5. Compare all three views. As you can see, the fourth view using the alpha channel for optimization produces the largest file size. The reason for this is that the Discrete Cosine Transformation (used by JPEG) requires some additional information that needs to be stored for each optimization setting. It never makes sense to use the alpha channel feature with JPEGs. Our recommendation is to use the Quality slider with a setting between 10-30.

Slicing

Slicing allows you to cut a design in pieces and export each piece individually. There are other uses for slicing:

- Slices can be exported with a matching HTML table that reassembles the image in the Web browser. This is also sometimes referred to as an Image table, because you have a table that is filled with images rather than text. This is an alternative to an Image map since each slice can be assigned a link to a specified URL (Uniform Resource Locator).

- Slices (particularly when used as an Image table) allow you to apply different format and compression options to different parts of the image, preserving full-color, high-quality JPEG detail in one part, while saving another slice as a GIF.

- If part of your image is animated, slicing it can reduce the file size.

- Slicing allows you to create rollover buttons.

Slice an Image

1. Open **sportezine.psd** from the **RF_Intro_Photoshop** folder. Let's isolate the elements in separate slices.

2. If it's visible, hide the Contents folder on the Layers palette. Choose the Slice tool (press the "K" key) and drag diagonally across the logo in the upper-left corner.

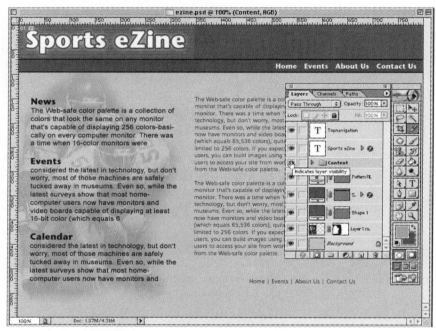

3. Precision is very important, so zoom into the lower-right corner of the slice and make sure the slice exactly matches the corner of the logo. If the rectangle does not closely frame the logo, use the Slice Select tool (press the "A" key) to resize the slice.

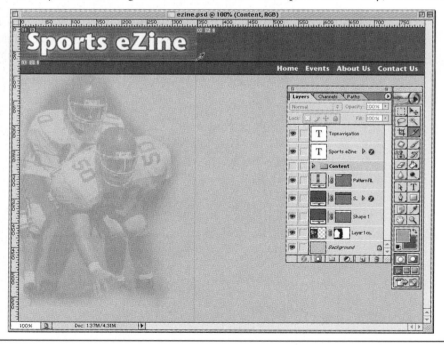

4. Create another slice that is 10 pixels wide that captures the grey horizontal bar with the black edges. Next, make individual slices for each of the navigation buttons on the right side of the grey bar. This can be a difficult process; you can move the slices around so you more easily select them, and then put them back in place after the slices have been created.

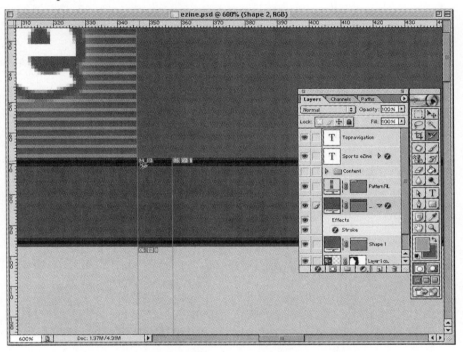

5. Choose the Slice Select tool from the dialog box. Double-click on the logo slice. In the Slice Options dialog box, name the slice "logo" and then close the slice. Name the slice for the horizontal grey navigation bar "navbar", and name the button slices "bttn_home", "bttn_events", "bttn_about", and "bttn_contact".

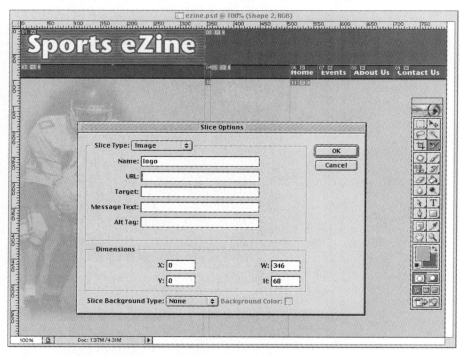

6. Save the file, and leave it open for the next exercise.

Assign Optimum Formats to Slices

1. With the document **sportsezine.psd** still open, select Save for Web from the File menu. In the dialog box that appears, select the Slice Select tool in the upper-left corner and click on the slice for the logo.

2. For this slice, select GIF format, Adaptive Color Reduction, 8 Colors, 30% Dithering, 0% Lossy.

3. Click on the slice for the grey navigation bar and all of the navigation button slices. Apply GIF format, Adaptive Color Reduction, 8 Colors, 0% Dithering, and 0% Lossy. The settings you pick are simultaneously applied to all of the slices.

4. Select the logo slice and click Save. In the dialog box that appears, select Images Only from the Format pop-up menu, and Selected Slices from the Slices pop-up menu. Save the image. Repeat this process for the grey navigation bar background.

5. Select all of the navigation button slices and click Save. This time, choose Images and HTML from the Format pop-up menu, and choose Selected Slices from the Slices pop-up menu. Photoshop saves the buttons in an Image table that can then later be used by an HTML programmer.

As you can see, by combining various compression methods for different file formats, and by using techniques such as slicing and the Save for Web features, you can reduce the weight of your images to a manageable level without a great deal of work.

Chapter Summary

In this chapter, you learned how to use Photoshop to create graphics that are suitable for use on the Web. Even though Photoshop isn't strictly a Web-authoring package – and doesn't offer many functions that are critical to complete site development – it can be used very effectively for the design of your overall site, as well as for creating the images, backgrounds, textures, navigation elements, and other objects.

You learned about bandwidth considerations and Web-compatible file formats. From there, you proceeded to work with Web-safe color palettes and custom colors, and learned how to optimize different types of images to ensure they download quickly.

Lastly, you worked with slicing – a technique that allows you to compress different portions of an image using more than one compression method.

Free-Form Project #2

Assignment

You work at a design firm that enjoys success in the niche market of book jackets. Your client, a major publishing house, is about to launch an outdoor life series featuring fishing, hiking, camping, and other activities.

Your assignment is to design a format that will work for the entire series with consistent title treatments, color schemes (which may differ from book to book), and treatment of photographs.

To create three high-quality concept proofs to show the client, you can pick two or three outdoor activities. Make up the titles for each of the three covers. If you want, you may obtain an appropriate photograph from the Web; but if you do so, be sure to credit the source. Alternately, you can use any of the photos supplied. Be sure to adjust the resolution appropriately.

Applying Your Skills

To design the book jackets, use the following functions, methods, and features:

- Create three new documents in Photoshop, meeting the size specifications. Be sure to allow for the back cover, the spine, and the front cover. Using the ruler and guides will help with this.
- Select images from the **project_assignments** folder found in the **RF_Intro_Photoshop** folder, or obtain others you like from the Web (making sure to credit your sources appropriately). Crop and size these images to fit on your front and back covers.
- Use a pattern, texture, or other filter-generated background, or a flat color to fill the space beyond the photos. The choice is yours.
- Set type for the front cover — the book title and author; the spine — book title, author, publisher; and the back cover — a sentence about the author or the series. You might fill the large cover type with color, texture, or a gradient; or you might consider using a drop shadow.
- Consider using masks to highlight or reveal only specific portions of the image. You should also consider using shapes – either predefined or custom – to enhance the project and provide high-resolution output.
- Prepare the file for printing on an RGB-savvy printer to show your client.
- Prepare a copy of the file for traditional lithographic printing to show your service provider.

Specifications

- Execute the designs as three comprehensive layouts, each approximately 15.5 in. × 9 in.
- The front and back cover size is 7.5 in. × 9 in. each. The book spine varies from ⅜″ to ⅝″.
- Laid flat, this printed piece (starting at the left) should be the back cover, the spine, and the front cover.
- The design should bleed on all four sides, allowing ⅛″ for the printer to use as trim. Use CMYK as the color mode, and check the color separations when you're done.
- The back cover may or may not have complicated design features. If a patterned background is used for the front cover, it should display on the back cover as well.

Included Files

There are a number of related images (skiing, cycling, boating, fishing, camping) contained within the **project_assignments** folder, which is inside the **RF_Intro_Photoshop** folder.

Publisher's Comments

For this assignment, it's important that you spend some time at the bookstore to see how the professionals approach book jacket design. Although it's said that you can't judge a book by its cover, many people do, in fact, make purchase decisions based upon cover appeal.

Don't let your design get cluttered — you only have so much space to work with. Look at book jackets created by the professionals to get ideas for your assignment.

Remember: spines are as important as covers. In most stores, shelf space dictates that books be displayed where only the spines are visible.

Most back covers include extracts of the text, or comments about the author and content. While the final version of this design would probably be prepared in a page-layout application, which would be more appropriate for setting detailed text like this, you can produce a concept proof in Photoshop to give your client an idea of what you plan to create with their actual photos and text. (It is also likely that you would prepare the final images in Photoshop for use in that page-layout application file.)

Review #2

Chapters 7 through 12

In Chapters 7–12, you learned how to convey your messages through strategic use of text elements that are combined with graphic images. You found that using Blending modes in conjunction with layers and transparency effects can lead to very powerful designs. You were introduced to the Pen tool, and learned how to use it to create borders and stencils, and to modify existing paths that were created with the tool. You discovered how Photoshop's powerful filters can add seemingly endless special effects to your artwork. You worked with various printing and publishing techniques, preparing you to correctly output your work to print or the Web. Information was presented on using Photoshop as a Web design tool, how you can effectively design Web objects and pages in the program, and then export to a dedicated Web-authoring tool for final production. Through this series of discussions, exercises, and projects, you should:

- Understand how to work with text elements so your messages are clearly seen and understood.

- Be familiar with the Blending modes, and know how to use them in conjunction with layers and transparency effects.

- Be comfortable using the pen tools to create and modify paths, and turn paths into selections.

- Know how to use filters to enhance your artwork without overusing them, which ends up detracting from the final design.

- Be capable of saving your print and Web projects for successful output, using the proper file format for each deliverable.

- Understand how to use Photoshop to create compelling Web objects and mock-up Web pages that can later be exported to a dedicated Web-authoring program for publishing on the Internet.

Project A: Gulls Poster

This project is typical of image editing and manipulation assignments. In this situation, you're part of a creative team which is developing a series of billboard images that will also be used in a print ad campaign for the Clearwater Tourist Board. The client wants to see five or six different ideas, and you're one of three art directors who have been asked to come up with some concepts.

In this project, you're going to take an existing photograph, and use various selection techniques and transformations — including cloning, scaling, and repositioning elements. You'll also be introduced to the concept of filters — something we'll cover in detail in Chapter 10.

Prepare the Image

1. Open the file named **gull.tif** from the **RF_Intro_Photoshop** folder.

2. Select the Magic Wand tool from the Toolbox (or press the "W" key). On the Options bar, set the Tolerance to 32, check Anti-aliased, check Contiguous, and leave Use All Layers unchecked.

3. Click once on the sky, a little above the gull. All the blue pixels that make up the sky are quickly selected. From the Select menu, choose Inverse, or press Shift-Command/Control-I to change the selection from the sky to the gull.

   As you can see, this photograph is tailor-made for the Magic Wand, as the entire sky is very close to the same blue color. The Magic Wand's Anti-aliased option helps to smooth the transition from the edge of the gull to the blue of the sky. A feather of 1-1.5 pixels would help to eliminate a slight blue edge surrounding the gull, but it would also eliminate the selection of a fine area of the bird's feathers. You are working against a blue background, so feathering is unnecessary.

4. Copy and then paste the gull back into the image. Doing so creates a new layer. Name this new layer "Gull 2". Press Command/Control-T (Free Transform) and make the second gull slightly smaller. Hold down the Shift key as you make the adjustment to maintain the same proportions.

Profile Mismatch Errors: When you're opening an image, you may get an error message that says that the embedded color profile contained in the image doesn't match the one you're currently using. If this happens, refer back to the Getting Started section to learn how to disable the warning. Color profiles will be discussed in Chapter 10.

5. Double-click the Background layer and rename it "Gull". This converts it to a normal Photoshop layer. (There are many commands that do not work on a Background layer because it is a locked layer; you must convert it before making modifictaions.)

6. From the Edit menu, select Transform>Flip Horizontal.

7. Select the Move tool, and activate the Gull 2 layer (click on it). Position the copied gull below and slightly to the left of the original gull.

It's a good idea to regularly save your documents to protect yourself against system failure or other unexpected occurrences.

8. Save the image as "gulls.psd" in your **Work_In_Progress** folder.

Add to the Composition

1. Select Image>Canvas Size and enter a value of 7 in. for the Width and 5 in. for the Height. Click OK, or press the Return/Enter key to accept the default position (the center box). Press Command/Control-0 (zero) to make the image fit the screen.

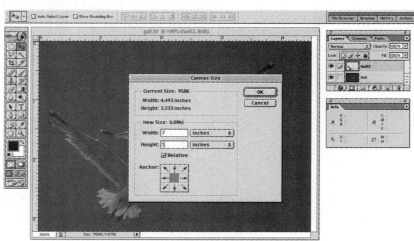

2. Click the New Layer icon to add a layer. Name it "Matte", and move it to the bottom of the stack.

3. Use the Eyedropper tool to sample some color from the blue sky. Fill the new layer (Edit>Fill>Foreground Color). On the Layers palette, the Blending Mode should be set to Normal and the Opacity set at 100%.

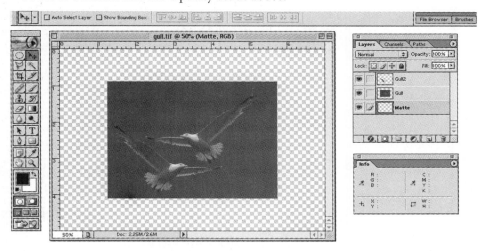

A complete chapter on working with filters appears later in this book. For now, just apply the filter as described in the instructions.

4. Apply a texture by selecting Texture>Texturizer>Sandstone (from the pop-up menu) from the Filter menu. Adjust the controls until you generate a texture you like, and then press Return/Enter or click OK. (We used a Scaling of 120%, Relief of 6, and Top Light Direction.)

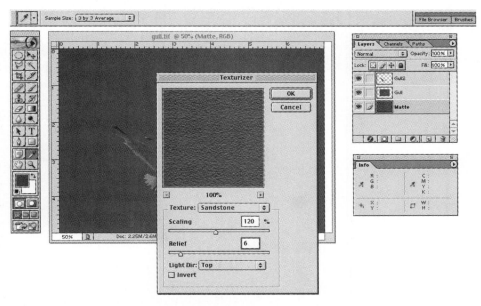

Command/Control-click on the layer to quickly select the gull.

Add Accent

Photoshop allows for quick and easy selection of pixels by holding down the Command/Control key and clicking on the layer that contains what you want to select. In this case, you need to select the second gull to make a drop shadow. We are going to create this shadow without using layer styles in order to allow for placement of the shadow between layers. To successfully create this effect, you also need to select the original image of the gull against the blue sky so you can add the white accent line around it.

1. Press the "D" key to reset the foreground and background colors to their defaults (black and white), and then press the "X" key to swap their positions.

2. Select the Gull 2 layer. Move the copied gull into its final position using the Move tool. Place it wherever you prefer, but allow the tip of the wing to extend beyond the smooth blue sky over the textured matte.

3. Add a new layer and position it below the Gull layer. The selection is still active. Fill it with Black (Edit>Fill>Black). Press Command/Control-D to deselect.

4. Be certain Lock Transparent Pixels is unchecked for the layer. From the Filter menu, select Blur>Gaussian Blur, and enter a value of 5, 6, or 7 to soften the edge of what will be the shadow. Use the Move tool or the Arrow keys to move the shadow down and slightly to the left. The shadow is positioned between the Matte layer and the Gull layer, so it appears that the gull is flying out of the frame.

5. Select the Gull layer, then Command/Control-click. Make a new layer for your accent line above the Gull layer. From the Edit menu, choose Stroke. Set the Width to 6 pixels, and choose Outside for the Location of your stroke. Press Return/Enter or click OK to apply the settings.

6. Deselect. Link all the layers except the Matte layer by clicking in the box to the left of the layer icon (a chain link appears), and then use the Move tool to position the image down and slightly to the right of center.

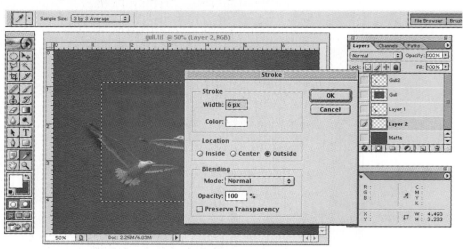

7. Save the document as **gull.psd** in your **Work_In_Progress** folder.

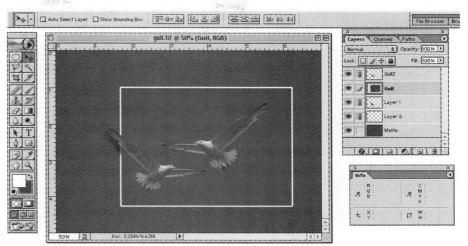

Prepare Files for RGB-Savvy Printing

1. For the purpose of the presentation, you will be preparing your file for output on your in-house RGB color printer. Flatten the file.

2. Select File>Save As>TIFF. Name the file "gulls.tif", and save it in your **Work_In_Progress** folder. Most desktop printers will print a .psd file, but it is a good idea to save both a .psd and a flat .tif (with no extra channels) to use as a printable file. Many professional lab printers return unpredictable results when they try to print files containing extra channels or .tif files containing layers.

3. Close the file.

The result of your effort is an image worthy of framing and proudly displaying in your home. It could be a testament to your growing skill with this powerful software. Perhaps you are already thinking of other images that you can enhance and prepare for display?

NOTES

Project B: Fallsbridge Menu Cover

Two friends have just purchased a lovely bed and breakfast inn near the White Mountains of New Hampshire. Since you're a designer, they've asked you to design the cover of the menu that captures the charm and ambience of the region. The finished piece should be nice enough to both inspire new visitors, as well as serving as a souvenir for people who have visited the inn.

You'll start the project with the quintessential image of a New England covered bridge photographed more than 25 years ago. Some work has already been done to the image, and you're going to finish the job. Doing so is going to require painting, adding foliage, repairing damaged portions, adding type, and compositing a line art image into the design.

Finish Our Painting

1. Open the image **bridge.psd** from the **RF_Intro_Photoshop** folder. The watercolor effect is believable and the overall appearance is acceptable, but it lacks excitement. Adding some fall foliage to the bare branches and some grass among the rocks on the banking will provide a brighter and cleaner look to the piece.

2. Select the Eyedropper tool (press the "I" key), sample two greens from within the image — one for the foreground color and one for the background color. Choose the Paintbrush tool from the Toolbox, and then open the Brushes palette from the Palette Well or the Window menu. Click Brush Presets and scroll down to the brush that resembles three blades of grass.

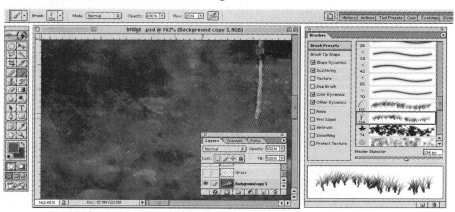

3. As you can see, this brush has been preset to help you create realistic-looking grass. If you wish, take some time to open each of the checked styles to see how they are set up. Create a new layer and name it "Grass". Change the size of your brush to between 25 and 40 pixels, and then paint over and around the rocks on the far banking. Experiment with the effect until you are satisfied with the results. Change brush sizes as needed for a natural look. You may want to zoom in to get a better view of what is happening — we find working at 100% works well. Save the file to your **Work_In_Progress** folder. Be sure to assign a unique name to the file. We used "inn_at_the_bridge.psd".

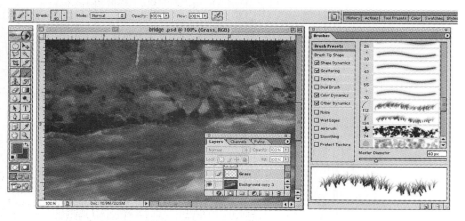

4. Toggle the visibility eyeball on and off to see the effect you are creating. It is not necessary that your version of the image exactly match the example. The essence of the painting process is to fulfill your own personal vision of the subject matter.

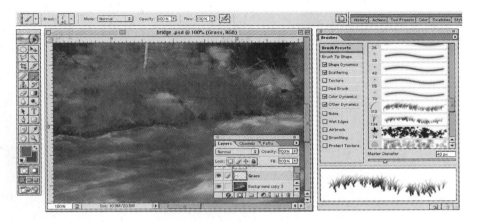

5. Create another layer. Use the same two green colors for the foreground and background colors. From the Brushes palette, select the brush that resembles a maple leaf.

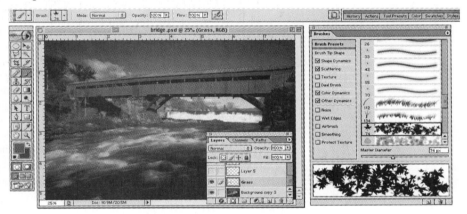

6. Paint some leaves on the branches of the tree in the lower-right corner of the image. Experiment with Opacity settings and brush sizes; alter the checked Brush Presets if you feel adventurous (although the presets work very well here). When you have created a believable bush, turn off the visibility icon, save your layered image, and then create a new layer. The green leaves improve the appearance of the image, but an Autumn motif would be better for the intended use of the image.

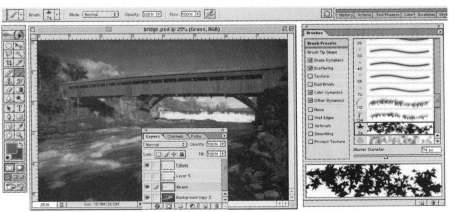

7. Choose some fall colors from the foliage below the bridge. Add a new layer, name it "Foliage", and continue painting. Move from place to place on the image, and add leaves of various sizes to areas that are bare. Experiment by switching foreground and background colors. Notice the different effects you can produce.

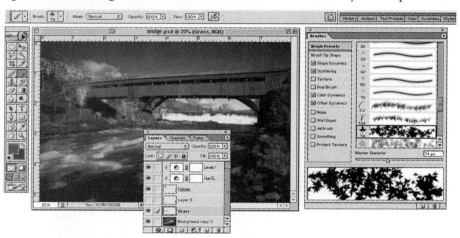

8. As an option for those with adventurous spirits, you can add levels, and hue and saturation adjustment layers; then you can link them to the foliage layer: hold down the Option/Alt key while clicking on the adjustment layer icon at the bottom of the layer stack, and then choose Link with Previous Layer.

9. Adjust the foliage until you are satisfied with the results. Although we have not discussed color and tone adjustment in this book, a little experimentation while you're working on this project will help prepare you for the section on color correction in the advanced Photoshop book. Proceed with caution and make small adjustments, raising the overall saturation just a bit, and using the middle Levels slider to brighten the foliage.

10. Use the visibility eyeball icons to switch back and forth from your new version to the original. Note how much better the image appears after making color and tonal adjustments. The added color enhances the overall image. An artist working with traditional media could have painted any version of this scene that he or she preferred. With Photoshop, we now have the same freedom.

11. When you are satisfied with your painting, save the layered file (note the size increase due to the new layers). Save another copy as a flat .tif using the Save As dialog box, accessed by pressing Shift-Command/Control-S.

Add Texture and Type

1. Open the file named **texture.psd** from the **RF_Intro_Photoshop** folder. This is a large file, so it might take a few seconds to open. (Most computers today have adequate power both in CPU speed and RAM; but if you are using an older machine, make sure you have plenty of free space on your hard drive and give your system adequate time to respond.) Open the flat .tif file of the bridge that you saved in the previous exercise.

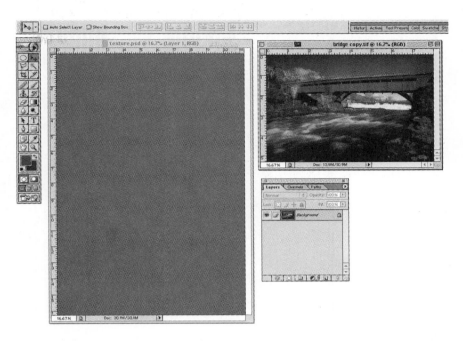

2. Select the Move tool (press the "V" key) and drag the **inn_at_the_bridge.psd** file into the **texture.psd** file. Hint: if you hold down the Shift key during this operation, the file comes in at the exact center of the image. Use the Up Arrow key to move the file to the top of the image as shown.

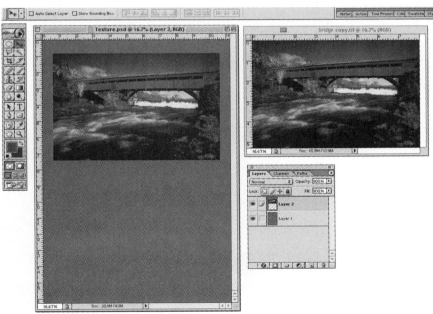

3. Close the file of the bridge to save RAM, and open the file called **pen_drawing_ of_bridge.psd**. Use the Move tool to drag the top layer into your

composite image. Position it as shown. Close the **pen_drawing_of_bridge.psd** file to save RAM.

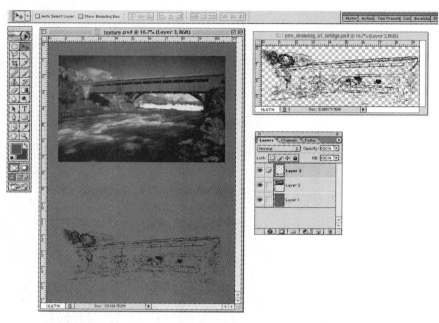

4. Select the Type tool from the Toolbox and choose the font called ATCJacaranda. Using the Eyedropper tool, sample a color from the side of the bridge. Set the font Size to about 175 pt. Enter the word "Fallsbridge" in the text box. Add layer styles for Drop Shadow and Bevel and Emboss to create a 3-D effect. Press Command/ Control-T to access Free Transform. Stretch the type up a little, and then compress it until it fits in the text box. Press Return/Enter to commit the type.

5. Enter the word "Tavern". Set the "T" slightly smaller than the rest of the word, and use Free Transform to adjust the size and shape until you are satisfied with the way it looks. Set the type for "Fine Dining Since 1902", leaving a space for the "T" in tavern (as shown). Use ATC Laurel Bold Italic at about 30 pt. Adjust using Free Transform. Drag the layer styles you used on Fallsbridge to the other type layers to set the same style for each of them.

6. Save your file as a .psd using any name you wish.

Finishing Touches

1. All that's left to do is create the beveled cut-out effect on the menu cover. Move the layer containing the painting (Layer 2) below the texture layer (Layer 1). Command/Control-click Layer 2. Select the texture layer, invert the selection, and add a Layer mask.

2. Add a new layer between the bridge and texture layers and fill it with White. Command/Control-click Layer 2 to create a selection marquee. From the Select menu, choose Modify>Contract, and set a value of 6 pixels. Be sure you are on the layer filled with white. Invert the selection and add a Layer mask by clicking the mask icon at the bottom of the layer stack. Don't worry if you forget to invert the selection, as you can invert the mask by pressing Command/Control-I.

3. Add a layer style for Bevel and Emboss with the settings shown below. Add another layer style to create a soft Drop Shadow; set the Distance and Size controls to suggest a feeling of depth. The file must be viewed at 100% to clearly see the effect. This is a subtle effect that works very well in print, creating the illusion of a beveled, hand-cut matte.

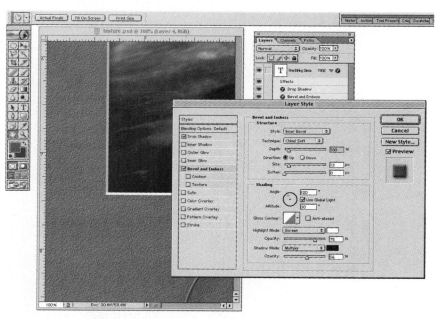

4. You have created a finished menu cover. With today's RGB-savvy printers, many small establishments are printing their own menus and covers. An Epson 1280 prints on 13 × 19-inch stock; since the total number of menus printed during each print run is usually quite small, this type of printer might be the perfect solution for the average restaurant. Larger runs can be printed as the need arises. Of course, the file could also be converted to CMYK for press output. Whenever you convert to CMYK, keep a close watch on the drop shadows, as they tend to darken during the conversion process.

5. Reproduction at this size doesn't do justice to the beveled edge effect. Printed full-size or viewed on a monitor at 100%, the edges look exactly like hand-cut mattes from a high-quality frame store.

6. Save two versions of the file — one as a .psd to allow for later edits, and one as a flat .tif for printing.

Congratulations! You completed a very attractive menu cover that any restaurant owner would be proud to present to customers. You began with a photo, applied some basic photo retouching techniques, and created an image that has a definite watercolor appeal. You learned that you can repurpose images such as this, and that you can print these images on in-house copiers to reduce reproduction costs and allow designers to create and reproduce graphics directly from their desktops.

NOTES

Project C: Jazz Postcard

This project is being done for a dinner/concert cruise that embarks from your town. The client is an upscale establishment, and draws customers both from local, repeat diners as well as from tourist-oriented local publications, often distributed at airport counters and rental car facilities.

The project will require extensive compositing, the addition of several different type layers, and the use of custom foreground and background colors. Retouching will also be part of the project, as you combine several photographic and line art elements into what will appear to be a hand-painted image. You will prepare the image for several different applications.

Create the Background

1. Create a new RGB document, 4.25-in. wide by 5.75-in. high at 100-ppi Resolution with White contents (background).

2. Click the foreground color swatch to bring up the Color Picker. Locate the area near the bottom of the swatch that lists R, G, and B (for the Red, Green, and Blue color spaces). Set Red at 50, Green at 65, and Blue at 135. Click OK.

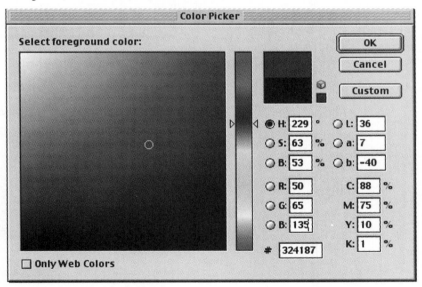

3. Press Option/Alt-Backspace/Delete to fill the Background layer with the blue color you just created.

4. Click the New Layer icon at the bottom of the Layers palette to add a new layer. Select Layer Properties from the layer Options menu, and name the new layer "Star Field".

5. Press the "D" key to reset the default colors, and then press Option/Alt-Backspace/Delete to fill the new layer with Black.

6. From the Filter menu, select Noise>Add Noise. Change the Amount to 100, and make the noise Gaussian and Monochromatic. Click OK.

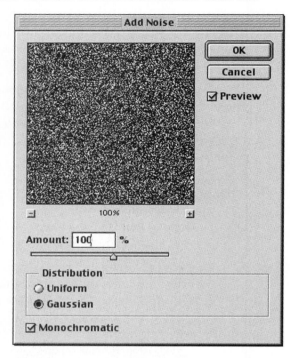

7. From the Filter menu, select Stylize>Diffuse. Click the Darken Only button. Click OK.

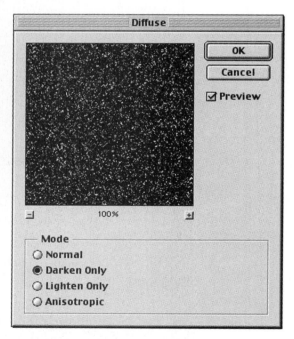

8. Press Command/Control-F twice to run the Diffuse filter 2 more times. Press Command/Control-L to display the Levels dialog box. Move the white Input Levels slider to about 70 so the stars become visible in the image. Click OK.

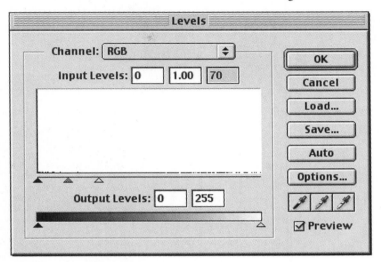

9. Set the layer Blending Mode for the Star Field layer to Lighten. The sky turns blue.

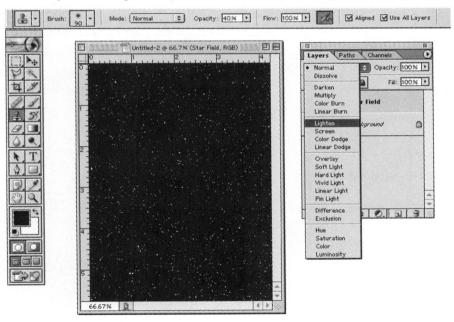

10. Add a new layer. Name it "Gradient". Place it above the Star Field layer in the Layers palette.

11. Click on the foreground color swatch. Set Red to 140, Green to 0, and Blue to 100. Click OK.

12. Click the Linear Gradient tool. Set the gradient to Foreground to Transparent, and click the Reverse box.

13. Hold down the Shift key, and start a gradient about one-fifth of the way down the image. Hold the Shift key to constrain the gradient to vertical. Extend it all the way down to the bottom of the image. If you wish, activate the rulers by choosing Show Rulers from the View menu (or press Command/Control-R).

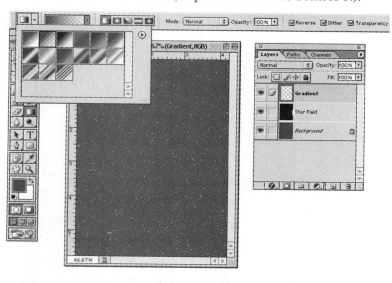

Command/Control-Option/Alt-F allows you to access the previously used filter, and allows you to change the filter settings.

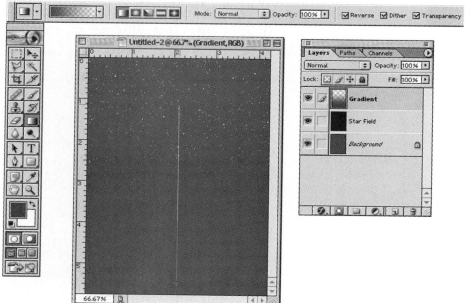

Create a Water Texture

1. Create a new layer called "Water". Position this layer above the Gradient layer in the Layers palette.

2. Press the "D" key, and then the "X" key to change the foreground color to White.

3. Select the Rectangular Marquee tool. On the Options toolbar, set Style to Fixed Size, Width to 425 pixels, and Height to 135 pixels.

4. Click on the image, and position the marquee at the bottom of the image. Fill the selection with White.

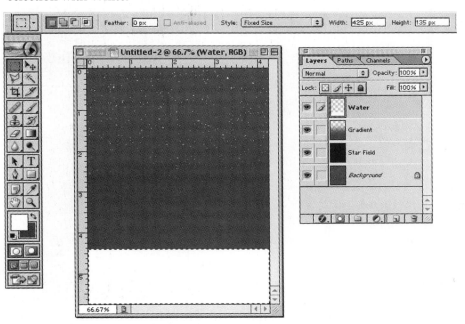

5. Select Noise>Add Noise from the Filter menu. Set the Amount to 400, and make the noise Gaussian and Monochromatic.

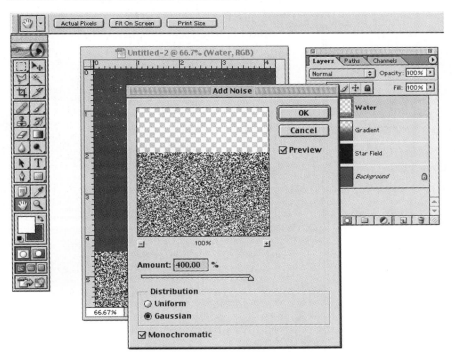

6. Select Blur>Motion Blur from the Filter menu. Set the Angle to 0 and the Distance to 40 pixels.

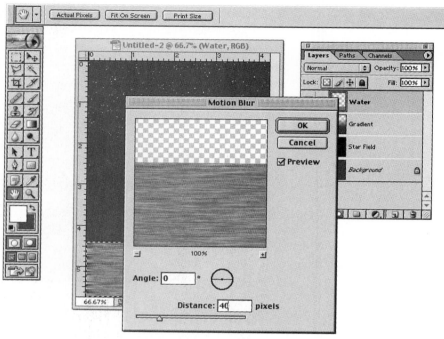

7. Select Adjustments>Auto Levels from the Image menu to allow Photoshop to automatically adjust the highlight, shadow, and midtone areas of the image. Then choose Adjustments>Hue and Saturation from the Image menu.

8. Click the Colorize and Preview check boxes. Set the Hue to 240, Saturation to 50, and Lightness to –45. Click OK.

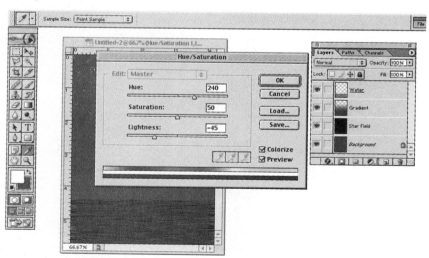

Image Adjustments are covered in depth in the advanced Photoshop book during the discussion on color correction. For now, follow the instructions for making image adjustments as they are presented in the project.

The Hue/Saturation dialog box may be accessed using Command/ Control-U.

9. Deselect what is selected. Notice that the water does not look quite right on the left and right edges of the canvas. Choose Canvas Size from the Image menu. Click the Relative box and set the Width and Height values to –50 pixels (make sure you set the values for pixels, not inches). Leave the placement grid (Anchor) in the center. Click OK.

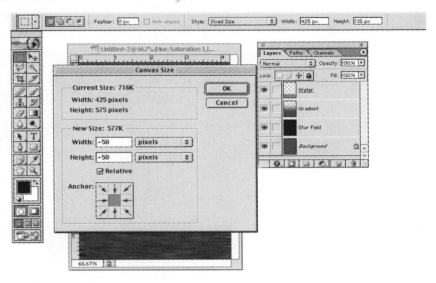

10. Click Proceed/OK when the clipping warning dialog box appears.

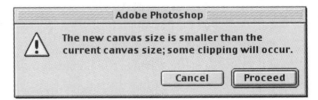

11. Save the document as a Photoshop document named "concert_postcard.psd" in your **Work_In_Progress** folder.

Add Artwork

1. Open the **palm_silhouette.tif** file located in the **RF_Intro_Photoshop** folder.

2. Select the Move tool from the Toolbox, or press the "V" key. Hold down the Shift key and drag the palm tree layer into your document. Close the **palm_silhouette.tif** file.

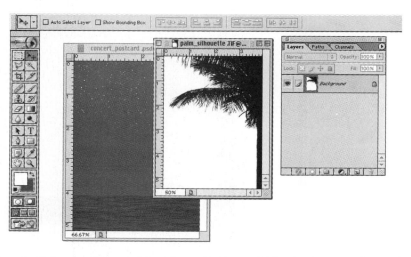

3. Using the Move tool, reposition the palm tree within the layer as shown below. Line it up on the right side of the image with no space showing at the top or right. Retain as much of the tree trunk as possible.

4. Make certain the palm tree layer (Layer 1) is above the Water layer in the Layers palette. Change the Blending mode for the palm tree layer to Multiply.

Holding the Shift key while drawing a gradient, while you are using most other tools, or while you are moving an item constrains the movement horizontally or vertically.

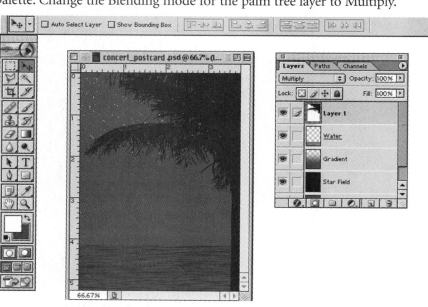

5. If you have limited RAM on your system, you might want to select Purge>Clipboard from the Edit menu to free up RAM. Click OK when the warning box appears.

6. Save the image.

Create a Sailboat Silhouette

1. Open the image **ship_silo.psd** located in the **RF_Intro_Photoshop** folder.

2. Use the Move tool to drag the top layer from this file to your postcard document. Position the ship on the horizon line.

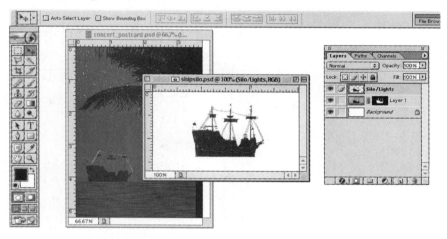

3. Set the Blending mode to Hard Light to blend any edges left over from the original background. Name the layer "Ship".

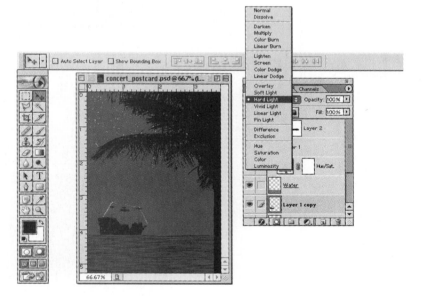

Create Reflections

1. Add a new layer to the image. Call it "Shoreline".

2. Position this layer just above the Water layer.

3. Use the Lasso tool to draw a rough land shape that is sloping into the water on the right horizon. Don't worry about the shape overlapping the water; we'll delete the overlapping image area later in the project.

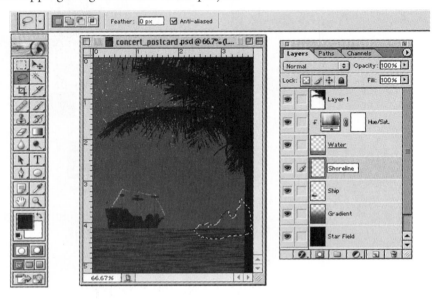

Be sure Auto Select Layer is not checked. Also remember to reset the Marquee tool to Normal (we set it to a fixed size earlier in the project).

4. Fill the selection with Black. Deselect.

5. Move the Shoreline layer under the Water layer as shown. The water now covers the lower part of the shoreline.

Cutting and pasting large objects ties up a lot of your system's memory (since the image is held in RAM). Purging the clip-board clears the memory for use.

6. Duplicate the Shoreline layer; accept the default name, Shoreline copy.

7. Select Transform>Flip Vertical from the Edit menu.

8. Move the Shoreline copy layer above the Water layer. With the Move tool, reposition the image immediately below the land.

9. Lower the Fill to about 44%. Draw a selection marquee as shown, and press the Delete key to remove any part of the shoreline reflection that shows above the waterline. Deselect the selection area.

10. Apply a Motion Blur filter of about 5-10 pixels to make the reflection look as though it's on the water.

Simplify the Image

1. The file has so many layers that it is getting rather large. We need to simplify the image.

2. Add a new layer at the top of the layer stack. Accept the default name.

3. Hold down the Option/Alt key, and select Merge Visible from the Layer menu. Continue to hold down the Option/Alt key until the new layer is filled with all of the other visible layers. (Watch the icon in the layer stack to view the process.)

4. Link all the other layers, but not link the new layer. Using the pop-up menu, make a new layer set from the linked layers. Accept the default name, Set 1. This action simplified the document, but enables you to return to the layered file if necessary.

Command/Control-I inverts (makes a negative) any layer in your image.

The Info palette is a very useful development tool. Whenever you're making adjustments to documents, you'll want to keep it visible on your screen.

If you know what layer opacity will be used, you may set the opacity and name the layer at the same time.

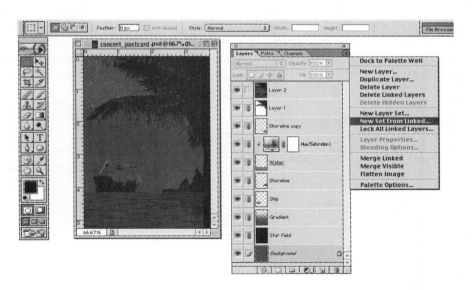

Add Type

1. Select the top layer of your document (the merged version of the image, Set 1).

2. Change the foreground color to White.

3. Click the Type tool near the trunk of the palm tree.

4. Set the Font to ATC Jacaranda and the Alignment to Right. The font Size is not critical at this point; about 14 pt. works well. Enter the following 4 lines of type (without the quotes):

    "Ride the Jazz Boat

    Friday & Saturday Evenings

    8:00 PM - Midnight

    Reservations 800.555.1234"

5. Use the typographic controls to modify the type until you are satisfied with its appearance. Use your own judgment as to point size, leading, and kerning (if needed). The example shows one idea, but you may have another. Do not be afraid to experiment with the design.

6. Using the Type tool, click away from the text and drag to reposition the type as shown in the graphic beneath Step #9.

7. Press Return/Enter to commit the text.

8. Open the file named **headline_copy.psd** from the **RF_Intro_Photoshop** folder. Use the Move tool to drag the shape layer (Jazz at the Beach) onto your postcard. Hold down the Shift key as you drag the layer to the center of the document. The typeface used in this file is not one of the fonts included on the Resource CD, but it adds interest to this postcard, so it is included as a shape layer. Close the **headline_copy.psd** file.

9. Add the layer effects as shown (Drop Shadow, and Bevel and Emboss). Adjust them to suit your preferences. Lower the Fill percentage. If you lower the Fill instead of the Opacity, the effects are not changed; as the Fill percentage is lowered, you can see the color of the sky start to show through the white shape layer.

With the fill set to 13%, the white headline begins to take on the color of the layer below. As the fill has been lowered instead of the opacity, the layer effects still show at 100%. The Character and Paragraph palettes are included to give you an idea of some (not all) of the typographic controls used to set the type block.

10. Open the file **moon.psd** from the **RF_Intro_Photoshop** folder. Load the selection provided using the Moon channel. Copy and paste the moon into your document. Use the Move tool to position it at the upper left. This adds the finishing touch to the card. Close the **moon.psd** file.

11. Another finishing touch is to make a reflection layer for the ship. Open the layer set, and make a copy of the Ship layer.

12. Drag the new layer up the layer stack until it is visible (just above the composite image, Layer 2, in the example).

13. From the Edit menu, select Transform to flip the layer vertically. Use the Move tool to position the layer as shown. Lower the Fill to 33%.

14. The project is ready to print on an RGB-savvy printer. Due to the nature of this image, you may find that increasing the resolution to about 240 dpi still allows acceptable detail in the image. The type and the shape layer will redraw perfectly at the higher resolution. As you can see in the layer stack, we turned off Drop Shadow and added an Outer Glow. The shadow seemed out of place against the sky; the glow draws attention to the headline. Save the document as a native Photoshop .psd file.

Prepare Files for RGB-Savvy Printers

1. Select File>Save As>Photoshop.eps. Name the file "concert.eps". The default settings are fine, but you should click Include Vector Data. Be sure to include a copy of all fonts when you send the file to an off-site PostScript-enabled printer. Save a copy of the file as a flat .tif to print on non-PostScript ink jet or other non-PostScript devices.

2. Leave the file open for the next operation.

You can print directly from the layered Photoshop file to most any printer attached to your computer or network. In this case, however, it might be better to create a version of the file that can be taken to a service bureau for output on a high-speed printer.

Prepare Files for the Newspaper

1. From the Image menu, select Mode>Grayscale. When prompted, do not flatten the file.

2. Save the file as a Photoshop EPS file with the name "concertg.eps". The default settings are fine, but you should click Include Vector Data. The "g" in the file name tells you it is a grayscale image. Include a copy of the fonts in the same folder as your document. Saving the file as an .eps allows the type to print with a sharp edge when processed through the PostScript RIP (used to prepare newspapers for press).

3. Close the file. Do not save the changes. This will save the color values in the .psd version of the file.

By completing this project, you have done more than simply invite people to a concert. You have conveyed the mood of this "Jazz at the Beach" event through the use of color, layers, filters, type, and other special effects. This will undoubtedly result in greater attendance, and heighten the appreciation of fine music throughout the community.

Project D: USA Poster

You're assignment in this project is to create a high-resolution, high-quality poster for a local patriotic celebration being held in honor of military, fire, police, and rescue personnel. The client is the town's celebratory committee, who are known to be demanding — and somewhat picky — about the quality of the artwork they commission.

This project is unique in the sense that it relies on the realistic simulation of a physical object — namely an American flag. Starting with a line-art illustration created in Adobe Illustrator, you're going to use advanced techniques such as displacement maps and displacement filters to convert a flat-colored graphic into extremely believable linen. Once the flag image is complete, you're going to use it as a backdrop for a high-resolution poster — incorporating scanned photographs of the people being honored, as well as other related imagery.

The Flag

This project is designed to produce a poster that can be printed at large sizes. With today's inexpensive RAM and hard drives, it should not be a problem for most users. If you want to work at lower resolution, feel free to do so; but remember that the additional files used later in the project must be reduced to the same resolution with which you start.

1. Open a new RGB Photoshop document with 10-in. Width and a 10-in. Height at a Resolution of 300 ppi. Check the Transparent option in the Contents section. Save the file as "Flag.psd" to your **Work_In_Progress** folder.

```
                                New
         Name: Untitled-2                              OK
    ─ Image Size: 25.7M                                Cancel
    Preset Sizes: Custom                     ⬍

              Width: 10        inches         ⬍
             Height: 10        inches         ⬍
         Resolution: 300       pixels/inch    ⬍
          Mode: RGB Color        ⬍

        ┌ Contents ─────────────────────────
        ○ White
        ○ Background Color
        ● Transparent
        └────────────────────────────────────
```

2. Select Place from the File menu and choose the Adobe Illustrator document **americanflag.ai** from the **RF_Intro_Photoshop** folder. The image comes with scalable handles. Adjust the size, if necessary, while holding down the Shift key to constrain the proportions until it almost fills the window from side to side. Press Return/Enter to rasterize the layer.

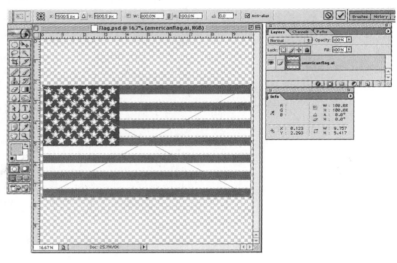

3. Add a new channel filled with Black, and use the Noise filter to add some background noise. Set the Amount to about 100, and check Gaussian and Monochromatic. Duplicate the channel. Compare your settings to the screen shot that follows.

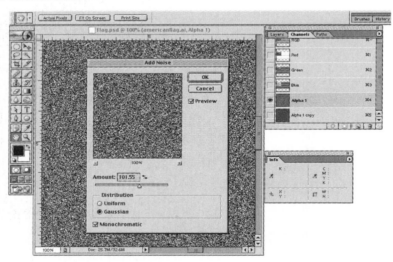

4. Apply the Motion Blur filter to each of these new channels. Set one Horizontal and one Vertical, both at 95 pixels. These channels are the basis for a linen texture we will add to the flag.

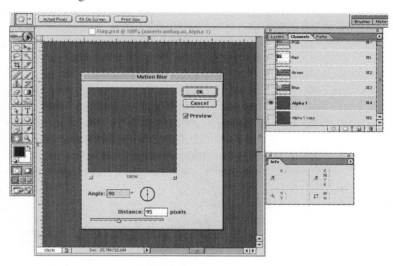

5. From the Image menu, select Calculations. Using the newly created channels, create another channel using Hard Light as the Blending mode. When the dialog box appears, set it as shown in the illustration that follows. Information from each channel will be used to calculate a third channel that has a cross-weave effect.

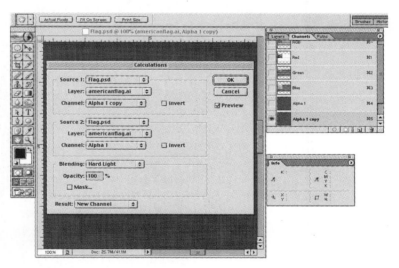

6. We need to increase the contrast of the new channel through the use of calculations. From the Image menu, select Adjustments>Levels and move the sliders to the ends of the curve as shown (set the Input Levels to 19, 1.00, and 100). These settings increase the contrast. (We will cover the use of the Levels and Curves controls in depth in the advanced Photoshop book. For now, apply the settings as shown.)

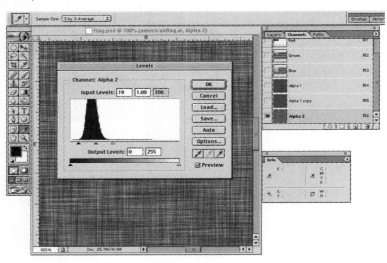

7. Copy and paste the channel into a new layer above the americanflag.ai layer. Start on the new channel (Alpha 2), and press Command/Control-A to select all. Press Command/Control-C to copy the information to the clipboard. Switch to the Layers palette and press Command/Control-V to paste the information.

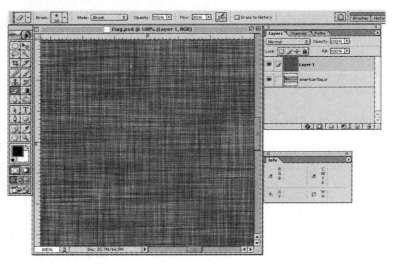

8. Change the Blend Mode to Luminosity and lower the Opacity to 21% to apply the linen texture to the flag. Turn off the visibility eyeball for the texture layer (Layer 1) to complete the next step.

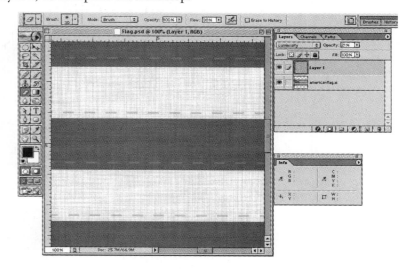

9. Activate the Channels palette and duplicate the Green channel (drag it to the New Layer icon at the bottom of the layer stack). Run the Threshold command on the copy by selecting Adjustments>Threshold from the Image menu. This forces pixels lighter than 50% gray to white, and pixels darker than 50% gray to black. The result is a mask that can be loaded as a selection.

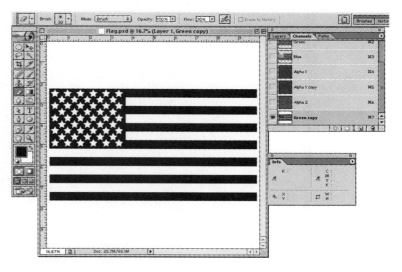

10. From the Select menu, choose Load Selection and choose the Green copy layer as the source. Invert the selection. From the Layers palette, select the texture layer (Layer 1). There should be only 2 layers at this point. Add a Layer mask to the texture layer (Layer 1). This removes the texture from the white areas of the flag. From the Image menu, select Adjustments>Levels to lower the density of the black areas of the mask to control how much texture shows in the white areas. Move the black Output slider to the right to about 100-150. This may seem like a very small detail, but it makes a significant difference in the appearance of the finished flag.

To see the effect, hold down the Shift key and click on the Layer mask to toggle it on and off. With the texture layer (Layer 1) selected, choose Merge Down from the pop-up menu. This applies the linen texture to the flag.

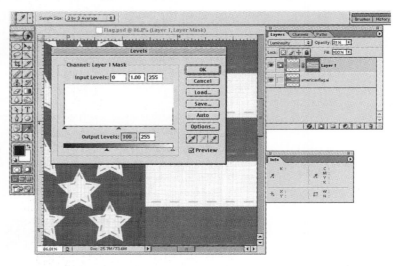

11. Create a new channel. Be sure the foreground and background colors are set to the defaults (press the "D" key) and fill the channel with clouds by selecting Render>Clouds from the Filter menu. Select the Distort>Wave filter and set the Number of Generators to 5, Wavelength to Minimum 314 and Maximum 866, Amplitude to Minimum 91 and Maximum 489, Scale to Horizontal 14% and Vertical 43%, click the Sine button in the Type section, click Repeat Edge Pixels in the Undefined Areas section, and then click OK.

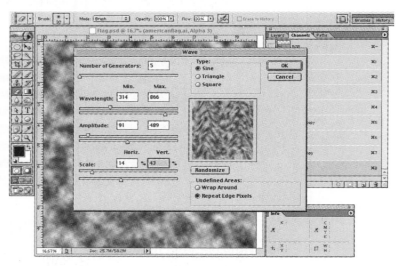

12. Copy this channel by selecting all, and then pressing Command/Control-C. Press Command/Control-N to make a new document. The new document defaults to the size of the clipboard, so your channel copy fits perfectly. Press Command/Control-V to paste the information. Be sure it is a grayscale document. Save the file as "d_map.psd" to your **Work_In_Progress** folder. Be sure to save it as a .psd file. Also, this is one of the times that you must remember to maximize compatibility, so check the box if it comes up. Close **d_map.psd**.

13. In the original file, make a duplicate of the americanflag.ai layer. We will apply the displacement map to the copy so we can see the difference. From the Filter menu, select Distort>Displace. Set the parameters to Horizontal Scale 20%, Vertical Scale 20%, Stretch to Fit, and Repeat Edge Pixels. Click OK. Choose **d_map.psd** as the displacement map file. You may have to navigate to your **Work_In_Progress** folder to find the file.

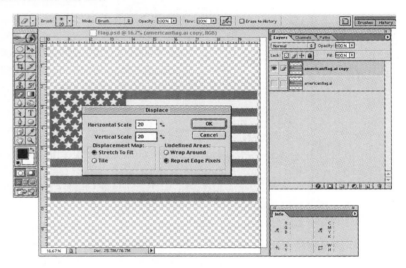

The displacement map moves the pixels in the image according to the grayscale values in the map. Light areas go up and to the left, while dark areas go down and to the right. The amount of displacement is controlled by the horizontal and vertical scales in the dialog box. Negative values reverse the pattern. Shades of gray move pixels proportionally to their light or dark value. As you can see, the flag takes on a very irregular shape and the linen texture is also distorted.

14. Press Command/Control-V to paste the displacement map (it should still be on the clipboard) as a layer above the flag. Change the Blending mode to Darken, and lower the Opacity to add shadows that correspond to the displaced pixels, creating realistic shadows on the flag. You may want to experiment with Levels or Curves to make the shadows stand out more clearly. (We haven't fully explained these tools in this Photoshop book, but you can experiment if you wish.)

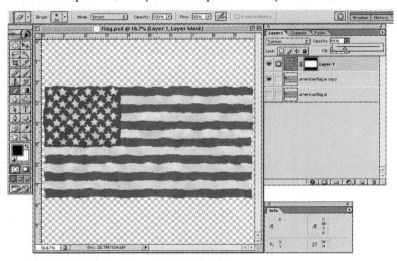

15. Select the outline of the displaced flag by Command/Control-clicking on the americanflag.ai copy layer. Then click on the shadow layer (Layer 1 in the illustration) and add a Layer mask (click on the mask icon at the bottom of the stack) to remove any stray pixels.

16. Turn off the original americanflag.ai layer by clicking its visibility icon. Add a new layer to the top of the stack. Hold down the Option/Alt key, and from the Layers menu, select Merge Visible. Hold down the key until a new icon shows up in the layer stack. This merges the shadows and the Layer mask with the flag, making it easier to use the new flag layer later. This technique is not the most efficient way to use your computer's resources, but it does result in a file that can be edited at any time. For a more resource-friendly technique, use the pop-up menu to Merge Down the shadow layer (Layer 1 in the illustration).

17. Select the Magic Wand tool and set the Tolerance to about 80. Shift-click on each of the stars. Copy and paste (Command/Control-C and then Command/Control-V) a new star field. Using the Move tool (press the "V" key to activate the tool), reposition the star field over the original stars, if necessary. Double-click on the new star field layer to access Layer Styles. Add a Drop Shadow and a slight Bevel and Emboss to help achieve a more 3-dimensional appearance. The default settings for these styles work fine; all you need to do is check the boxes. Name the layer "3D Stars".

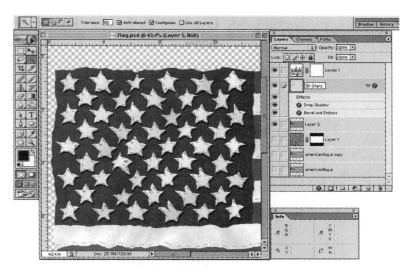

18. Press Command/Control-L to access the Layers palette. You're going to slightly increase the contrast of this image by reducing the tonal range. Underneath the Histogram, you'll see the three sliders (shadow on the left, midtones in the center, and highlights on the right). Grab the shadow slider and move it slightly to the right. Then pull the Highlight slider a small amount to the left. This action reduces the overall tonal range, and increases the apparent contrast. Make sure you don't overdo it – keep your eye on the flag to make sure you don't reduce the details in the image.

This part of the project is now complete. Save it to your **Work_In_Progress** folder as "flag.psd".

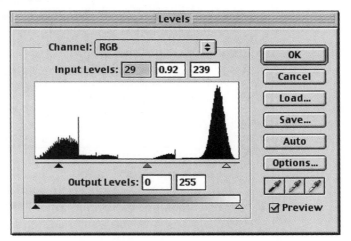

During the second part of the project, we will create the map of the USA and fill it with images. The techniques used here are similar to those we used in the "Twelve Angry Jurors" exercise presented earlier in the book. The skills are basic to creating artwork in Photoshop.

In order to provide for some artistic input from the user, this part of the project will not be presented in a step-by-step fashion. Instead, you are asked to create your own interpretation of the graphic using the images provided. The map is included as a .psd file to make it easy to import it into the final document. Our version of the USA map is available in the **RF_Intro_Photoshop** folder in the **Shortcuts** folder for those who wish to shorten the project. We strongly recommend, however, that every user create a unique version of the design.

USA

1. Open the **usa_map.psd** file from the **usa_composite_images** folder in the **RF_Intro_Photoshop** folder. Use the Move tool (press the "V" key to access the tool) and drag the map onto the **flag.psd** file (it should be open from the previous exercise; if not, re-open the **flag.psd** file). Be sure the top layer of the **flag.psd** document is highlighted so the map layer (Layer 5) will be placed above it.

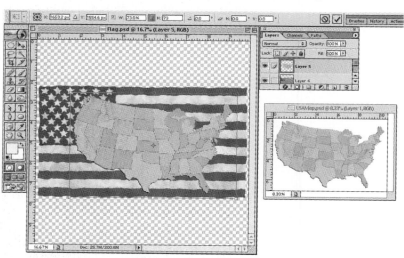

2. Press Command/Control-T to access the Free Transform controls. Click on the chain icon between the Width and Height boxes on the Options toolbar to constrain the proportions. Enter 73% in both Width and Height boxes. Position the map where you want it and press Return/Enter to accept the transformation (you may have to press Return/Enter twice). Close the **usa_map.psd** file

3. Open **liberty_fireworks.psd** from the **usa_composite_images** folder and drag it into the flag file. Position it above the map image in the layer stack. Use Free Transform to scale it to about 70%. Remember to click on the chain icon to link the layers. Command/Control-click on the layer that contains the map to load it as a selection.

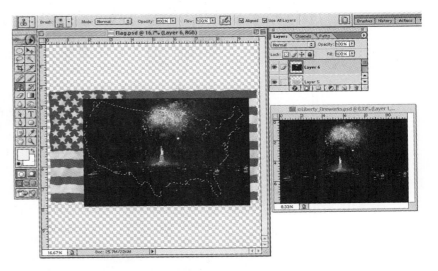

4. Add a Layer mask to the liberty fireworks layer by clicking the mask icon at the bottom of the layer stack. Unlink the mask from the image by clicking on the chain icon between the image icon and the mask icon. Position the image using the Move tool. When the chain icon is not visible, the image and mask can be moved independently. Be careful not to move the mask; it is lined up with the map that is positioned beneath it. Click in the link box to turn the chain back on. Close the **liberty_fireworks.psd** file.

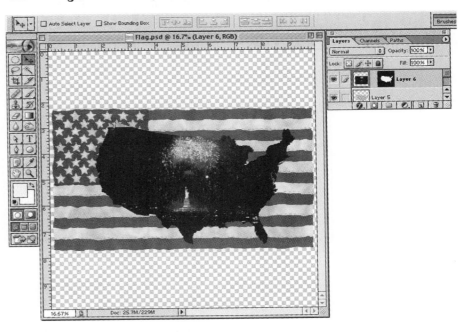

5. Open the **sunset_silo.psd** image from the **usa_composite_images** folder. Using the same procedure from the previous steps, position the image toward the left of the map. Add another Layer mask as before, and reposition the image as necessary. Close the **sunset_silo.psd** file.

6. Use the Gradient Fill tool set to Darken and blend the areas inside the USA outline. Apply the gradient to the Layer mask, white-to-black and left-to-right. Experiment until you get a satisfactory effect. If you prefer, use the Paintbrush tool to further modify your mask.

7. Continue adding the images from the **usa_composite_images** folder until you are satisfied with your version of the USA composite. At this point, you may choose to add personal images. A common addition is a family member in uniform. When you are done, save the image in your **Work_In_Progress** folder. A trick to remember when working with the image of the Preamble to

the Constitution is to apply a Blending mode (use the Blend sliders to blend away the dark areas) to remove the dark background, and then apply a Layer mask to complete the effect. The following illustration highlights these controls.

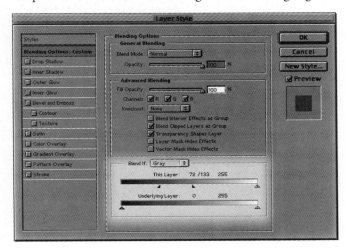

8. When you are finished, merge the layers used to build the composite map by high-lighting the USA map layer, clicking between the visibility eyeball and the layer icon of each of the component layers to link them, and using the pop-up menu to Merge Linked Layers. If you wish, add a layer style — perhaps Bevel and Emboss and/or Drop Shadow.

The third part of this project prepares the image for framing and display. Using colors from within the image to promote color harmony, we will create a canvas background and a textured matte board, complete with beveled edge and white core. The final image will then be ready to frame, complete with the look of an expensive custom matte. Before we start the final steps of the project, we need to alter the canvas size to the final dimensions.

Mount and Matte

1. From the Image menu, select Canvas Size. Set the Width to 12 in. and the Height to 8 in. (Click Proceed when the warning dialog box appears.) This size canvas provides the room needed to frame the project.

2. Add a new layer to your document and position it just below the layer that contains the flag (americanflag.ai copy). Name the new layer "Canvas". Using the Eyedropper tool, sample an appropriate color from within the document (we used a color from the sunset sky) and fill the new layer (Edit>Fill>Foreground or Option/Alt-Delete). If you prefer, temporarily turn off the layers above the Canvas layer to make the document less visually complex. Remember to turn them on again after the Canvas layer is complete. The next few illustrations display a 100% view to show the texture effects.

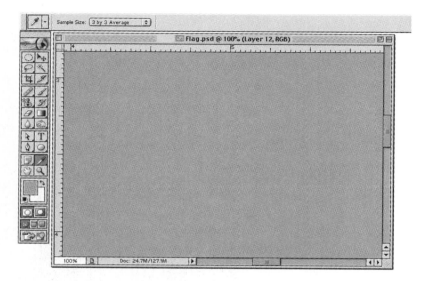

3. From the Filter menu, select Texture>Texturizer>Canvas. Set the Scaling to 100%, the Relief to 4, and the Light Direction to Top Left. Apply the filter by clicking OK.

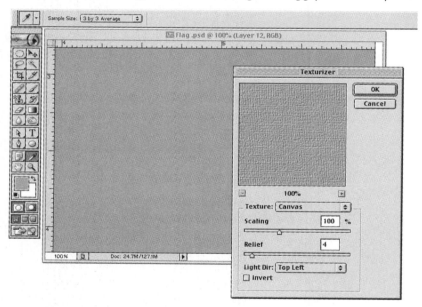

4. From the Filter menu, select Pattern Maker.

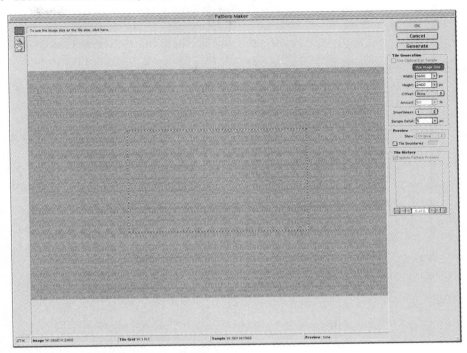

5. Select an area in the middle of the display with the Marquee tool. In order to create one tile the size of our document, click on Use Image Size, and then click Generate. The process may take a few seconds to complete. Once the pattern has been generated, use the built-in Zoom tool to view it at 100%. If you are satisfied with the results, save it by clicking the disk icon at the bottom of the dialog box (the button on the far left under the Tile History box). Give the new pattern the name of your choice. It will be available for use as a fill or by the Pattern Stamp tool. Click OK to apply the new pattern to your document.

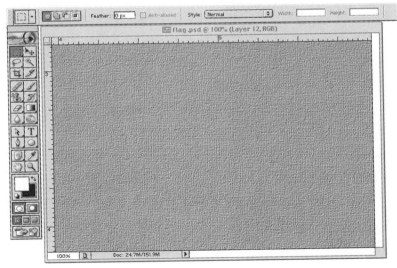

This 100% view shows the more random effect achieved by using the Pattern Maker tool.

6. Set your document to 100%, and toggle Command/Control-Z to see the pattern change. As an option (and since you know how to do it) you might want to apply a small displacement to the Canvas layer to make it even more random. You can use the displacement map (**displacement_map_a.psd**) included with the images for this project in the **Shortcuts** folder. We set the displacement map to 20% Horizontal and 20% Vertical and reduced the effect to about 68% using the Edit>Fade command.

7. The next step is to create the matte board surrounding the image. Make a new layer at the top of the layer stack and fill it with a color sampled from within the **USAcomposite_map** layer (we chose a medium brown). Name the new layer "Matte". Lower the Opacity of this new layer so you can see through to the layers below. Use the Marquee tool to draw a selection around the flag and USA image.

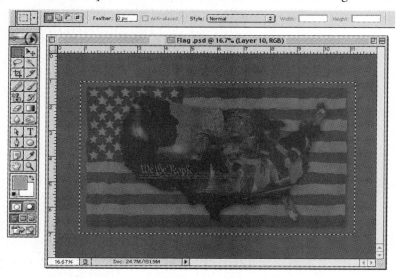

8. Invert the selection and add a Layer mask to the Matte layer. Set the Opacity at 100%. Switch from the mask to the paint layer (click on the icon of the matte board). From the Filter menu, select Texture>Texturizer>Sandstone. Set the parameters to create a pleasing appearance. Set the Light Direction to Top Left, and apply the setting. You will most likely have to drag the image in the dialog box down several times to see a complete preview, as the mask has eliminated the middle section of the image.

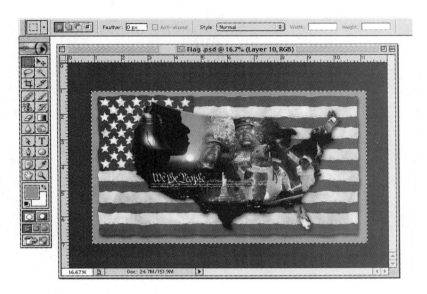

9. Command/Control-click on the Layer mask to restore the selection. From the Select menu, select Modify>Expand, and enter a value of 5 pixels. Make a new layer and position it just below the Matte layer. Fill the selection with White and deselect.

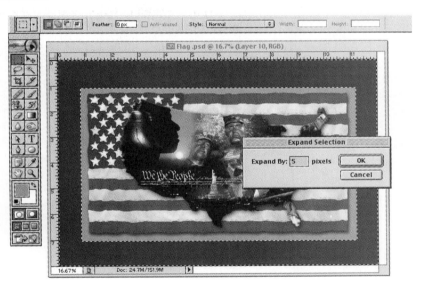

10. Using the Layer Styles dialog box, apply a Bevel and Emboss effect and a gentle Drop Shadow to create the beveled edge of your new matte board. These are the settings we used, but you can experiment to discover what settings you like best.

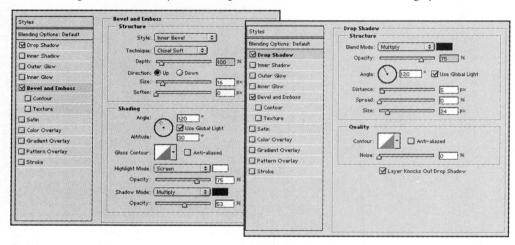

Be sure to remove any extra channels from the file if you send it out to be printed — extra channels can cause output problems.

11. As a final touch, set a line of type across the bottom of the flag. We used 48-pt. ATCJacaranda. The blue was sampled from the flag with the Eyedropper tool. Enter the following text: "In honor of those who sacrifice to keep us free." Layer effects of Drop Shadow and Bevel and Emboss can be added to your personal preference.

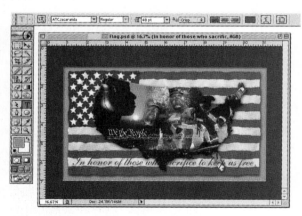

12. Save and close the file.

The finished piece is now ready to print. There is enough resolution to print up to a 24-in. piece on many ink jet printers, as they typically require only 150 dpi at final size. Photographic printers require more resolution, so the size will be smaller. Save the master file in a .psd format, and save a flat .tif file for printing.

If you want to sign your work, create your signature using block letters, scan it, use the Magic Wand tool to select the white paper, and invert the selection. Copy and paste the signature into your document, positioning the new layer just above the Canvas background layer. Add layer effects for Bevel and Emboss and a small Drop Shadow, and then lower the fill opacity until the texture begins to show through. Even if you lower the fill opacity all the way, the effects remain, leaving an interesting way to personalize your work.

Achromatic

By definition, having no color; therefore, completely black or white or some shade of gray.

Acrobat

This program by Adobe Systems, Inc. allows the conversion (using Acrobat Distiller) of any document from any Macintosh or Windows application to PDF format, which retains the page layout, graphics, color, and typography of the original document. It is widely used for distributing documents online because it is independent of computer hardware. The only software needed is a copy of Acrobat Reader, which can be downloaded free.

Adaptive Palette

A sampling of colors taken from an image, and used in a special compression process usually used to prepare images for the World Wide Web.

Additive Color Process

The additive color process is the process of mixing red, green, and blue light to achieve a wide range of colors, as on a color television screen. See Subtractive Color.

Adjacent Color

The eye will respond to a strong adjacent color in such a way as to affect the perception of the particular color in question. That is, a color having different adjacent colors may look different than it does in isolation.

Algorithm

A specific sequence of mathematical steps to process data. A portion of a computer program that calculates a specific result.

Alpha Channel

An 8-bit channel of data that provides additional graphic information, such as colors or masking. Alpha channels are found in some illustration or graphics programs, and are used in video production.

Anti-Aliasing

A graphics software feature that eliminates or softens the jaggedness of low-resolution curved edges.

ATM (Adobe Type Manager)

A utility which causes fonts to appear smooth on screen at any point size. It's also used to manage font libraries.

Background Eraser

This tool erases areas over which it is dragged to transparency.

Banding

A visible stair-stepping of shades in a gradient.

Bézier Curves

Curves that are defined mathematically (vectors), in contrast to those drawn as a collection of dots or pixels (raster). The advantage of these curves is that they can be scaled without the "jaggies" inherent in enlarging bitmapped fonts or graphics.

Bit (Binary Digit)

A computer's smallest unit of information. Bits can have only two values: 0 or 1. This can represent the black and white (1-bit) pixel values in a line art image. Or in combination with other bits, it can represent 16 tones or colors (4-bit), 256 tones or colors (8-bit), 16.8 million colors (24-bit), or a billion colors (30-bit). These numbers derive from counting all the possible combinations (permutations) of 0 or 1 settings of each bit: $2 \times 2 \times 2 = 16$ colors; $2 \times 2 \times 2 \times 2 \times 2 \times 2 \times 2 \times 2 = 256$ colors; $2 \times 2 = 16.8$ million colors.

Bitmap Image

An image constructed from individual dots or pixels set to a grid-like mosaic. Each pixel can be represented by more than one bit. A 1-bit image is black and white because each bit can have only two values (for example, 0 for white and 1 for black). For 256 colors, each pixel needs eight bits (2^8). A 24-bit image refers to an image with 24 bits per pixel (2^{24}), so it may contain as many as 16,777,216 colors. Because the file must contain information about the color and position of each pixel, the disk space needed for bitmap images is usually quite significant. Most digital photographs and screen captures are bitmap images.

Bitmapped

Forming an image by a grid of pixels whose curved edges have discrete steps because of the approximation of the curve by a finite number of pixels.

Bleed

Page data that extends beyond the trim marks on a page. Illustrations that spread to the edge of the paper without margins are referred to as "bled off."

Blend

See Graduated fill.

Blind Emboss

A raised impression in paper made by a die, but without being inked. It is visible only by its relief characteristic.

Blow Up

An enlargement, usually of a graphic element such as a photograph.

Brightness

1. A measure of the amount of light reflected from a surface. 2. A paper property, defined as the percentage reflection of 457-nanometer (nm) radiation. 3. The intensity of a light source. 4. The overall percentage of lightness in an image.

Burn

1. To expose an image onto a plate. 2. To make copies of ROM chips or CD-ROMs. 3. To darken a specific portion of an image through photographic exposure.

Byte

A unit of measure equal to eight bits (decimal 256) of digital information, sufficient to represent one text character. It is the standard unit measure of file size. (See also Megabyte, Kilobyte, and Gigabyte).

Calibration

Making adjustments to a color monitor and other hardware and software to make the monitor represent as closely as possible the colors of the final printed piece.

Calibration Bars

A strip of reference blocks of color or tonal values on film, proofs, and press sheets, used to check the accuracy of color registration, quality, density, and ink coverage during a print run.

Camera Ready

A completely finished mechanical, ready to be photographed to produce a negative from which a printing plate will be made.

Choke

See Trapping

Chroma

The degree of saturation of a surface color in the Munsell color space model.

Chromalin

A single-sheet color proofing system introduced by DuPont in 1971 and still quite popular in the industry. It uses a series of overlaid colorants and varnish to simulate the results of a press run.

Chromaticity Diagram

A graphical representation of two of the three dimensions of color. Intended for plotting light sources rather than surface colors. Often called the CIE diagram.

Cloning

Duplication of pixels from one part of an image to another.

CMYK

Acronym for cyan, magenta, yellow, and black, the four process color inks which, when properly overprinted, can simulate a subset of the visible spectrum. See also Color Separation. Also refers to digital artwork that contains information necessary for creating color separations.

Color Balance

The combination of yellow, magenta, and cyan needed to produce a neutral gray. Determined through a gray balance analysis.

Color Cast

The modification of a hue by the addition of a trace of another hue, such as yellowish green, or pinkish blue. Normally, an unwanted effect that can be corrected.

Color Chart

A printed chart of various combinations of CMYK colors used as an aid for the selection of "legal" colors during the design phase of a project.

Color Control Strip

A printed strip of various reference colors used to control printing quality. This strip is normally placed outside the "trim" area of a project, as a guide and visual aid for the pressman.

Color Conversion

Changing the color "mode" of an image. Converting an image from RGB to CMYK for purposes of preparing the image for conventional printing.

Color Correction

The process of removing casts or unwanted tints in a scanned image, in an effort to improve the appearance of the scan or to correct obvious deficiencies, such as green skies or yellowish skin tones.

Color Gamut

The range of colors that can be formed by all possible combinations of the colorants of a given reproduction system (printing press) on a given type of paper.

Color Management System (CMS)

A process or utility that attempts to manage color of input and output devices in such a way that the monitor will match the output of any CMS-managed printer.

Color Model

A system for describing color, such as RGB, HLS, CIE L*a*b, or CMYK.

Color Overlay

A sheet of film or paper whose text and art correspond to one spot color or process color. Each color overlay becomes the basis for a single printing plate that will apply that color to paper.

Color Picker

A function within a graphics application that assists in selecting a color.

Color Proof

A printed or simulated printed image of the color separations intended to produce a close visual representation of the final reproduction for approval purposes and as a guide for press.

Color Separation

The process of transforming color artwork into four components corresponding to the four process colors. If spot colors are used, additional components may be created

containing only those items that will appear in the corresponding spot color layer. Each component is imaged to film or paper in preparation for making printing plates that correspond to each ink.

Color Sequence

The color order of printing the cyan, magenta, yellow, and black inks on a printing press. Sometimes called rotation or color rotation.

Color Space

Because a color must be represented by three basic characteristics depending on the color model, the color space is a three-dimensional coordinate system in which any color can be represented as a point.

Color Temperature

The temperature, in degrees Kelvin, to which a blackbody would have to be heated to produce a certain color radiation. (A "blackbody" is an ideal body or surface that completely absorbs or radiates energy.) The graphic arts viewing standard is 5,000 K. The degree symbol is not used in the Kelvin scale. The higher the color temperature, the bluer the light.

Color Transparency

A positive color photographic image on a clear film base that must be viewed by transmitted light. It is preferred for original photographic art because it has higher resolution than a color print. Transparency sizes range from 35mm color slides up to 8 × 10 in. (203 × 254 mm).

Colorimeter

An optical measuring instrument designed to measure and quantify color. It is often used to match digital image values to those of cloth and other physical samples.

Composer

Photoshop will use either the Single-Line Composer, which composes every line using the parameters you have programmed into Preferences, or it will use the Every-Line Composer, which considers several lines when making hyphenation and justification decisions.

Composite Proof

A version of an illustration or page in which the process colors appear together to represent full color. When produced on a monochrome output device, colors are represented as shades of gray.

Compression

A digital technique used to reduce the size of a file by analyzing occurrences of similar data. Compressed files occupy less physical space, and their use improves digital transmission speeds. Compression can sometimes result in a loss of image quality and/or resolution.

Continuous Tone

An image such as an original photograph in which the subject has continuous shades of color or gray tones through the use of an emulsion process. Continuous tone images must be screened to create halftone images in order to be printed.

Contrast

The relationship between the dark and light areas of an image.

Copyright

Ownership of a work by the originator, such as an author, publisher, artist, or photographer. The right of copyright permits the originator of material to prevent its use without express permission or acknowledgment of the originator. Copyright may be sold, transferred, or given up contractually.

Creep

The progressive extension of interior pages of the folded signature beyond the image area of the outside pages. Shingling is applied to correct for creep.

Crop Marks

Printed short, fine lines used as guides for final trimming of the pages within a press sheet.

Cropping

The elimination of parts of a photograph or other original that are not required to be printed.

Custom Printer Description File

A file containing information specific to a type of output device; used in conjunction with a standard PPD file to customize the printing process.

DCS (Desktop Color Separation)

Acronym for Desktop Color Separation, a version of the EPS file format. DCS 1.0 files are composed of five PostScript files for each color image: cyan, magenta, yellow, and black, plus a separate low-resolution FPO image to place in a digital file. In contrast, DCS 2.0 files have one file that stores process color and spot color information.

Default

A specification for a mode of computer operation that operates if no other is selected. The default font size might be 12 point, or a default color for an object might be white with a black border.

Densitometer

An electronic instrument used to measure optical density. Reflective (for paper) and transmissive (for film).

Die Line

In a digital file, the outline used to mark where cutting, stamping, or embossing the finished printed piece will occur. Used to create a particular shape, such as a rolodex card.

Digital

The use of a series of discrete electronic pulses to represent data. In digital imaging systems, 256 steps (8 bits, or 1 byte) are normally used to characterize the gray scale or the properties of one color.

Digital Camera

A camera which produces images directly into an electronic file format for transfer to a computer.

Digital Proofs

Digital proofs are representations of what a specific mechanical will look like when output and reproduced on a specific type of printing press. The difference with a digital proof is that it is created without the use of conventional film processes and output directly from computer files.

Dingbat

A font character that displays a picture instead of a letter, number, or punctuation mark. There are entire font families of pictographic dingbats; the most commonly used dingbat font is Zapf Dingbats. There are dingbats for everything from the little airplanes used to represent airports on a map, to telephones, fish, stars, balloons — just about anything.

Dithering

A technique used in images wherein a color is represented using dots of two different colors displayed or printed very close together. Dithering is often used to compress digital images, in special screening algorithms (see Stochastic Screening) and to produce higher quality output on low-end color printers.

Dot Gain

The growth of a halftone dot that occurs whenever ink soaks into paper. This growth can vary from being very small (on a high-speed press with fast-drying ink and very non-porous paper) to quite dramatic, as is the case in newspaper printing, where a dot can expand 30% from its size on the film to the size at which it dries. Failure to compensate for this gain in the generation of digital images can result in very poor results on press. Generally speaking, the finer the screen (and therefore, the smaller the dot) the more noticeable dot gain will be.

Downloadable Fonts

Typefaces that can be stored on disk and then downloaded to the printer when required for printing.

DPI (Dots Per Inch)

The measurement of resolution for page printers, phototypesetting machines, and graphics screens. Currently graphics screens use resolutions of 60 to 100 dpi, standard desktop laser printers work at 600 dpi, and imagesetters operate at more than 1,500 dpi.

Drop Shadow

A duplicate of a graphic element or type placed behind and slightly offset from it, giving the effect of a shadow.

Drum Scanner

A color scanner on which the original is wrapped around a rotary scanning drum. See Scanner.

DSC

Acronym for the Adobe Document Structure Conventions, designed to provide a standard order and format for information so applications that process PostScript, such as PressWise, can easily find information about a document's structure and imaging requirements. These conventions allow specially formatted PostScript comments to be added to the page description; applications can search for these comments, but PostScript interpreters usually ignore them. TrapWise requires that the PostScript in incoming files is formatted using conventional DSC comments, so certain functions may not work properly if the file is not DSC-conforming.

Duotone

The separation of a black-and-white photograph into black and a second color having different tonal values and screen angles. Duotones are used to enhance photographic reproduction in two-, three-, or sometimes four-color work. Often the second, third, and fourth colors are not standard CMYK inks.

Dye

A soluble coloring material, normally used as the colorant in color photographs.

Dye Transfer

A photographic color print using special coated papers to produce a full color image. Can serve as an inexpensive proof.

Electrostatic

The method by which dry toner is transferred to paper in a copier or laser printer, and liquid toners are bonded to paper on some large-format color plotters.

Elliptical Dot Screen

A halftone screen having an elliptical dot structure.

Embedding

1. Placing control codes in the body of a document. 2. Including a complete copy of a text file or image within a desktop publishing document, with or without a link (see Linking).

Emulsion

The coating of light-sensitive material (silver halide) on a piece of film or photographic paper.

EPS (Encapsulated PostScript)

Acronym for file format used to transfer PostScript data within compatible applications. An EPS file normally contains a small preview image that displays in position within a mechanical or used by another program. EPS files can contain text, vector artwork, and images.

Export

To save a file generated in one application in a format that is readable in another application.

Extension

A modular software program that extends or expands the functions of a larger program. A folder of extensions is found in the Macintosh System folder.

Faux

When creating type, Photoshop allows you to artificially make letters bold or oblique. This is called "faux bold" and "faux italic." You should always use real bold and italic when they are available.

Fill

To add a tone or color to the area inside a closed object in a graphic illustration program.

Film

Non-paper output of an imagesetter or phototypesetter.

Filter

In image-editing applications, a small program that creates a special effect or performs some other function within an image.

Flat Color

Color that lacks contrast or tonal variation. Also, flat tint.

Flatbed Scanner

A scanner on which the original is mounted on a flat scanning glass. See Scanner.

Flexographic Printing

A rotary letterpress process printing on a press using a rubber plate that stretches around a cylinder making it necessary to compensate by distorting the plate image. Flexography is used most often in label printing, often on metal or other non-paper material.

Font

A font is the complete collection of all the characters (numbers, uppercase and lowercase letters and, in some cases, small caps and symbols) of a given typeface in a specific style; for example, Helvetica Bold.

Four-Color Process

See Process Colors

FPO

Acronym for For Position Only, a term applied to low-quality art reproductions or simple shapes used to indicate placement and scaling of an art element on mechanicals or camera-ready artwork. In digital publishing, an FPO can be low-resolution TIFF files that are later replaced with high-resolution versions. An FPO is not intended for reproduction but only as a guide and placeholder for the prepress service provider.

Gamma

A measure of the contrast, or range of tonal variation, of the midtones in a photographic image

Gamma Correction

1. Adjusting the contrast of the midtones in an image. 2. Calibrating a monitor so that midtones are correctly displayed on screen.

Gamut

See Color Gamut

GASP

Acronym for Graphic Arts Service Provider, a firm that provides a range of services somewhere on the continuum from design to fulfillment.

Gigabyte (G)

One billion (1,073,741,824) bytes (230) or 1,048,576 kilobytes.

Global Preferences

Preference settings which affect all newly created files within an application.

Glyph Scaling

Photoshop will automatically scale individual letters in order to achieve appropriate hyphenation and justification.

Graduated Fill

An area in which two colors (or shades of gray or the same color) are blended to create a gradual change from one to the other. Graduated fills are also known as blends, gradations, gradient fills, and vignettes.

Grain

Silver salts clumped together in differing amounts in different types of photographic emulsions. Generally speaking, faster emulsions have larger grain sizes.

Graininess

Visual impression of the irregularly distributed silver grain clumps in a photographic image, or the ink film in a printed image.

Graphics Interface File (GIF)

A CompuServe graphics file format that is used widely for graphic elements in Web pages.

Gray Balance

The values for the yellow, magenta, and cyan inks that are needed to produce a neutral gray when printed at a normal density.

Gray Component Replacement (GCR)

A technique for adding detail by reducing the amount of cyan, magenta, and yellow in chromatic or colored areas, replacing them with black.

Grayscale

1. An image composed in grays ranging from black to white, usually using 256 different tones of gray. 2. A tint ramp used to measure and control the accuracy of screen percentages on press. 3. An accessory used to define neutral density in a photographic image.

Greeking

1. A software technique by which areas of gray are used to simulate lines of text below a certain point size. 2. Nonsense text use to define a layout before copy is available.

Grid

A division of a page by horizontal and vertical guides into areas into which text or graphics may be accurately placed.

Group

To collect graphic elements so an operation may be simultaneously applied to all of them.

GUI

Acronym for Graphical User Interface, the basis of the Macintosh and Windows operating systems.

Gutter

Extra space between pages in a layout. Sometimes used interchangeably with Alley to describe the space between columns on a page. Gutters can appear either between the top and bottom of two adjacent pages or between two sides of adjacent pages. Gutters are often used because of the binding or layout requirements of a job — for example, to add space at the top or bottom of each page or to allow for the grind-off taken when a book is perfect bound.

Hairline Rule

The thinnest rule that can be printed on a given device. A hairline rule on a 1200 dpi imagesetter is 1/1200 of an inch; on a 300 dpi laser printer, the same rule would print at 1/300 of an inch.

Halftone

An image generated for use in printing in which a range of continuous tones is simulated by an array of dots that create the illusion of continuous tone when seen at a distance.

Halftone Tint

An area covered with a uniform halftone dot size to produce an even tone or color. Also called flat tint or screen tint.

High Key

A photographic or printed image in which the main interest area lies in the highlight end of the scale.

High Resolution File

An image file that typically contains four pixels for every dot in the printed reproduction. High-resolution files are often linked to a page layout file, but not actually embedded in it, due to their large size.

Highlights

The lightest areas in a photograph or illustration.

History Brush

A tool that allows you to paint to a specific state in the History palette.

HLS

Color model based on three coordinates: hue, lightness (or luminance), and saturation.

HSV

A color model based on three coordinates: hue, saturation, and value (or luminance).

Hue

The wavelength of light of a color in its purest state (without adding white or black).

Hyperlink

An HTML tag directs the computer to a different Anchor or URL (Uniform Resource Locator). The linked data may be on the same page, or on a computer anywhere in the world.

HyperText Markup Language (HTML)

The language, written in plain (ASCII) text using simple tags, that is used to create Web pages, and which Web browsers are designed to read and display. HTML focuses more on the logical structure of a page than its appearance.

Hyphenation Zone

The space at the end of a line of text in which the hyphenation function will examine the word to determine whether or not it should be hyphenated and wrapped to the next line.

Imagesetter

A raster-based device used to output a computer page-layout file or composition at high resolution (usually 1000 - 3000 dpi) onto photographic paper or film, from which to make printing plates.

Imaging

The process of producing a film or paper copy of a digital file from an output device.

Import

To bring a file generated within one application into another application.

Imposition

The arrangement of pages on a printed sheet, which, when the sheet is finally printed, folded and trimmed, will place the pages in their correct order.

Indexed Color Image

An image which uses a limited, predetermined number of colors; often used in Web images. See also GIF.

Indexing

Marking certain words within a document with hidden codes so an index may be automatically generated.

Inline Graphic

A graphic that is inserted within a body of text, and may be formatted using normal text commands for justification and leading; inline graphics will move with the body of text in which they are placed.

Intensity

Synonym for degree of color saturation.

Jaggies

Visible steps in the curved edge of a graphic or text character that result from enlarging a bitmapped image.

JPG or JPEG

A compression algorithm that reduces the file size of bitmapped images, named for the Joint Photographic Experts Group; JPEG is a "lossy" compression method, and image quality will be reduced in direct proportion to the amount of compression.

Kelvin (K)

Unit of temperature measurement based on Celsius degrees, starting from absolute zero, which is equivalent to -273 Celsius (centigrade); used to indicate the color temperature of a light source.

Kerning

Moving a pair of letters closer together or farther apart, to achieve a better fit or appearance.

Key (Black Plate)

In early four-color printing, the black plate was printed first and the other three colors were aligned (or registered) to it. Thus, the black plate was the "key" to the result.

Keyline

A thin, often black border around a picture or a box indicating where to place pictures. In digital files, the keylines are often vector objects while photographs are usually bitmap images.

Kilobyte (K, KB)

1,024 (210) bytes, the nearest binary equivalent to decimal 1,000 bytes. Abbreviated and referred to as K.

Knockout

A printing technique that represents overlapping objects without mixing inks. The ink for the underlying element does not print (knocks out) in the area where the objects overlap. Opposite of overprinting.

L*a*b

The lightness, red-green attribute, and yellow-blue attribute in the CIE Color Space, a three-dimensional color mapping system.

Layer

A function of graphics applications in which elements may be isolated from each other, so a group of elements may be hidden from view, locked, reordered or otherwise manipulated as a unit, without affecting other elements on the page.

Leading ("Ledding")

Space added between lines of type. Usually measured in points or fractions of points. Named after the strips of lead which used to be inserted between lines of metal type. In specifying type, lines of 12-pt. type separated by a 14-pt. space is abbreviated "12/14," or "twelve over fourteen."

Letterspacing

The insertion or addition of white space between the letters of words.

Library

In the computer world, a collection of files having a similar purpose or function.

Ligatures

When this type option is selected, Photoshop will substitute the ligature (for example, ffi would be rendered using the ligature ffi). Ligatures are used when Open Type fonts are available.

Lightness

The property that distinguishes white from gray or black, and light from dark color tones on a surface.

Line Art

A drawing or piece of black and white artwork, with no screens. Line art can be represented by a graphic file having only 1-bit resolution.

Line Screen

The number of lines per inch used when converting a photograph to a halftone. Typical values range from 85 for newspaper work to 150 or higher for high-quality reproduction on smooth or coated paper.

Linking

An association through software of a graphic or text file on disk with its location in a document. That location may be represented by a "placeholder" rectangle, or a low-resolution copy of the graphic.

Lithography

A mechanical printing process used for centuries based on the principle of the natural aversion of water (in this case, ink) to grease. In modern offset lithography, the image on a photosensitive plate is first transferred to the blanket of a rotating drum, and then to the paper.

Lossy

A data compression method characterized by the loss of some data.

Loupe

A small free-standing magnifier used to see fine detail on a page.

LPI

Lines per inch. See Line Screen.

Luminosity

The amount of light, or brightness, in an image. Part of the HLS color model.

LZW

The acronym for the Lempel-Ziv-Welch lossless data- and image-compression algorithm.

Macro

A set of keystrokes that is saved as a named computer file. When accessed, the keystrokes will be performed. Macros are used to perform repetitive tasks.

Magic Eraser

This tool converts solid colors within a tolerance range to transparency with a single click.

Mask

To conform the shape of a photograph or illustration to another shape such as a circle or polygon.

Masking

A technique that blocks an area of an image from reproduction by superimposing an opaque object of any shape.

Match Print

A color proofing system used for the final quality check.

Mechanical Dot Gain

See Dot Gain

Medium

A physical carrier of data such as a CD-ROM, video cassette, or floppy disk, or a carrier of electronic data such as fiber optic cable or electric wires.

Megabyte (M, MB)

A unit of measure of stored data equaling 1,024 kilobytes, or 1,048,576 bytes (1020).

Megahertz(mHz)

An analog signal frequency of one million cycles per second, or a data rate of one million bits per second. Used in specifying CPU speed.

Menu

A list of choices of functions, or of items such as fonts. In contemporary software design, there is often a fixed menu of basic functions at the top of the page that have pull-down menus associated with each of the fixed choices.

Metafile

A class of graphics that combines the characteristics of raster and vector graphics formats; not recommended for high-quality output.

Metallic Ink

Printing inks which produce gold, silver, bronze, or metallic colors.

Midtones or Middletones

The tonal range between highlights and shadows.

Misregistration

The unwanted result of incorrectly aligned process inks and spot colors on a finished printed piece. Misregistration can be caused by many factors, including paper stretch and improper plate alignment. Trapping can compensate for misregistration.

Moiré

An interference pattern caused by the out-of-register overlap of two or more regular patterns such as dots or lines. In process-color printing, screen angles are selected to minimize this pattern.

Monochrome

An image or computer monitor in which all information is represented in black and white, or with a range of grays.

Montage

A single image formed by assembling or compositing several images.

Neutral

Any color that has no hue, such as white, gray, or black.

Neutral Density

A measurement of the lightness or darkness of a color. A neutral density of zero (0.00) is the lightest value possible and is equivalent to pure white; 3.294 is roughly equivalent to 100% of each of the CMYK components.

Noise

Unwanted signals or data that may reduce the quality of the output.

Non-Reproducible Colors

Colors in an original scene or photograph that are impossible to reproduce using process inks. Also called out-of-gamut colors.

Normal Key

A description of an image in which the main interest area is in the middle range of the tone scale or distributed throughout the entire tonal range.

Notes

The Notes and Audio Annotated Notes tools allow you to attach comments to an image.

Object-Oriented Art

Vector-based artwork composed of separate elements or shapes described mathematically rather than by specifying the color and position of every point. This contrasts to bitmap images, composed of individual pixels.

Offset

In graphics manipulation, to move a copy or clone of an image slightly to the side and/or back; used for a drop-shadow effect.

Old Style Numbers

When this type option is selected, Photoshop will substitute the old style number for the regular numbers. Old Style numbers are used when Open Type fonts are available.

Opacity

1. The degree to which paper will show print through it. 2. Settings in certain graphics applications that allow images or text below the object whose opacity has been adjusted, to show through.

OPI

1. Open Prepress Interface. 2. A set of PostScript language comments originally developed by Aldus Corporation for defining and specifying the placement of high-resolution images in PostScript files on an electronic page layout. 3. Incorporation of a low resolution preview image within a graphic file format (TIF, EPS, DCS) that is intended for display only.

Output Device

Any hardware equipment, such as a monitor, laser printer, or imagesetter, that depicts text or graphics created on a computer.

Overlay

A transparent sheet used in the preparation of multicolor mechanical artwork showing the color breakdown.

Overprint

A printing technique that lays down one ink on top of another ink. The overprinted inks can combine to make a new color. The opposite of knockout.

Overprint Color

A color made by overprinting any two or more of the primary yellow, magenta, and cyan process colors.

Overprinting

Allowing an element to print over the top of underlying elements, rather than knocking them out (see Knockout). Often used with black type.

Page Description Language (PDL)

A special form of programming language that describes both text and graphics (object or bit-image) in mathematical form. The main benefit of a PDL is that it makes the application software independent of the physical printing device. PostScript is a PDL, for example.

Palette Well

An area in Photoshop's Menu bar to which often-used palettes may be stored for quick and easy access.

Pantone Matching System (PMS)

A system for specifying colors by number for both coated and uncoated paper; used by print services and in color desktop publishing to assure uniform color matching.

PCX

Bitmap image format produced by paint programs.

PDF (Portable Document Format)

Developed by Adobe Systems, Inc. (and read by Adobe Acrobat Reader), this format has become a de facto standard for document transfer across platforms.

Perspective

The effect of distance in an image achieved by aligning the edges of elements with imaginary lines directed toward one to three "vanishing points" on the horizon.

PICT/PICT2

A common format for defining bitmapped images on the Macintosh. The more recent PICT2 format supports 24-bit color.

Pixel

Abbreviation for picture element, one of the tiny rectangular areas or dots generated by a computer or output device to constitute images.

PMT

Photo Mechanical Transfer - positive prints of text or images used for paste-up to mechanicals.

Positive

A true photographic image of the original made on paper or film.

Posterize, Posterization

The deliberate constraint of a gradient or image into visible steps as a special effect; or the unintentional creation of steps in an image due to a high lpi value used with a low printer dpi.

PostScript

1. A page description language developed by Adobe Systems, Inc. that describes type and/or images and their positional relationships upon the page. 2. An interpreter or RIP (see Raster Image Processor) that can process the PostScript page description into a format for laser printer or imagesetter output. 3. A computer programming language.

PPD

Acronym for PostScript Printer Description; device-specific information enabling software to produce the best results possible for each type of designated printer.

PPI

Pixels per inch; used to denote the resolution of an image.

Primary Colors

Colors that can be used to generate secondary colors. For the additive system (i.e., a computer monitor), these colors are red, green, and blue. For the subtractive system (i.e., the printing process), these colors are yellow, magenta, and cyan.

Printer Fonts

The image outlines for type in PostScript that are sent to the printer.

Process Colors

The four transparent inks (cyan, magenta, yellow, and black) used in four-color process printing. See also Color Separation; CMYK.

RAM

Random Access Memory, the "working" memory of a computer that holds files in process. Files in RAM are lost when the computer is turned off, whereas files stored on the hard drive or floppy disks remain available.

Raster

A bitmapped representation of graphic data.

Raster Graphics

A class of graphics created and organized in a rectangular array of bitmaps. Often created by paint software, fax machines, or scanners for display and printing.

Raster Image Processor (RIP)

That part of a PostScript printer or imagesetting device that converts the page information from the PostScript Page Description Language into the bitmap pattern that is applied to the film or paper output.

Rasterize

The process of converting digital information into pixels at the resolution of the output device. For example, the process used by an imagesetter to translate PostScript files before they are imaged to film or paper. See also Raster Image Processor.

Reflective Art

Artwork that is opaque, as opposed to transparent, that can be scanned for input to a computer.

Registration

Aligning plates on a multicolor printing press so that the images will superimpose properly to produce the required composite output.

Registration Color

A color designation that prints on all four or more printing plates and is used to create alignment, or registration marks.

Resolution

The density of graphic information expressed in dots per inch (dpi) or pixels per inch (ppi).

Retouching

Making selective manual or electronic corrections to images.

Reverse Out

To reproduce an object as white, or paper, within a solid background, such as white letters in a black rectangle.

RGB

Acronym for red, green, blue, the colors of projected light from a computer monitor that, when combined, simulate a subset of the visual spectrum. When a color image is scanned, RGB data is collected by the scanner and then converted to CMYK data at some later step in the process. Also refers to the color model of most digital artwork. See also CMYK.

Rich Black

A process color consisting of solid black with one or more layers of cyan, magenta, or yellow.

ROM

Read Only Memory, a semiconductor chip in the computer that retains startup information for use the next time the computer is turned on.

Roman Hanging Punctuation

With the Roman Hanging Punctuation option selected, certain characters will be placed to the left or right of the escapement of a text frame, "hanging" into the margin.

Rosette

The pattern created when color halftone screens are printed at traditional screen angles.

RTF

Rich Text Format, a text format that retains formatting information lost in pure ASCII text.

Rubylith

A two-layer acetate film having a red or amber emulsion on a clear base used in non-computer stripping and separation operations.

Saturation

The intensity or purity of a particular color; a color with no saturation is gray.

Scaling

To reduce or enlarge the amount of space an image will occupy by multi-plying the data by a scale factor. Scaling can be proportional, or in one dimension only.

Scanner

A device that electronically digitizes images point-by-point through circuits that can correct color, manipulate tones, and enhance detail. Color scanners will usually produce a minimum of 24 bits for each pixel, with 8 bits each for red, green, and blue.

Screen

To create a halftone of a continuous tone image (See Halftone).

Screen Angle

The angle at which the rulings of a halftone screen are set when making screened images for halftone process-color printing. The equivalent effect can be obtained electronically through selection of the desired angle from a menu.

Screen Frequency

The number of lines per inch in a halftone screen, which may vary from 85 to 300.

Screen Tint

A halftone screen pattern of all the same dot size that creates an even tone at some percentage of solid color.

Shape Layer

A special vector layer is created whenever the special shape tools are used.

Shape Tools

These vector-based tools include the Rectangle, Rounded Rectangle, Ellipse, Polygon, Line, and Custom Shape tools. They allow you to create and edit vector shapes in Photoshop.

Sharpness

The subjective impression of the density difference between two tones at their boundary, interpreted as fineness of detail.

Silhouette

To remove part of the background of a photograph or illustration, leaving only the desired portion.

Slice and Slice Select Tool

Allows you to create and edit user-defined slices of an image for creation of Web graphics.

Snap-To (Guides or Rulers)

An optional feature in page-layout programs that drives objects to line up with guides or margins if they are within a pixel range that can be set. This eliminates the need for very precise, manual placement of an object with the mouse.

Specular Highlight

The lightest highlight area that does not carry any detail, such as reflections from glass or polished metal. Normally, these areas are reproduced as unprinted white paper.

Spot Color

Any pre-mixed ink that is not one of or a combination of the four process color inks, often specified by a Pantone swatch number.

Stochastic Screening

A method of creating halftones in which the size of the dots remains constant but their density is varied; also known as frequency-modulated (or FM) screening.

Subtractive Color

Color which is observed when light strikes pigments or dyes, which absorb certain wavelengths of light; the light that is reflected back is perceived as a color. See CMYK and Process Color.

Tagged Image File Format (TIFF)

A common format for use with scanned or computer-generated bitmapped images.

Tint

1. A halftone area that contains dots of uniform size; that is, no modeling or texture. 2. The mixture of a color with white.

Toolbar

This toolbar automatically displays in the menu bar area of your Photoshop window, revealing the options available for the tool in use.

Tracking

Adjusting the spacing of letters in a line of text to achieve proper justification or general appearance.

Transfer Curve

A curve depicting the adjustment to be made to a particular printing plate when an image is printed.

Transparency

A full-color photographically-produced image on transparent film.

Transparent Ink

An ink that allows light to be transmitted through it.

Trapping

The process of creating an overlap between abutting inks to compensate for imprecise registration in the printing process.

TrueType

An outline font format used in both Macintosh and Windows systems that can be used both on the screen and on a printer.

Type 1 Fonts

PostScript fonts based on Bézier curves encrypted for compactness that are compatible with Adobe Type Manager.

Type Family

A set of typefaces created from the same basic design but in different weights, such as bold, light, italic, book, and heavy.

Undercolor Removal (UCR)

A technique for reducing the amount of magenta, cyan, and yellow inks in neutral or shadow areas and replacing them with black.

Undertone

Color of ink printed in a thin film.

Unsharp Masking

A digital technique performed after scanning that locates the edge between sections of differing lightness and alters the values of the adjoining pixels to exaggerate the difference across the edge, thereby increasing edge contrast.

Varnish Plate

The plate on a printing press that applies varnish after the other colors have been applied.

Vector Graphics

Graphics defined using coordinate points, and mathematically-drawn lines and curves, which may be freely scaled and rotated without image degradation in the final output. Fonts (such as PostScript and TrueType), and illustrations from drawing applications are common examples of vector objects. Two commonly used vector drawing programs are Illustrator and FreeHand. A class of graphics that overcomes the resolution limitation of bitmapped graphics.

Vignette

An illustration in which the background gradually fades into the paper; that is, without a definite edge or border.

Visible Spectrum

The wavelengths of light between about 380 nm (violet) and 700 nm (red) that are visible to the human eye.

Warped Text

The appearance of the text itself can be distorted through horizontally and vertically bending and distorting the text. The Create Warped Text button is located in the Text Options toolbar.

White Light

Light containing all wavelengths of the visible spectrum.

White Space

Areas on the page which contain no images or type. Proper use of white space is critical to a well-balanced design.

Wizard

A utility attached to an application or operating system that aids you in setting up a piece of hardware, software, or document.

WYSIWYG

An acronym for "What You See Is What You Get," (pronounced "wizzywig") meaning that what you see on your computer screen bears a strong resemblance to what the job will look like when it is printed.

measurement units 49
megapixels 11-12
menu bar 43
midtones 31
mode effects 182
modems 265-266
move tool 57
multichannel 167, 169
multiply 104

N

native Photoshop format 95
navigation 52, 54
  keyboard 54
navigation bars 94
navigational structures 263
navigator palette 43
nearest neighbor 244
Netscape 264-265
newspaper 247
newsprint 11
no break 171
noise 203, 224, 229, 231

O

old style numbers 170
opacity 103-104, 140
opacity slider 140
opacity value 86
open type 170
optimization 275-276, 282, 285
option dialogs 42
option key 54
option-delete 54
options 56
options palette 43
orientation 166, 168, 170, 173, 244-246
output 163, 179-180
  requirements 11

P

page geometry 244
page setup 245-246
paint bucket tool 149-151
paint engine 139-141, 145, 160
paint tools, 66
paintbrush tool 58, 139-140, 143, 146
painterly effects 140
painting tools 58, 98, 140, 182-183, 188
palette well 43, 47
palettes 42
paragraph palette 169, 171, 173
parallel 263, 267

paste into 66
patch tools 58
path (component) selection 59
path selection tool 191
paths 189-201
paths palette 43, 191-192, 197-198, 200-201
pattern dither 27
pattern maker 203, 205, 221-222, 235
pattern stamp tools 58
patterns 28, 141, 221-224, 235
pdf 261-262
pen tools 60, 109, 189-192, 194
pencil tool 58, 139, 145-146
perceptual and selective 276
perspective 82
photomultiplier 14
physical dimensions 17
picas 48
pixelate 102
pixels 48, 66, 164
pixels per inch 237, 239
plug-in 205
png 14, 16, 265-267, 275-276
point text 163, 168-169
points 48, 264
polygonal lasso tool 57, 73
portrait 244-246
ppi 18, 237, 239-242
preferences 49
premiere 12
preset sizes 48
print with preview 237, 246, 253, 255-256
printers 16, 24, 30
printing 237-262
process color 34, 237
profiles 256-258, 261
proof setup 256

Q

quality factor 18, 239
quick mask 116, 135

R

radius 243
ram 18
ramp 166
raster 163-165, 180
rasterize 167
rectangular marquee tool 69
red, green, and blue 116
reflective copy 13

regular lasso tool 72
render 203, 205, 224, 230-231
resample 237, 244
reset palette locations 44
resize 237, 239-240, 244, 255, 259
resolution 11, 17, 164, 178-179, 237-242, 244, 246, 255, 259, 262
rgb 16, 24, 48, 116, 247, 249-250, 261
rollover 108
rotate 82
rotate character option 173
roundness 142
rulers 43

S

sample 154, 156
save as a copy 103
save for web 263, 273, 275-276, 279-280, 282-284, 288-289
save workspace 48
scale 82
scanners 13
  transparency 14
screening 18, 238-239, 247, 254
scroll bars 43
selection techniques 66
selection tools 57
selections 56, 190, 201
separations 237, 247-248, 254, 256
set painting cursors to brush size 44
shades of gray 28
shadows 31, 122, 184-187
shape 141
shape layers 109
shape tools 56, 60, 189-190
sharp 166
sharpening 203, 239, 243
sheet-fed 13
shift key 54
single-line composer 172-173
skew and distort 82
slice 275, 285-289
slice and slice select tools 57
slicing 285, 289
smooth 166
soft-edged channel 117
spacing 142
spot color channel 252
spot colors 237, 251-253
stack 264
status bar 44
stock photography 12
style 264

subtract from selection 88
subtractive color 23
swap foreground and background
    colors 63
swatches 146
swatches palette 43
system resources 95

T

table formatting 265
tables 264-265, 275
tabloid 244
text boxes 163, 169
text elements 163-164, 180
text formatting 264
tiff 14, 18, 95, 103, 259
titles 166
tolerance 149, 151-152, 154-156
tonal values 31
tones 26
tool behavior settings 67
tool options 56

toolbox 42, 43, 55
torque 197
transform tools 81
transparency 94, 266-267, 277, 279-281
true color 24
type 189, 192, 198, 200
type layers 96, 163, 167-168, 177, 179
type mask 166, 174
type palette 169
type tool 163, 166-169, 174, 178-180
type tools 59

U

underline 170
underlying image 141
units of measurement 49
unsharp mask 243

V

varnish 252
vector 163-165, 167-168, 174, 179-180
vector objects 189

video capture 14
views 62
visibility icon 186-187

W

warping text 177
web objects 263-264
web snap 276-277
web-safe color palette 272-273
web-safe colors 263, 273, 275-277
wet edges 147
windows 42, 264-265, 267, 272
word spacing 172
workspace 44
world wide web 16

Z

zoom tool 52, 62

Resource CD-ROM
ADOBE® PHOTOSHOP® 7
Introduction to Digital Images
AGAINST THE CLOCK

System Requirements

Windows:

- Intel® Pentium® III, or 4 Processor.

- Microsoft® Windows® 98, Windows 98 Special Edition, Windows Millennium Edition, Windows NT® with Service Pack 6a, Windows 2000 with Service Pack 2, Windows XP

- 128 MB of RAM (192 recommended)

- 280 MB of available hard-disk space

- Color monitor capable of 800 × 600 pixel resolution

- CD-ROM drive

Macintosh:

- PowerPC® processor (G3, G4, or G4 Dual)

- Mac OS software version 9.1, 9.2, or Mac OS X version 10.1.3

- 128 MB of RAM (192 recommended)

- 320 MB of available hard-disk space

- Color monitor capable of 800 × 600 pixel resolution

- CD-ROM drive

To use the additional resources available on this CD-ROM, you will need to have the appropriate applications installed on your system and enough free space available if you copy the files to your hard drive. This product does not come with the application software required to use the data files on this CD-ROM.